EMBERS OF THE PAST

A book in the series Latin America Otherwise: Languages, Empires, Nations

SERIES EDITORS
Walter D. Mignolo, Duke University
Irene Silverblatt, Duke University
Sonia Saldívar-Hull, University of Texas, San Antonio

EMBERS OF THE PAST

Essays in Times of Decolonization

JAVIER SANJINÉS C.

WITH A FOREWORD BY WALTER D. MIGNOLO   Translated by David Frye

Duke University Press   Durham and London   2013

© 2013 Duke University Press
All rights reserved
Designed by Courtney Leigh Baker
Typeset in Dante and Trade Gothic by Keystone Typesetting, Inc.

Library of Congress Cataloging-in-Publication Data
Sanjinés C., Javier, 1948–
[Rescoldos del pasado. English]
Embers of the past : essays in times of decolonization /
Javier Sanjinés C. ; translated by David Frye ;
with a foreword by Walter D. Mignolo.
pages cm. — (Latin america otherwise)
ISBN 978-0-8223-5444-4 (cloth)
ISBN 978-0-8223-5476-5 (pbk.)
1. Multiculturalism. 2. Cultural pluralism. 3. Ethnic relations.
4. Postcolonialism. I. Title. II. Series: Latin America otherwise.
HM1271.S36613 2013
305.8—dc23
2013010156

Duke University Press gratefully acknowledges the support of the
Office of the Vice President for Research at the University of Michigan,
which provided funds toward the publication of the book.

IN MEMORY OF FERNANDO CORONIL (1943–2011)

Contents

ABOUT THE SERIES ix
ACKNOWLEDGMENTS xi
FOREWORD BY WALTER D. MIGNOLO xiii

INTRODUCTION
MODERNITY IN THE BALANCE, THE "TRANSGRESSIVE" ESSAY, AND DECOLONIZATION 1

Modernity in the Balance 2
The "Leftward Turn" in Our Societies 6
The Conflict over Time and the "Decolonial Turn" 11
The Essay as a Transgressive Proposition 15
The Embers of the Past 24

ONE
THE CHANGING FACES OF HISTORICAL TIME 29

Tradition and Revolution 36
The Experience of the Past 38
The Horizon of Expectations 42
The Resource of the "Other" 46

TWO
IS THE NATION AN IMAGINED COMMUNITY? 57

Nationalism, Nation, and Ethnicity 59
The Nation: A Contested Concept 62
Lettered Culture 66

The Brazil of Euclides da Cunha 69
Mariátegui and the Case of Peru 74
The Persistence of "Then" within "Now" 81
On Negativity: "Multitude," "Subalternity," and "Pueblo" 84

THREE
"NOW TIME": SUBALTERN PASTS AND CONTESTED HISTORICISM 97

The Hidden Face of Modernity 98
The Need to "Provincialize" Europe 103
The "Time of the Now": Messianism and Redemption 107
The Secular and the Supernatural 113
On Complementarity and Reciprocity 118
The Problems of Translation 127
A "Culture of Integration" 133
By Way of Conclusion 138

FOUR
THE DIMENSIONS OF THE NATION AND THE DISPLACEMENTS OF SOCIAL METAPHOR IN BOLIVIA 143

The Nation's Developmentalist and Pedagogical Dimension 144
The Nation's Two Faces 146
Metaphors about "National Pedagogy" 149
Deterritorialization and Metaphors of Flowing 158
The Metaphor of the Amphibian 168
Plurinational State or Intractable State? 172

NOTES 183   REFERENCES 197   INDEX 209

About the Series

Latin America Otherwise: Languages, Empires, Nations is a critical series. It aims to explore the emergence and consequences of concepts used to define "Latin America" while at the same time exploring the broad interplay of political, economic, and cultural practices that have shaped Latin American worlds. Latin America, at the crossroads of competing imperial designs and local responses, has been construed as a geocultural and geopolitical entity since the nineteenth century. This series provides a starting point to redefine Latin America as a configuration of political, linguistic, cultural, and economic intersections that demands a continuous reappraisal of the role of the Americas in history and of the ongoing process of globalization and the relocation of people and cultures that have characterized Latin America's experience. *Latin America Otherwise: Languages, Empires, Nations* is a forum that confronts established geocultural constructions, rethinks area studies and disciplinary boundaries, assesses convictions of the academy and of public policy, and correspondingly demands that the practices through which we produce knowledge and understanding about and from Latin America be subject to rigorous and critical scrutiny.

Acknowledgments

I warmly thank Walter Mignolo, Valerie Millholland, and Gisela Fosado for accepting this book for the Latin America Otherwise series at Duke University Press.

I would also like to thank the Academy of Latinity, particularly its General Secretary, Candido Mendes, for his several invitations to participate at conferences in Amman (2007), Yucatán (2007), Rabat (2008), Lima (2008), Cairo (2009), and Oslo (2009). The ideas developed in this book were tested at these meetings, and the Academy of Latinity provided stimulating forums for reflection and for fruitful dialogues in the Middle East, South and North America, and Europe.

I express my gratitude to Stephen R. Forrest, Vice President for Research at the University of Michigan, for the partial funding provided for this publication.

My gratitude also goes to David Frye for his excellent translation of the original version in Spanish. The manuscript was first published in Bolivia by Proyecto de Investigación Estratégica (PIEB) with the title *Rescoldos del pasado: Conflictos sociales en sociedades poscoloniales* (2009). With the new subtitle *Essays in Times of Decolonization*, *Embers of the Past* has substantially changed the original version. The book has a new introduction and a new final chapter.

Finally, I thank the two anonymous readers of *Rescoldos del pasado*. Their observations have been very helpful for the gestation of the presently revised version.

Foreword
WALTER D. MIGNOLO

I

Embers of the Past confronts the blind spot of modernity: the myth of a better future that, detached from tradition, doesn't need to look back to go forward. Progress and development, coupled with concepts such as innovation, excellence, and efficiency, dethrone any other possibility of living and conceiving life and society. The hidden side of the triumphal rhetoric of the narrative is that in both its earlier and its current versions, European modernity relies on its own past, the past of Western civilization. The affirmation of the European past as universal allows for the sustained rhetoric of modernity that disavow any other tradition and any other past as sustainable.

Javier Sanjinés takes issue with this myth from the memories of colonial legacies, which are alien to the European experience. Western European states (monarchic and secular) were not colonized; they enacted imperial expansion and colonialism. He confronts the myths of modernity tracing the genealogy of two critical trajectories. One trajectory is found within Europe itself and Euro-America. Walter Benjamin and Charles Sanders Peirce are two examples that call our attention to the "embers of the Euro-American past." The other trajectory is found in the local histories of European colonies. The points of origination of both trajectories are grounded in different local histories. The first trajectory offers critiques of modernity within modernity itself. The second trajectory advances critiques of modernity from its colonial underside. In the first trajectory, modernity itself, not coloniality, is a problem. In the second the problem is coloniality, the darker side of modernity. It is the compound of modernity / coloniality that calls for decoloniality. Sanjinés brilliantly connects both trajectories, offering clear analysis of the first and exploring the second in sophisticated ways. Basing his analysis on the Bolivian and Andean past, he delinks from the discipline of history. Sanjinés opts to reinscribe the past in the present.

Published first in Spanish, the book was a clear intervention in the heated and creative political and epistemic debates that have flourished in Bolivia in the past twenty years. The English version has been substantially modified with an introductory chapter reflecting on the "essay" and a final chapter dwelling on what Sanjinés sees as two co-existing metaphors: the metaphor of progress and the metaphor of decolonization.

THE MAIN THRUST of the book remains in both versions. Taking sides with the arguments advanced by many Aymara and Quechua scholars and intellectuals, Sanjinés's book confronts the current politics of the Bolivian state. "Decolonization" is a word that in today's Bolivia has three different sources and is inscribed in three different projects. One is the project advanced and enacted, since colonial times, by Aymaras and Quechuas. Decolonization is not a novelty to them. They knew it before all of us who are neither Quechua nor Aymara. Second, the word is used in official discourse of the state. Decolonization as a discourse of the state hides what it means when used in indigenous projects: it hides the fact that the state itself is a product and consequence of coloniality. We encounter the third use of the concept within the project of modernity / coloniality, a project that emerged from a group of dissidents of European descent, mestizas / os and immigrants. Sanjinés's book is squarely located in this third project, in conflictive dialogue with the state and in solidary dialogue with indigenous decolonial projects.

II

Javier Sanjinés was born and raised in Bolivia. Educated in France and the United States, he obtained his PhD at the University of Minnesota and taught at the University of Maryland before returning to Bolivia in the early 1990s, when Bolivia elected a neoliberal president, Gonzalo Sánchez de Losada, who invited the Aymara scholar and politician, Victor Hugo Cárdenas, to run as vice president. The seeds of change were planted: neoliberalism is today in decay, while Indianism is on the move. *Embers of the Past* (first published in La Paz with the title of *Rescoldos del pasado*) was written not so much as a study of Bolivian past and present but as an intervention in the intellectual and political debates that have been mounting in Bolivia since the surprising (for many) presidency of a wealthy neoliberal president and an Aymara educator vice president. Obviously, the surprising combination did not emerge out of the blue but had been in the air, developing gradually, since the revolution of 1952 and perhaps even since Francisco Pizarro's execution of Atahualpa in 1533. *Embers of the Past* reflects on the present (and the future) by retrieving the silences of the past. Sanjinés returned to the United States in 1998 and joined the Department of Romances Languages and Literatures at the University of Michigan in Ann Arbor.

Certainly, this is not the first book to reflect on Bolivia's colonial past. What matters is the "way" Sanjinés addresses it. Several features highlight Sanjinés's reflections on the past in comparison with historical accounts of today's Bolivia. The nation-state territory of today is filled with millenarian memories of the former civilization of Tiwanaco and Tawantinsuyu. The first sentences of the book are questions. Beginning a book with questions rather than with affirmations engages the reader to take part in the conversation. Sanjinés is not affirming; he is questioning, and the questions will not be answered once and for all, but are left open. What counts, then, are the questions rather than the answers. Not, of course, that Sanjinés's answers should be dismissed, but they should be read as what they are: a series of "essays" dealing with pressing questions.

> Must we always fixate on progress and "building the future," never stopping to consider why we are going through a crisis in the historical project of modernity?

The first sentence of *Embers of the Past* opens a fissure in the unquestioned dream of progress, development, and growth assumed as the necessary conditions to happiness, and the premise that being happy is more important than living in harmony and in plenitude. Modernity doesn't need to go back to the past except to glorify its own glories, because the idea of modernity is built on the *very modern idea* of its own past. But that past is regional, local; it is European, adopted and adapted by the United States—it is the past of perhaps 20 percent of the planet's population, not the past of the remaining 80 percent. And the magic trick of the idea of modernity is that it makes us believe that all pasts that are not European have to be superseded by the march of European modernity, sold as universal modernity. Sanjinés's argument dismantles that fairy tale, grounding itself in the local history of Bolivia and the Andes.

Questioning from the beginning is inherent to the "essay" as a genre.

Instead of the affirmation of the social sciences supported with statistics or that of the historian claiming the authority of the archives, Sanjinés returns to a powerful but derogated genre devalued by the myth of "scientificity" inherent to the idea and the fable of modernity. "The essays think": that is, she or he who writes thinks through the essays. It is not that the social scientists basing their work on statistics or the historians hiding behind the authority of *the* archive do not think. They simply think differently. They think professionally, that is, disciplinarily. The essayist thinks on his or her own, like the poet or the storyteller. While the poet thinks through the articulation of words, sounds, rhythm, and cadence, the storyteller through characters and situations, the essayist thinks through and across ideas, situations, statistics, literature, poetry, metaphors, and other rhetorical figures.

The essay has a prestigious genealogy. Michel de Montaigne embraced and conceptualized it in the process of delinking it from grammar, rhetoric, and the rules of writing history that, in the European tradition, were handed down from the European Middle Ages to the European Renaissance. It spread through the world, reaching into Spain and into Latin America. In the colonies the form-essay, particularly in the first half of the twentieth century, was the genre in which history, sociology, philosophy, political theory, political economy, aesthetics, and psychology coalesced. From Domingo Faustino Samiento's *Facundo: Civilización y barbarie* (1845) to Ezequiel Martinez Estrada's *Radiografía de la pampa* (1933) and Octavio Paz's *El laberinto de la soledad* (1955), the essay was and is an "undisciplinary" genre. Not every essay is decolonial, but Sanjinés makes the explicit connection between the essay and decolonial thinking.

A second important move made by Sanjinés is the parallel he builds between Latin American and Eastern European thinkers and intellectuals, such as the Rumanian Emil Cioran and the Hungarian Georg Lukàcs, to whom Sanjinés owes in part his own reconsideration of the form-essay. What distinguishes Sanjinés's argument from many great studies of the past, of Bolivia and the Andes, is the "saying" rather than the "said." Or, to be more explicit, it is the "said" through the form-essay that brings decolonial thinking to the foreground. Why? Because disciplinary thinking is entrenched and built into the very idea of modernity, from its Renaissance and theological-humanist versions (*les anciens et les modernes*) to its secular-humanist version (progress and the civilizing mission). In Latin America the social sciences "arrived" around 1960, together with the project of development and modernization launched by the United States. To be modern meant to be scientific, and the form-essay was relegated to the past, to tradition, superseded by the excellence and objective truth promised in the discourse that justified the social sciences.

The last memorable essays in Latin America were written before the 1960s and were replaced by the alleged "scientificity" of the social sciences. Sanjinés breaks away and delinks from that myth and retrieves the past, bringing it into the present through a discursive form that was relegated to the past. That is, delinking not only critiques the content (the enunciated) by the means of the social sciences, but shifts from disciplinary norms (the enunciation) toward a personal way of understanding and knowing, where sensing and reason go hand in hand. Jewish thinkers such as Theodor Adorno and Walter Benjamin, who, within Europe, struggled against the positivist and rationalist conceptions of history and the modern colonization of time (or, if you wish, the control of time within and by the colonial matrix of power), could be favorably compared, in Sanjinés's argument, with thinkers and intellectuals in European colonies. Sanjinés clarifies that it is not a question of adopting and adapting Adorno or Benjamin, for the priorities they had in Europe are not the same priorities that move thinkers in the colonies. They are parallel histories, so to speak, that in their own unfolding deny the privilege and denounce the dangers of a single story and a single time.

In contradistinction with Adorno, Benjamin, and Lukàcs, Sanjinés claims the form-essay for a global process of decoloniality, located in the singular time of Bolivia and the Andes: a particular entanglement of imperial modernity / coloniality. The response to this entanglement was, from its very inception in the sixteenth century, decolonial thinking and doing, as Guamán Poma de Ayala did in the Andes. Sanjinés sees in his essay a current option to advance processes of decolonization of knowledge and being: "I propose"—he writes in the introduction—"that the essay be considered an aesthetic transgression linked to decolonization. Having observed modernity 'from the outside,' I can vouch for the fact that Western historical time shatters when it meets the life of our peoples."

Sanjinés's argument does not, of course, "represent" all Bolivian citizens, scholars, or intellectuals. His argument intervenes in current debates in Bolivia. And although he is not addressing issues in Ecuador, his arguments resonate with similar issues in the neighboring country. The reason is simple: what is today Ecuador was the extreme North of the Incanate. Atahualpa was the Inca ruling in Quito located in Chinchaysuyu, while his brother Huascar was the Inca ruling in Cuzco (today

Peru), the center of the Incanate. What is today Bolivia, as I mentioned before, was the Collasuyu. This may sound like a digression, since these issues are not explicitly addressed in Sanjinés's argument. However, they are "embers of the past" very much alive in the memories, the theoretical and political thinking, of Aymara and Quechuas in Bolivia and Peru as well as among Quechuas in Ecuador.

Sanjinés addresses issues related to the memories of the Incanate in chapter 1, when he discusses José María Arguedas, and in chapter 2 when he takes on Benedict Anderson's concept of the nation as an imagined community. Anderson's work was celebrated in Latin America shortly after its publication because his narrative suggested that the emergence of a national consciousness and the formation of the nation-state preceded Europe's. It did not take long until less satisfied readers confronted Anderson's thesis. Sanjinés disregards the celebration of the modern myth of newness and who came first and focuses, instead, on why the *nation* became the *nation-state* and why it worked in Europe (and in the United States) but it was more problematic in the Spanish American colonies after independence. National consciousness may have emerged in the Spanish colonies after independence (which were not yet "Latin America"), but the state is no doubt a European institution that became the model for the Spanish American Creole elite in building their own dependent and colonial nation-state.

The emerging bourgeoisie that created the nation-state in Europe did not have to deal with the challenge of a diversity of indigenous and African populations facing the Creole elite of European descent, in the Americas from North to Central and South America. How do you fit them into the "state" if they belong to another "nation"? "Nation," it should be remembered, comes from the Latin *natio*, translated into English in the family of "birth and born." That is, "nation" is a community of birth and therefore an ethno-community. But it so happened that in the colonies the "nations" of Europeans, Indians, and Africans did not belong. The solution was either to subsume local ethnicities under the nation-state constructed by the Creole elite or to marginalize them from the nation-state.

The history and destiny of each nation-state in the Americas vary according to local history. In the Andes, particularly in Bolivia and Ecuador, their local history brought the principle of "plurinational state" into their respective constitutions. The idea of a "plurinational state," Sanjinés argues, radically questions the nation as an "imagined community." In Europe, the "imagined community" was possible because of the homogeneous national composition of each state. Today, increasing immigration suggests that at some time in the future the idea of plurinational states could also reach Europe. In many of the colonies, and certainly in Bolivia and Ecuador, the plurinationality of each state was an unavoidable consequence of postcolonial nation building. Furthermore, by bringing this issue to the foreground, Sanjinés unveils another weakness of Anderson's analysis: the need to uncouple nation from state. Nations are ethno-class communities; states are legal and administrative machines. After the concept of a plurinational state was introduced in the Andes, the original European nation-state should be properly called a "mono national state."

Questioning the modern state that served well the purposes of the emerging European bourgeoisie goes hand in hand with calling into question the secularization and disenchantment of society. It worked well in Europe because the institutionalization of Christianity had already done a good job in disenchanting the world. The formation of the secular state that marginalized the Christian church paved the way to the triumphal promotion of secular reason and reasoning, together with its civilizing mission and with the idea of progress. However, when the secular nation-state was exported to the rest of the globe, to South America and the Spanish, French, British, and Dutch Caribbean colonies, the non-European enchanted world met with suspicion the disenchanted idea embedded in the secular state. The Andes is a region where the enchanted world never receded and now, more than ever, is gaining ground. Ideas such as the right of Pachamama, the right to live in harmony (some would say "to live well"), and the plurinational state are all ideas no longer coming from the European legacy but from legacies of the great Andean civilizations.

Sanjinés devotes the last chapters to exploring in detail both the processes of disenchantment in the formation of the colonial states (the triumphal rhetoric of modernity and the repressive logic of coloniality) and the processes of re-enchantment (decolonization) that are under way in Andean countries nowadays. In this regard, and following the thoughts of Walter Benjamin and Charles Sanders Peirce, Sanjinés shows in chapter 3 how within Europe and the United States, the disenchantment of the world encountered its radical critics. His analysis follows, although indirectly, the philosophical and epistemological battle fought by the Argentinian philosopher Rodolfo Kusch between 1960 and 1979. Kusch's immersion in the Aymara world, his critique of development and what he called "el patio de los objetos," refers to a world in which the multiplication of objects repressed spirituality while at the same time showed that the enchanted world never vanished from the Aymara consciousness.

In chapter 4 Sanjinés explores one of the most enduring myths of modernity: the assumption that the modern structure of government, the nation-state, is of global currency and the guarantee of democratic processes. Sanjinés begins his discussion with two basic European ideas of the nation: the civic and the ethnic. The civic brings forward the idea of the state; the ethnic the idea of the nation (from Latin *natio*, communities of birth). The confusion of nation with state allowed the European ethnoclass, the bourgeoisie, to build states of homogeneous nations by disavowing and hiding national minorities. In the histories of European colonies, however, the myth that states were configured by homogeneous nations did not work. In Latin America, the foundation of modern / colonial states in the nineteenth century was founded in an oxymoron: that the homogeneity of the nation was composed of "mestizos / as": mixed in blood but of European mentality. "First nations" fall outside or at the margin of the "mestizo" state. After almost two centuries of tense relations between colonial legacies—the nation and the state—the recent Constitution of Bolivia dealt with the issue by stating that Bolivia is indeed a "plurinational" state. This was indeed a revolutionary constitutional change. However, constitutions are not necessarily followed *ad pedem litterae* by their governments. And indeed, Sanjinés closes the chapter reflecting on the march of the TIPNIS, in which "first nations" were legally enacting the constitution that the state was violating when they repressed the march and attempted to implement economic developmental decisions contrary to the constitution and to the rights of first nations to participate in the decisions of the state. The book thus closes bringing forward the force and visibility of a major actor in global political transformation: the emerging global political society of which Bolivia has been at the forefront. By connecting Colombian sociologist Orlando Fals Borda's conceptualization of porous, "amphibian" societies, with Bolivian sociologist René Zavaleta Mercado's notion of the form-multitude, Sanjinés demonstrates that specific social movements such as the March for Territory and Dignity, in 2000, and the present March in Defense of TIPNIS, are not only fighting for the rights of Amazonian first peoples, as well as for those of nature, but also marching toward a radical transformation of governmentality, not only showing that the nation-state has run its course, but that the plurinational state is also in need of radical mutations.

The force of the political society is to reinvest the "embers of the past" into the present in search of more humane global futures no longer regulated by the state in complicity with foreign or nationalized corporations, striving for one only global future sustained by the myth of development created by Western modernity.

III

Sanjinés's work and this book in particular carries the traces of his active participation in important politically oriented research collective projects. He was closely associated with the formation of the Latin American Subaltern Studies project, collaborating with Ileana Rodríguez, John Beverley, and José Rabasa. Later he joined the Modernity / Coloniality / Decoloniality project. The first was a follow-up to the groundbreaking work of the well-known South Asian Subaltern Studies Group. This project was initiated by Spanish American scholars based in the United States (Ileana Rodríguez, José Rabasa, and Javier Sanjinés himself, among others) and U.S. Latinamericanists (such as John Beverley). The second was initiated by Spanish American scholars based in the South, in Peru, México, and Venezuela (Aníbal Quijano, Enrique Dussel, and Edgardo Lander) and South American scholars based in the United States (Arturo Escobar, Fernando Coronil, and Walter D. Mignolo), The second project, based in South America, unfolded after the introduction of two key concepts in political, intellectual, and scholarly debate in the subcontinent: "coloniality," introduced by Aníbal Quijano, and "transmodernity," introduced by Enrique Dussel. Sanjinés blends these two theoretical strands. The "Otherwise" in the name of the book series "Latin America Otherwise" was intended to signal a shift in the geography of reasoning that is by now globally irreversible. *Embers of the Past* makes a significant contribution to this book series, which has grown and consolidated through the years.

Walter D. Mignolo
Durham, May 2013

Introduction

MODERNITY IN THE BALANCE, THE "TRANSGRESSIVE" ESSAY, AND DECOLONIZATION

Must we always fixate on progress and "building the future," never stopping to consider why we are going through a crisis in the historical project of modernity? Aren't we facing a historical impasse because we have no map to tell us which routes to the future might work? Aren't "peripheral" societies—the ones that the dominant systems of knowledge have forgotten or left in the dust—precisely the societies that now reject, sometimes violently, the moral and philosophical systems that modernity thought were universal? Doubt seems to have corroded and dissolved every certainty that once shored up our lives and conveniently blinded us so we could go on living in a world that had lost its aim, its sure direction.

What can we do in the face of such pervasive doubt? Dissociating ourselves from humanity would mean forgetting that we are never so human as when we regret it. What holds us in doubt now is not so much the death of the old era as the birth of a new one, an event we can no longer look forward to with the same confidence we had when we waited for modernity to finally arrive. For vast groups who have found their voice in the key of voicelessness itself, consciousness has arrived uninvited, mired in virtual reality, rejoicing in the empty plenitude of a self, an identity that must negotiate the thorny pathways that will lead it to delve into a "ruinous" past, into a "self" that predates the modern self. There, in that space —better yet, in that space-time—will be what E. M. Cioran called "the light of pure anteriority" (Cioran 1970: 48). Unable to take refuge in animal howling or mineral senselessness, we humans find ourselves forced to come up with a new project inspired more by the past and by a continuing, constantly expanding present than by a perfectible future. Its "rhythm" demands a new state, a new disposition of the soul, not conditioned exclusively by the philosophical assumptions of Western temporality, particularly those that govern the modern philosophy of history. Today, social dynamics in our countries has destroyed the prestige of many of our formerly cherished concepts and has forced us to reconsider the space-time structure of our thinking. It isn't that we should be indifferent bystanders, just watching the problematic historical time that it has been our lot to live through. Quite the contrary: we must be observers free of all illusion, critics of the utopian goal of modernity. Since we can no longer refrain from questioning it, I think it useful to cover some controversial aspects of this goal that we now find dubious.

1. MODERNITY IN THE BALANCE

Seen from the European perspective, from the point of view of supposedly universal thought, modernity—the historical project that began in the Renaissance with the "discovery" of America—acquired its philosophical foundations with seventeenth-century Rationalism and the eighteenth-century Enlightenment.

If we stick to dictionary definitions and call anything referring to Greco-Roman antiquity "classical," it is clear that the seventeenth century, which is taken to be foundational for modern culture and modern civilization, was France's classical century, given that, while its great writers wanted to continue imitating the Greeks and Romans, its scientists, followers of Galileo, made progress the basis for Western culture and civilization. It was precisely the notion of change, of progress, that influenced science so profoundly. Thus, the modernity of Descartes was based on the imposition of a mathematical model founded on the principle that only logic, with its forms and categories, was capable of deciphering the world. Thanks to this model, long chains of reasoning arose that made it possible to have, on the one hand, deductive philosophy, and, on the other, observations of measurements on which an inductive science could be built. Thus, the application of the Cartesian method had a revolutionary impact on progress and on change.

But could the dominated, the subjugated, peacefully accept a rectilinear modernity that was imposed on them from the outside, that defined them without caring about the particularities of their own being? Complicated by intellectuals from the former colonies of Spain, Portugal, and France, the victorious gaze of modernity could not be taken into account unless it was associated with "coloniality," that is, with its complementary concept, with the historical-structural violence that Walter Mignolo has called, after Frantz Fanon, the "colonial wound" (Mignolo 2005: 5–8), which even today constitutes modernity's dark side. Well, this "wound," which introduces doubt into the cocksure course of modernity, is nothing but the physical and psychological consequence of racism, of the hegemonic discourse that denied and still denies the humanity of the dispossessed, that assumes it alone can encompass everything and can classify everyone else's stage of evolution and of knowledge.

If modernity is the name of the historical process by which imperial Europe began to build its worldwide hegemony, its mantle of knowledge also covers "coloniality," a set of events that, as I have said, has oppressed vast human groups. Coloniality thus explains the logic that has imposed control, exploitation, and domination on the rest of humankind and that masks this subjugation with the language of salvation, of progress, of modernization. If "colonialism" refers to a specific period of imperial domination, "coloniality" is the logical structure of domination that colonialism has imposed since America was "discovered." Coloniality explains the logic of economic, political, and social domination of the whole world, above and beyond the concrete fact that in the past the colonizing country may have been Spain, Britain, or more recently the United States. Therefore, dressed up in "civilization" and "progress," the rhetoric of modernity created an imaginary, a conceptual coherence that derives from the abstract principles of equality and fraternity, as fashioned in the French Revolution. This imaginary generally corresponded to the political, economic, and social configuration from which the three great ideologies of the modern world emerged: conservatism, liberalism, and socialism.

From the viewpoint of the triumphal march of modernity, these three great ideologies seem to express the development of reality well. However, what all three leave out—willfully, it must be said—is any genuine expression of the injustices suffered by the dominated. We therefore think that the colonial experience can only be articulated from the "colonial wound," not from the sensitivities of the imperial victors. Triumphant modernity and its opposite, "modernity / coloniality," are perspectives organized from two different paradigms that intertwine in the colonial matrix of power[1] and that are articulated under structurally heterogeneous histories of language and knowledge; later in the book we call this, after Ernst Bloch, "the contemporaneity of the non-contemporaneous" (Bloch 1991 [1935]: 106). In this way, the paradigm of the "dispossessed," those whom Fanon and Sartre termed "the wretched of the earth," came about due to the diversity of the noncoeval, structurally heterogeneous histories of those who had to live under the burden of imperial languages and the civilizing process imposed by the lineal and future-directed view of History. This colonial history is what obliges us to distinguish between the colonizer's discourse and the discourse of national resistance. So placing yourself within the rhetoric of the French *mission civilisatrice* isn't the same as doing so from the point of view of *négritude* or Indian identity. When we enunciate from the viewpoint of coloniality, we do so from a different consciousness, an alternative consciousness, made invisible by the dominant thought of the West, which Frantz Fanon relates to C. L. R. James, W. E. B. Du Bois, Walter Rodney, Aimé Césaire, and José Carlos Mariátegui. All of these writers, unquestionably metropolitan in their thinking, are "ex-centrics," because their writings purvey a different consciousness, distant from and profoundly critical of the prevailing consciousness in Europe and the United States.

History, a field created in the eighteenth century by the rise of the analytic method itself, remains a privilege of modernity, which subordinate peoples can also have if they adapt to the perspective imposed by European knowledge. This perspective governs life, economy, subjectivity, family, and religion in nations that have been subjugated and modeled on the organizing principles of the dominant nations.

From the viewpoint of the dominated, History is an institution that legitimates the silence of other histories; that obscures the testimony of the dispossessed. Thus, the Hegelian philosophy of History is the best example of how the West made any other possible view of the world unrealizable. The West held on to the categories of thought by which the rest of the world could be described, interpreted, and classified. Hegel's "Occidentalism" was located, geohistorically and geopolitically, in the heart of modernity.

Now, the so-called colonial matrix of power—of which the Hegelian philosophy of History is a fundamental element—could be observed critically only if a new paradigm were constructed that could understand the difference of the dispossessed, that is, the "colonial difference." As Mignolo has rightly observed (2000), this is a remarkably important geopolitical turn within knowledge itself. Thanks to it, we now realize that only when we abandon the natural belief that History is a chronological succession of events, ordered linearly (past, present, future) in pursuit of the progressive development of humanity, can we comprehend that History is actually interwoven with coloniality in a spatial distribution of nodules that fill a "structural" space, not merely a time line. It is even more important to become aware that every historical milestone, in addition to having a structure and not a linear location, is also profoundly heterogeneous. Therefore, if we bear in mind that we are facing not the "end of history," as Francis Fukuyama prematurely declared, but merely the demise of the Hegelian concept of History, we can also comprehend the spatial-temporal intricacies that make up our modernity, fraught with coloniality.

"Historical-structural complexity" removes us from Hegelian-style secular narratives. Instead of accepting history as a linear succession of events, I speak of "the contemporaneity of the non-contemporaneous" in our peoples because history, viewed from a local vantage point, far from Western macronarratives, obliges us to see that social space is full of multiple and contrasting perspectives and historical processes. Thus we can look at history as a set of historical-structural heterogeneities that must be interpreted using both the rhetoric of modernity (progress, happiness, wealth) and the logic that constitutes coloniality (backwardness, death, poverty). Instead of observing modernity from the historical process that brings happiness, historical-structural heterogeneity springs from the fact that the "utopian dreams" of modernity were achieved at an enormous human cost that our dependent societies have suffered, and that they will continue to suffer so long as the annoying rhetoric of modernity maintains its hegemony. Dating from the seventeenth century, this rhetoric is based on the idea that history is a linear process, with progress as the driving force propelling it into the future.

Given that the rectilinear time organized in the West according to abstract universals conflicts with the historical-structural reality of the former colonies, this conflict shows that the differences between our peoples and the Europeans are not merely spatial; they are also temporal. As I argue in this book, Euclides da Cunha, the peerless Brazilian writer of the early twentieth century, observed this historical-structural impasse with particular keenness. And observing it led the author of *Os sertões* (1902) to doubt the rectilinear meaning of history. It also caused him to suggest the need for our peoples, who lacked their own histories, to reactivate their memories (of slavery, oppression, racism, marginalization) and to project the embers of the past onto the present. Today we are experiencing a situation already captured by da Cunha's essay: that the philosophy of history has been turned upside down by the growing organization of "societies on the move" (Zibechi 2006). Doubts have also been planted by the increasing self-analysis undertaken by the peoples of the Caribbean and South America—particularly those in the Andean and Amazonian regions—who have been making a troublesome and uncertain "leftward turn."

2. THE "LEFTWARD TURN" IN OUR SOCIETIES

A keen and level-headed critic of the changing faces of modernity and historical time, the Venezuelan anthropologist Fernando Coronil, argued in a recent essay (2011b) that, after a euphoric embrace of neoliberalism, more than 300 million Latin Americans are now ruled by governments that promote nationalist ideologies associated with socialist principles. What should we infer from this surprising leftward turn? How should we conceptualize it in social and cultural terms? What image of the future has guided it? Coronil is careful to point out that, before we ask whether or not the Left has a future, the work of theory is to clarify what notion of the future has led to such a turn. In other words, he is guided by the same interest that orients my work here: to illuminate the future that the Left is imagining right now, thus constructing what Coronil calls the "imaginary future of the present" (2011b: 232). Regardless of the different and contradictory forms to which this leftward turn is giving rise, then, the question is to investigate how the course of history has been reoriented over the past three or four decades.

As we know, the tremor that shook History (once again with a capital H) was less turbulent in some countries and regions of Latin America than in others. The leftward turn in the Southern Cone countries (Argentina, Uruguay, Chile) was basically pragmatic and reformist, eschewing the revolutionary radicalism that marked the processes that took place in Venezuela, Ecuador, and especially Bolivia. With actions on the ground, the Andean and Amazonian regions are shifting beyond the homogenizing idea of a single, universal modernity. We might speak of a shift to a "postliberal stage," if by "postliberal" we understand, to put it succinctly, the decentering of capitalism on the economic plane, of liberalism on the political plane, and of the nation-state as the matrix that defines social organization. This doesn't mean that capitalism, liberalism, and the nation-state have ceased to exist; it simply means that the discursive and social centrality of these "universal" concepts has been significantly supplanted,[2] so that a wide range of social experiences are being considered as possible alternatives, thus constituting an unknown, and a problematic unknown at that, which nonetheless has thrown modernity into question.

There can be no doubt that Latin America has reached an uncertain historical crossroads. Here we see the growth and unfolding of critical theories at least as complex as those that dominated modernity, and richer in every aspect in both advantages and dangers, which point to different trajectories, from Marxist political economy and poststructuralism to what is now called "border thinking and decolonization thinking,"[3] of particular importance in Bolivia.

Looming on the horizon, which is no longer the exclusive property of a uniform modernity and its expectations, we can see new theoretical intertwinings, giving rise to multiple histories and futures, to diverse political and cultural projects, all converging on the same space or territory. So the present conjuncture can be defined based on two processes: the crisis of the neoliberal project of the past three decades, and the crisis of the project that has been unfolding since Conquest and colonization, which brought modernity to our America.

In the Bolivian case, the neoliberal reformers who initiated the free-market turn in 1985 had privatized state industries, deregulated production, increased labor flexibility, and encouraged foreign investment in natural resource extraction and exportation. As Bret Gustafson and Nicole Fabricant have argued recently (2011), neoliberals also embraced the rhetoric of "interculturalism," a gesture that offered some recognition to indigenous peoples. Yet interculturalism, among other well-meaning reforms, did not ameliorate the dislocation of rural people into urban peripheries and informal economies. Indeed, the economic restructuring of the 1980s led to the relocation of both the ex-miners from highland communities and small-scale subsistence farmers moving from the Amazonian lowlands to the urban peripheral spaces. Migrants to cities like El Alto, one of the highest major cities in the world, above the city of La Paz, found jobs in the expanding informal economy as domestic servants and street vendors, and frequently moved in search of employment. The social and economic fragmentation and intensified poverty produced by the reterritorialization of miners and peasants had much to do with the rise of the powerful social movements that ended up debunking the neoliberal state.

The neoliberal disruption and its attendant reforms, most crucially municipal decentralization or "Popular Participation" (1994), led to the emergence of multiple new types of groups that mobilized around renewed concerns about territory and space. These territorially based organizations, such as the Federation of Neighborhood Councils (FEJUVE) in El Alto; the coca-grower movement in Cochabamba, where Evo Morales acquired power as a trade union leader; and the Landless Peasant Movement (MST) in Santa Cruz all multiplied and coexisted with new municipal indigenous organizations like the National Council of Ayllus and Markas of Qullasuyu (CONAMAQ), the new peasant Confederation from the Andean altiplano. In this sense, hybrid spaces and dispossessed peoples became forums in which distinct ethnic and cultural groups forged new political identities around territorializing logics and agendas. Urban satellite cities like El Alto now house informal workers, ex-miners, mestizos, and indigenous Aymara. Against liberal theorists of *mestizaje*, I have argued before (2004) and continue arguing that these social changes are not representative of some modernizing rupture with indigeneities rooted in the past, but, to the contrary, are the result of the crisis of both the neoliberal project and of the racial project of domination that has persisted since Conquest and colonization.

The Bolivian case is revealing with regard to this double crisis, between "productivist nationalism and indigenous decolonization," as Gustafson and Fabricant have described it (2011: 17). What is going on in Bolivia today is a dogged fight between differing political and cultural projects—a fight between two logics at loggerheads with one another, the results of which are manifested here in the tension between the projects put forward by indigenous movements and those developed by the state itself. I call this "tension" because the former are decidedly at a "postliberal" stage, while the state proposes an alternative modernization project that does not entail the wholesale transformation of liberal society (Escobar 2009). Let me elaborate on this tension.

With the demise of neoliberalism in 2005, the leftward turn was put forward by the vice president of the Plurinational State himself, Álvaro García Linera, who stated that the current MAS (Movimiento al Socialismo) administration of Evo Morales should achieve a high level of state control over the production of wealth and the distribution of the surplus. Moving beyond the "structural adjustments" of neoliberalism, and convinced that the country should enter a new stage of postcapitalist development, the vice president was arguing for a pluralist process that would articulate the modernization of three key economic sectors: industry, small urban craft businesses, and the indigenous/peasant rural sector. By speaking of the need for building a "satisfactory modernity" (2007), García Linera advocates an alternative form of modernity characterized by hybrid practices that decenter modernity via decolonizing projects such as "pluriversality" and "interculturality." For this leftward turn, "postliberalism" signifies a space/time in which social life isn't completely dominated by either the economy or individualist instrumental rationality, a pair of aspects fundamental to liberal modernity as seen from the Western perspective.

Though still modernizing and developmentalist, this leftward turn conceives of "postcapitalism" as an economic process that melds the hybrid practices of capitalism, alternative capitalism, and indigenous communalism.[4] In this way, liberal capitalism has ceased to be the hegemonic form of modernization, because it no longer occupies the field of the economy entirely on its own but, rather, has to share it with alternative economic systems. In other words, the prefix "post-" means, for this alternative modernity, the decentering that I have already discussed above: the economy is not "essentially" or "naturally" capitalist, nor are societies "naturally" liberal, and the state is no longer the only way in which social power can be instituted. These facts amplify the function of movements that emerge from the heart of civil society.

In sum, "postliberalism," "postcapitalism," and "poststatism," taken all together, constitute alternative forms that clash with the projects of modernity as thought from Western liberalism. These new movements support the hybrid practices of alternative modernity that best express this leftward turn (Escobar 2010).

But the leftward turn of productivist nationalism that Bolivia is undergoing is being resisted and questioned by a more radical proposal: the decolonial communal forms of exercising politics. For this "communalism," alternative modernization still maintains a teleological view of reality that is preserved within the confines of Eurocentrism and that reactualizes, in its expectation of a promising future, developmentalist imaginaries. Therefore this alternative modernization is being questioned by certain communal ways of practicing politics, which, from their radical decolonial enunciation, suggest the possibility of building forms of political and social organization that reject capitalism and the state itself. This is a radical philosophy that, starting from a different place of enunciation and from a different epistemology, renews the dynamics of certain popular movements in the present. Let me lay them out here briefly.

Popular uprisings in Bolivia during the first five years of the twenty-first century were characterized by a heavy decolonizing indigenous presence. The "water war" in Cochabamba in 2000 and the nationwide "natural gas war" of 2003 are the two best-known moments in this wave of uprisings, which, by rejecting the liberal system founded on representative democracy, introduced embers of past indigenous worlds into the present. This way of thinking has been reinforced since 2003 by the growth, not only demographic but also theoretical, of the great working-class urban concentration of El Alto, a city of nearly a million people that took in huge numbers of indigenous people displaced from mining and agricultural enclaves by the neoliberal reforms of the late 1980s. It was precisely in this urban conglomeration that a new kind of politics made its appearance, with significant influences from indigenous communal practices. This popular-communal and national-popular world is based on an epistemological position that, instead of rebuilding the social order from the heights of the state, as is now occurring with the alternative modernizing project of MAS, opts for a popular-indigenous project that views reality beyond the limits of the state. From this perspective, states "do not seem to be the appropriate tools for creating emancipatory social relations" (Zibechi 2006: 25). Another result of this is that the popular projects generated by indigenous-style poststate postliberalism go well beyond the kind of modernization centered on the power of the state: they express the actions of common people mobilized as a "multitude," as "a communitarian social machine that breaks up the power of the state" (Zibechi 2006: 161; see also Rabasa 2010: 138–147).

The communal decolonial practices that took place in Bolivia from 2000 to 2005 included the struggle for municipal autonomy for the city of El Alto, indigenous uprisings in rural communities, and uprisings of coca farmers and indigenous groups in the eastern half of the country. In my opinion, all of this is also related to the epistemological changes and the evolving view of life that have caused the state, as a form, to shatter when confronted with everyday activities, with the "here" and the "now" of a society on the move. Likewise, it is not surprising that the state has begun to recede in the face of new and unprecedented forms of self-government, which now include constituent assemblies, horizontal organizations, and carrying out civic tasks and duties by rotation.

So how should a sociocultural process as complex as the one I have been describing be approached? Should this process be examined exclusively from the theoretical space opened up by the social sciences? Wouldn't it be appropriate to involve other forms of knowledge as well, such as the aesthetic forms and concrete experiences of the "lifeworlds" (*Lebenswelten*) opened up by historical agents that are developing in daily life itself?[5] It seems to me that questions about aesthetic forms, about the place from which this complex reality should be considered, and about the temporal conditioning that guides our thought, are important elements that this investigation must incorporate into our analysis of reality.

3. THE CONFLICT OVER TIME AND THE "DECOLONIAL TURN"

Could a society as diverse and regionally complex as Bolivia—with its indigenous and nonindigenous populations, its individual and collective subjects, living their lives according to both liberal and communal logics —possibly respond to a single, unified historical time? It seems to me that research on time must be particularly sensitive to the fact that today we are living through a conflict that has erupted between liberal modernity on the one hand, and the communal systems and "alternative modernities" promoted by the state on the other. The conflict between such dissimilar spatial-temporal logics has given rise to a range of contrasts: between neoliberal developmentalist models that are firmly rooted in modernity, and anti-neoliberal political movements that have adopted a hybrid modernizing outlook; between the nation-state as conceived under the republic that has been built over the past two centuries, and our current Plurinational State; between the national *criollo-mestizo* culture and interculturality; between capitalist development and the socialism that is being constructed today and is still hard to define; between the leftward turn and the more radical decolonial turn.

These are sharp contrasts; the novelty of the two different turns is disconcerting. The background theme, however, is the crisis of modernity. This is a crisis of discourses, practices, structures, and institutions that are closely related to the growth of the social sciences and that have dominated the fields of knowledge over the past two hundred years, as modernity has clung to the cultural and ontological assumptions of the dominant European societies. In this way, modernity brought about a convergence between philosophy, biology, and the construction of the social sciences. This produced a modern ontology that established a separation between nature and culture; the racist supremacy of some human beings over others; the notion that the autonomous individual forges his own existence with no help from the community; the belief that for knowledge to be valid it must be objective, rational, and scientific; and the certainty that the cultural construction of the economy is an independent social practice, self-regulated by the invisible hand of the market, unrelated to social relationships (Escobar 2009).

The fact that the dominant form of imperial modernity has not seduced all European thinkers has been crucially important to my research. A very important tradition of decentered, "ex-centric" thinking exists in Europe, devoted to revealing the downfall of the fictions that we have been living up to now. This is a tradition of heterodox thought, stripped of illusions, dissenting from the dominant systems, which harasses people of good conscience and confronts them with the necessity of accepting the fall of a civilization whose universal validity is being questioned. I see a possibility of engaging a dialogue between this thought, disenchanted with modernity and its idea of progress, and the decolonizing projects we find in Latin America, particularly those of indigenous intellectuals who are thinking from their own needs. I conceive of decolonization as a local effort that has emerged from the struggle against colonial domination but cannot and should not disregard the tremendous critical contribution from Europe that questions Eurocentrism and the historical time that constitutes it. I think of José Carlos Mariátegui, an important early twentieth-century Peruvian essayist, as a revelatory and mature example of how to think from Latin America, how to imagine it beyond Western contributions in the various fields of knowledge and life, incorporating it into an epistemological and political project that, like Mariátegui's, will affirm the difference of those peoples who have been subjected to colonial domination for so long.[6] When it creates its own genealogy and its own history, decolonization cannot abandon those critical ex-centric thinkers who wrote in Europe and whose works are cited throughout this book.

I am speaking, then, of the possible formulation of "a paradigm other,"[7] to be articulated while bearing in mind not only the diversity of colonial histories that are now establishing the "South-South dialogue" (Latin America, Africa, Asia), but also the outstanding "place of enunciation" that is Southern and Eastern Europe, which has been undervalued as much by the geopolitics of knowledge as by the philosophy of history derived from Hegel's thought, which promotes progress and development (Mignolo 2000: 164). This decentered Europe occupies an important place in my research, particularly the thinking of those Europeans who question historicism and who, as we will see, have reclaimed an old mission of the essay: to doubt, to meditate, to attain the wise old aspiration of living with dignity, in accordance with nature.

For essayists as diverse, heterodox, and subversive as the Rumanian philosopher E. M. Cioran or the German Jewish intellectual Walter Benjamin (1968 [1940]), whose critical reading of the philosophy of history is fundamental to my work, history is nothing but "an imbalance, a swift, intense dislocation of time itself, a rush towards a future where nothing ever *becomes* again" (Cioran 1983: 33). In his ruthless attack on historical time, Cioran conceives of it as a time so taut that it is hard to see how it won't shatter when it comes into contact with concrete reality. If people make history, history, a veritable shredder of human beings, unmakes people. Modernity thought it had subjugated history, but we now know that it has escaped and bloomed, as Cioran puts it, "into the insoluble and the intolerable: a lunatic epic, whose conclusion implies no notion of finality" (1983: 37). With the "future" eliminated, what goal can now be assigned to historical time? Discredited, historical time has turned into a nightmare, dropping as many capital letters as the illusions we have known (who would be so naive today as to write "progress" with a capital *P*?).

Is this view too pessimistic? Perhaps, given that it runs a risk of being taken as an apology for irrationality. In the same way that we affirm our need to explore our identity by regressing to an earlier self than the one modernity has constructed for us, we also postulate the existence of "an other" time within historical time—what Bloch referred to as "persistence of 'then' within 'now'"—and we argue that, by introducing the past into the present, this "other time" is incapable of projecting itself "forward," unable to escape into the future, the hereafter.[8] Its disappearance is related to the fact that it is impossible to measure social life with the yardstick of the future; the criterion we should follow is that social life belongs to the present because it is always in construction, while the future plays a lesser role.

As I have just argued, the crisis of modernity and its historical time also imply that economy is not essentially or naturally capitalist, that societies do not have to be governed exclusively by liberalism, and that the state is not the only way to institute social power. In short, the crisis of teleological, linear, and progressive historical time is linked to the decentering of capitalism, of liberalism, and of the state, the last of which has traditionally been taken as the matrix of social organization. The discursive centrality of all these categories formed by modernity has been seriously contested.

In his observation on future utopias, Coronil correctly notes a theme that I will cover later as a fundamental element in my own interpretation of the contemporary essay: the crisis of historical time and uncertainty about the shape of the future clash with the contents of political activism in the present (2011b). Given that political activism has no given a priori form, being mutable in nature, the heterogeneity of Latin America and of the Andean region in particular oblige us to think about reality from different conceptions of history and from a variety of cosmogonies. We must face the fact that our nations contain many nations, that a new diversity of internal communities must give rise to multiple views of the world. Thus, the appearance of "societies on the move" (Zibechi 2006) has placed in the public arena a wide range of social actors and times that overlap each other and give rise to diverse concepts of life.

Coronil also observes that the crisis of capitalism, of liberalism, and of the state form will not necessarily lead to a redemptive future that lies "beyond" the concepts pointed out here. For this reason, Coronil argues, "utopian dreams" are adopting new forms, related to the crossing of two trends of thought: one is the transformational politics of the "here and now"; the other is our lack of certainty about the future (2011b: 234). Both tendencies are staking out the tense social panorama in which we act, and are creating the situation that Coronil defines as a "crisis 'of' the present and 'about' the future" (2011b: 235). This crisis leads us to wonder whether the future is the positive "horizon of expectation" envisioned by the German historian Reinhart Koselleck (1985), or whether it is instead an uncertain, dubious construct, not expanding but shrinking. Is the future the visionary and perfectible event imagined by liberalism? Or won't this event be, rather, a stage of deterioration, social anomie, and depression?

The seed of doubt planted here about the future is not only the result of the crisis of liberalism and its free-trade practices; it is also linked to the deterioration and disparagement of socialism and its collapse at the end of the twentieth century, a fact that gave rise to the widely trumpeted victory of capitalism and to the so-called "end of history."

The effects of the crises of capitalism and socialism are quite revealing: today we are witnessing a growing polarization in our societies as well as growing global inequality, the ecological destruction of the planet, the mass exclusion of vast social sectors and human groups that have never had access to development, the predominance of financial speculation over production, and exacerbated consumerism and individualism. How can we be optimistic about the future when the outlook is so unsettling?

Though the pernicious effects of the crisis of modernity occurred first in the nations of the South, unleashing protests against the "structural adjustments" imposed by neoliberal regimes, the limitations of the capitalist system became visible worldwide only when they affected the heart of Empire, in 2008. Today it is clear that we are not witnessing the failure of financial institutions in poor nations that have proved incapable of reaping the benefits of a globalized marketplace, but the deep crisis of a whole financial system that has put its failures and limitations on display.

So, then, the political changes produced by the crisis in the capitalist system, and in particular the controversial leftward turn that Coronil mentions in his essay, have a clear result: history has not ended; on the contrary, it has returned with unprecedented strength. But how should we think of it now? What kind of history governs us? What future inspires it? Is it possible to imagine aesthetic forms that can interpret this new reality?

4. THE ESSAY AS A TRANSGRESSIVE PROPOSITION

My aim in this section is to probe the category and even the status of the "foundational essays" that oriented the construction of the nation-state in the century after independence, comparing them and questioning them with my version of what the essay could be as a transgressive genre confronting the current rationalizing state of modernization. My version of the essay—a very subjective one, undoubtedly, and one I find useful for introducing the four essays that make up this book—is tied to the critical processes of the historical time that gives the essay its subversive, transgressive function, very much as recent ex-centric thinkers conceptualized it in the past, including the Palestinian critic Edward Said and the German philosopher Theodor W. Adorno, whose critical theory of society abandons the historical, rectilinear time of modernity.

I think it is necessary to clarify the place of the essay in relation to other literary genres, especially the novel. There can be no doubt that the transgressive role I have given to the essay is also characteristic of essay-novels such as *El zorro de arriba y el zorro de abajo* (translated as *The Fox from Up Above and the Fox from Down Below*) by the Peruvian writer José María Arguedas, which I briefly analyze in chapter 1. In this novel, as in others by Arguedas, we are clearly observing a writer of dialogistic orality, who, by interweaving Spanish with Quechua, has created one of the most accomplished examples of transculturation in literature.

Without scorning or underestimating the ability of any genre to subvert reality, I emphasize the role of the essay because I find in it a particularly keen capacity to think in fragments and against the grain of the historical time set up by the totalizing linearity of modernity.[9] The essay, a literary practice known for brevity, interests me because it is a genre that introduces doubt into its aesthetic form, refusing to situate itself as the beginning or end of the reality it describes and studies. For Adorno, whose critical thinking has helped me conceive of the essay as subversive, it was neither science nor art but an all-out effort on the part of youthful will to set fire to any totalizing scientific possibility. Luck and play are thus the essential characteristics of the essay, which, unlike the epic, has no utopian origin. The essay begins and ends with what it means to discuss or analyze; it says just enough, then stops when it is done with what it meant to say, unconcerned with whether it has exhausted or resolved its topic. In the process, the essay leaves questions unanswered.

The essay, then, is provisional in character, and doubt is its fundamental characteristic. In Latin America, however, there is a close relationship between the essay and the rationalist nature of the nation-building project, with its Enlightenment roots. This close relationship between "literary Americanism" and the European Enlightenment would complicate any possible connection between the essay and the aesthetic representation of decolonization. Aware of this situation, I still think it is worth looking into the relationship between the loss of the unity, the homogeneity, the perfectibility of the historical project of modernity, and my approach to the nature of the essay as an appropriate transgression for uncertain times such as these, with the crisis now developing about the theme of decolonization.

The close relationship between the essay and nation building in Latin America is beyond question. "Literary Americanism," the trend behind the most important essays of "our América," as José Martí called it (I will take a more detailed look at this "Americanism" in chapter 2), followed the historicist tradition that intellectuals such as Andrés Bello and Domingo Faustino Sarmiento began in the mid-nineteenth century. A project that gave expression to free-trade economics and political liberalism, this "Americanism" tightly linked local culture with Western culture. In attempting to construct their vision of a new American cosmos, the "men of letters" of that historical moment integrated local nature and human groups into the social program fashioned by the nascent liberal bourgeoisie, and subjugated them to it. By connecting the essay with another specific narrative genre, the epic of the conquest of the national hinterlands, "literary Americanism" functioned as an ideological practice of the booming commercial bourgeoisie, turning their practice into a national enterprise. In this sense, essays from the nineteenth century, and from the early decades of the twentieth had little or nothing to do with any sort of decolonizing emancipation; instead, they reinforced the new nations' "colonizing postcolonial" nature, fashioned from the perspective of European historicism, which, under its view of social perfectibility and of confidence in the future, was incapable of harboring the doubts and uncertainties that arose from the unrestricted application of foreign theories to profoundly different and contrasting local realities. Disseminated by the lettered culture of the era, these essays were the result of efforts by intellectuals who, in Edward Said's happy observation about the intellectual face of all colonizing enterprises, were "in symbolic relationship with their time" (1994: 43).

This project, "foreshadowed" by European historicism, came to include the very theories of *indigenismo* and mestizaje that Latin American essayists elaborated, beginning with Martí in the late nineteenth century, through José Vasconcelos in Mexico and, among others, the Bolivians Alcides Arguedas and Franz Tamayo in the early twentieth century, all the way to the more modern and liberating proposals of intellectuals such as Agustín Cueva of Ecuador. Reflections on the same, such as the theory of mestizaje, which seems to be a genuinely autochthonous development, still did not question the European historicist trajectory that would link America to ancient Greece, an inheritance which, even if it didn't pass probate, continued unrestrictedly reproducing rationalistic historiographical categories from the eighteenth and nineteenth centuries that had the ultimate effect of silencing and utterly displacing local cultures.

Given the profoundly rationalist and historicist nature of the Latin American essay, one has to ask whether it wouldn't be unfruitful to rethink it at a decolonizing moment that is struggling against the current of the Europeanizing project that gave birth to the foundational Latin American essay, as I have briefly argued here. I think there are powerful reasons to reclaim this genre for the needed liberatory ends; to rethink it against the current of the instrumental rationality introduced by modern culture; and to connect it with the conflicts raised by that "other America" about which Said has spoken (2003). Looking at it from the renovating viewpoint of contemporary thinkers such as the Martinique-born French psychoanalyst Frantz Fanon, I believe the fragmentary character of the essay—I am thinking of Pascal, Adorno, Benjamin—can also be made to carry out the task of dismantling the identity image that local elites have constructed, making way for the "silent" subjectivities that are thought from different epistemological suppositions. Beyond the fundamentalisms of the Right and the Left, it seems to me that Latin American pluralism cannot be reduced to the proposition of a homogenizing ethnic identity, which, like the ocular centrism introduced by the metaphor of mestizaje (Sanjinés 2004), forgets that diversity cannot be reduced to a Hegelian-style synthesis, but rather should open up, widen itself into a diversity that cannot be thought of as identical with one's self. There is, in this insistence that attention must be paid to the lists of diversity, a way of thinking that departs from the history on the move toward a synthetic unity, toward a resurrection of a lost wholeness. Seen from Europe, which has also had its thinkers in exile, ex-centric essayists, critics of instrumental reason, this complete rejection of the Hegelian concept of history as progress, as the identity of subject and object, appears in the construction of history in fragments that was advanced by Adorno, whose conception of the essay "rubs history against the grain," struggles against the spirit of the era, and, by introducing the "embers of the past" into the present, focuses history backward rather than forward (Adorno 2000 [1958]). Let me be clear: rather than following Adorno's arguments as if they were prescriptions for today's Latin America, I want to put them to use in organizing the argument of transgression. We must construct a "border epistemology" that will let us talk from various systems of knowledge, one of which is European ex-centric critical thought about modernity and its historical time.

To think the local from the past, I must reclaim the essay as the form that makes it possible to question the four "narratemes" (to use Vladimir Propp's 1968 [1927] neologism for the narrative equivalent of a morpheme, that is, a minimal narrative unit) that constitute the set of narrative structures that package and control modernity and that dress up reality in an appearance of variety and diversity.

The first of these narratemes is the preconception that the nation is a collective "we" (this common "we" deriving from the imaginary of European history) that can overcome differences by using an all-encompassing rhetoric that pays only lip service to the rightful claims of diversity.

The second narrateme relates to the difficulty that the rhetoric of modernity has in accepting the controversial nature of historicism, supporting its homogenizing view with the concept that history obeys "objective" laws. The critique of this view brings us to the basic argument of Adorno, who, as Susan Buck-Morss has observed, rejected any "ontological, positive definition of history's philosophical meaning" (1977: 49). There can thus be no "objective" law of history that is independent of human actions and that can guarantee the progress of society.

Without stopping to consider the origin of its enunciation (who speaks, and for whom), the historicist project sets up a third stumbling block: its radical intolerance for anyone who dissents from power, conceiving any kind of dissent as a complaint coming from the irrational "anti-nation."

Finally, the dominant narrative declares unacceptable any sort of knowledge that does not come from what has been formulated "from above" by the authorities who hold power. Since the essay is thought of as a counter-memory linked to subaltern groups, to critical collectivities that operate "outside" Europeanizing historicism and from the "outskirts" of modernity, its transgressive role must cling to a principle of "non-identity" (Adorno 2000 [1958]: 98), which, moving beyond the rationalizations of an elitist discourse that ties the nation to power, would be able to place the essay as a privileged form of resistance, of the nation's struggle with itself (Courville 2010). This "nonidentity principle" on which Adorno's "negative dialectic" is based is a theoretical tool that can be used to demythify the ideological web of discourse that is woven from power. In this sense, it seems to me that Adorno's process of nonidentity dialectics can help us conceptualize transgression, because it will allow us to read against the grain the discourse that has been referring to the nation over the past two centuries in order to turn it into the exclusive, hegemonic form of collective identity of modernity (hence the felt need to use "we" in its narrative), and the principal if not the only source of legitimacy for political power. Therefore, when a transgressive essay takes up this nation-building narrative, its point is to show that the narrative is nothing but a myth concealing the monadic, isolated, elitist nature of national construction. This transgressive process, which denies an identity-based synthesis, thus sets forth the existence of multiple subjectivities that complicate the seemingly collective nature of the "we" that was delivered "from up above." By emphasizing the fragmentary nature of social reality, the transgressive essay also demonstrates the double character of the concepts "modernity / coloniality" and "archaism / modernity." The constant use of antithetical pairs doesn't transform them into a synthesis; rather, it demythifies both concepts and the realities that they try to define.

By thinking, after Adorno and Said, more about "beginnings" (in which the past manages things so that it can return to the present, to question it and trouble it) than about "origins" (taken as utopian, as arcadian), the essay distances itself from poiesis, the construction of literary images; recall that in *Beginnings: Intention and Method* (1975), Said established, in the best Platonic style, the difference between the essay and literature. The essay is tied to the world of values, while literature is tied to the world of images and the senses—to reinforce a secular mysticism similar to what Said himself developed in the 1990s, and what the Peruvian José Carlos Mariátegui before him developed in the early twentieth century (I will analyze this in chapter 2). I am thinking, then, of a transgressive essay that, as an aesthetic proposition tied to the world of values, and as an advocate of the self-determination of nations, of peoples, will seek a nonidentity dialectic to mark the struggle of the nation against itself (in reality, its struggle to free itself) in order to gain recognition and respect for its "first nature" as diverse and pluriversal. Therefore, I refer to the essay, in the best Adornian sense of the term, as the most appropriate form of resistance and transgression: a renewed restart for the struggle in the interior of society itself that gave rise to the essay as the foundational form par excellence. This form, tied to the construction of the nation-state, depicts the mental horizon of modern humankind as an inescapable reality, one that shapes and determines all aspects of collective life, from people's characters to their forms of artistic expression. Treating this idea of the nation as ontological necessity "against the grain," it would appear that, were our way and manner of being in the world completely determined, transgressive thought should insist on the fact that only the nation can fight to liberate itself, to overcome the "hard boundaries" (Duara 1996: 169) that it has constructed from the vantage point of power. So my vision of the essay, which naturally does not implicate the views of other critics on the subject, revolves around Adorno's declaration, in *Minima Moralia* (2005 [1951]: 39), that "it is part of morality not to be at home in one's home."

But reflecting on the theme of transgression as seen by two thinkers in exile, Adorno and Said, I ask myself whether the essay can recover what was sacrificed and lost by homogenizing unity. I do not have the answer, but I think life itself, filled with twists and turns, creates decentered and fragmentary aesthetic forms, without any historicist a priori principles at all. So I opt for the essay as a transgression that can express "the turbulent richness of life." In tension between the lyrical expression of the poetic and the narrative demands of the mundane, the essay is the genre that conveys the lost, strayed, arcane flow of life. It organizes a new conceptual ordering of life, an arrangement of ideas that might cast doubt on the congealed and definitive solutions contained in the abstract values of philosophy. Perhaps because we now need art more than science itself, I again call my reader's attention to the proposition that the essay gives meaning to ex-centric, transgressive human events, a signification that they cannot attain by themselves, examining them and connecting them with the ultimate problems of life and fate.

Since empirical daily life thus needs the essay, this genre is an unimpeachably mundane historical experience because it implies an intellectual opening devoted to connecting the formal with the complex folds of life. The historical experience of the essay thus provides for a particularly interesting exploration of topics connected with ex-centric problems such as the everyday experiences of migration and exile. In this way, the essay opens up to the invigorating presence of topics too often made invisible by historicism. This new historical experience presented by the essay would not be exclusively concerned with the "imagined communities" of the dominant cultures; rather, it should also reclaim alternative communal experiences, that is, the formerly marginalized and little-explored experiences of ethnic groups.

But this new aesthetic experience presented by the essay is not exclusively political. Indeed, it would be wrong to think of it as one long political message. The essay, as an experience linked to the vicissitudes of life, should revive our senses. At the end of his introduction to *Reflections on Exile* (2002), Said argues that exile should sharpen our view of things, not keep us bound up in mourning or, even less, in hatred, which corrodes everything. What is forgotten, what is made invisible, should provide new motives to understand that although there is no return to the past that can be brought fully home in the present, the present must necessarily pay attention to the past if it wants to break with what Cioran called "the quietude of Unity" promoted by European historicism and by its most intimate nationalist aspiration: to construct the modern self. Opposed to this historicist perspective, the essay as I envision it must necessarily reinsert the discontinuity of the invisible past into the *longue durée* of history. As a turbulent experience of the empirical world, the essay is better prepared today to tackle the problems of active communities, of communities "on the move," than the pretentious gesture of the national epics, which, by forgetting the asynchronic experiences of the other, tended to homogenize and equalize everything.

Given that the question of the essay was, and remains, one of the subjects that most interests me intellectually, Xavier Albó is absolutely correct, in his prologue to the Spanish version of this book (2009: xi), to identify my research here with the proposition of the essay. Indeed, in this book, our doubts concerning the meaning of history run remarkably parallel to the uncertainties that the essay raises for us as an aesthetic experience of transgression.

Confined neither to science nor to philosophy, both of which cling to "abstract universals" as their goals, the essay is, as I put it at the beginning of this section, the literary expression best suited to posing doubts and conjectures about the concrete lives of human beings. To keep from turning into an abstract framework for universals disconnected from the life at hand, the essay delves into experience, into perceptible and concrete life. For the investigation I propose, it is very important to bear in mind one key limitation of the essay: it raises problems connected to the future of humanity, but it gives no definitive answers. In other words, the responses in an essay do not provide solutions like those that science or, in the higher regions, religion and philosophy aspire to offer. The irony of the essay rests on the fact that the essayist claims familiarity with the ultimate problems of life in a way that leads us to believe that these are merely passing incidents in life (Lukács 1974 [1910]: 15–39).

There is, then, a clear difference between the philosopher of history and the essayist. The former acts on the level of ideas; the latter seeks connections with complex, concrete reality. Whereas the philosopher of history always has answers, the essayist projects only doubts and conjectures. For the essayist, what is exceptional is not that History may have ended or definitively left, but that it is returning today at full strength, in so particular and sui generis a way that it has ceased to be progressive, because it has dispensed with the route dictated by the rectilinear character of national histories. The essay thus captures the uncertain course of that history. So, as Coronil noted, today neither the Right nor the Left can project a clear, sure, epic fate that might express how human beings might adapt to the community and to the universe. With all totalizing possibilities shattered, with any ability to explain the world in which we are living vanished, aesthetics can no longer double for ethics, an ability that, in the Hegelian sense of the term, could have been conferred in better times upon the national epics. I therefore hazard to pose the necessity of the essay as a transgression, because it is the literary genre that best expresses, along with paradox and fragmentary writing, the current rupture between humans and their social universe. The attempt to return once more to the Eurocentered modernity that covers up this dysfunction is, then, one of the most controversial utopias of our time.

Ever since European conquest and colonization, the elites of Latin America have followed the Western guidelines in having an ordering sense of the future. The problem now is that the horizons of expectation have grown murky and unpredictable. Indeed, the arbitration of those who were traditionally prepared to partake of the banquet of modernity, which consigned large groups of people to an uncertain "not yet," postponed the desires of the "noncontemporary" identities that are bursting into history with such force today. These are the huge sectors of postcolonial Latin American society that were forced for centuries to sit in the "waiting room of history" (Chakrabarty 2000: 8–10).

It seems to me that it isn't for the philosophy of history, which is fundamentally teleological and progress-oriented, but rather for what I call the "transgressive" essay, to capture the revolt of these sectors of Latin American society, which up to now have had a past of great economic and political instability, a chronic uncertainty that has deepened the inequality between the modern and the nonmodern, between the modern and the anachronistic, and that has given rise to "the contemporaneity of the noncontemporaneous." And this has a lot to do with the examples of Venezuela, Ecuador, and Bolivia. These countries are now displaying a much more confrontational "decolonizing turn" (socialist, *indigenista*, and revolutionary) than the societies where the Left has tended to establish political alliances and compacts based on formally democratic procedures. These cases demonstrate a historical modality for which the future appears ethereal and ghostly, like a space inhabited by the specters of the past. We are living through a turbulent present that is stretching on and on in time, occupying the space and time usually taken up by the future, yet it is not the future, which has turned into a kind of waiting period that should not be confused with modernity's much more solid horizon of expectations.

Pushed beyond the horizon of expectations promoted by modernity, the future takes on a spectral form, a ghostly appearance that stalks the paths of our lives. What are these specters from the past? They are specters formed by colonialism—events that, despite independence and nearly two hundred years of republican life, continue to influence (and to disturb) our present. Recognizing and overcoming them is the most important task for our decolonizing enterprise. I therefore put forward this new transgressive model of the essay as an aesthetic contribution to decolonization, as an aesthetic practice located at the margins of historical temporality, a practice that embodies the displacement, even the rupture of the time-form, which ought to be dealing with the empirical experience of the modern/colonial world. Decolonizing means reinscribing the suppressed, the ruinous, in the present. So reclaiming the essence of the essay means showing how the time-form—historical time; the national epic; the narratemes linked to modernity—shatters on contact with real life. In other words, I wonder whether it wasn't a peculiarly mestizo-criollo gesture to adopt a modernity that had no notion of the infinite precariousness of the local. Doesn't the imaginary of the dominant intelligentsia clash with the empirical experience of the modern/colonial world, with the place where the subaltern localization of Latin America is inscribed?

Again, I propose that the essay be considered an aesthetic transgression linked to decolonization. Having observed modernity "from the outside," I can vouch for the fact that Western historical time shatters when it meets the life of our peoples. After two long centuries of homogenizing projects, guided by cultural and political elites identified with the Western notion of progress, today's movements appear to be changing the rules of the game, making "the noncontemporaneous" possible in multiple nations whose respective cosmogonies can disrupt the spatial-temporal form of the nation-state. Thus, the "ruins of the past"—I prefer to call them "embers," a means of reinscribing the past (refusing to turn back the clock) in the debate over the new plurinational states—can set the imaginaries of the present afire. The need to reclaim icons of the past is a symptom that reveals our anxiety over learning that the future is uncertain and that we need to make the present more stable. This is why I prefer to talk about "embers" that illuminate our present-day struggles; this is a new image that reveals the presence now of flames that seemed to be extinguished but can be brought back to life to feed our utopian dreams.

5. THE EMBERS OF THE PAST

The four essays I have collected in this book as an exercise in the critique of historicism and modernity were thought through from the vantage point of an illusion-free need to study the conflict between the cultures and movements of indigenous peoples, on the one hand, and the modern nation-state in its contemporary Latin American manifestation, on the other.

As the reader can see from this introduction, I find the Bolivian case to be a particularly important example of this conflict, one that might even be taken as a contemporary model for other nations whose construction of modernity remains incomplete and problematic. But this book is also, above and beyond any argument it presents, a set of four essays on sociocultural temporality: the persistence in the present of the "embers of the past," which, buried and smoldering, are still capable of lighting new conflagrations.

These essays were inspired by the idea that questions of time have been relatively forgotten in cultural studies—roughly speaking, ever since Michel Foucault declared that "certain ideological conflicts animating present-day polemics take place between the pious descendants of time and the fierce inhabitants of space" (Foucault 2008 [1967]: 14). Following Foucault, the category of time was relegated to nineteenth-century philosophies of history, while space was understood as the category from which cultural otherness was to be approached.

Rejecting this dichotomous conception of the categories of time and space, in this book I argue that the current process of incorporating indigenous peoples and cultures obliges us to rethink our temporal categories. In "The Changing Faces of Historical Time," the first essay in the book, I contrast the cases of the Peruvian novelist José María Arguedas and the Bolivian essayist Carlos Montenegro. Following Arguedas, I argue that the inclusion of indigenous peoples and cultures in the modern nation has been accompanied by a renewal of temporal categories. Indigenous cultures experience time in a very different way from how it has been employed in the construction of the modern nation and from how it has maintained a continuity between tradition and progress, as painstakingly examined by the German historian Koselleck (2002). Indigenous migrations, dramatically represented in Arguedas's posthumous novel *The Fox from Up Above and the Fox from Down Below* (2000 [1973]), demand their place in modernity, but as I argue in this essay, they bear a completely different temporal relationship than the one that governs the axis between conservatism and progressivism, between tradition and revolution, which characterizes modernity. These migrations (and the cultural texts associated with them) force us to bear in mind that the state is somewhat more than a modern institution: that is, the state includes multiple forms of relating to time and history; it contains multiple twists and turns that cannot be simplified by a linear narrative like the one Carlos Montenegro constructed in his essay *Nacionalismo y coloniaje* (1994 [1943]), in which the noetic experiences of tragedy and comedy are revitalized by the novel and the catastrophic conflicts of the historical past lead to an epic beginning of the new social order introduced by the modern nation-state.

In the second essay, "Is the Nation an Imagined Community?" I express my doubts about how appropriate Benedict Anderson's well-known image of the nation as an "imagined community" is for the study of postcolonial societies. The newly independent nineteenth-century nations of Latin America are especially important in Anderson's study, but though he mentions the difficulty of building these national communities due to the marked economic inequalities the new nations faced, he doesn't take into account the irreducible specificity of the indigenous communities; instead he concentrates exclusively on the lettered culture of the criollo elites who organized the imagined construction of the nation-state. Isn't Anderson's own study a homogenizing view of the reality that was only consolidated in part in the hinterlands of our countries? My essay also illustrates this conjecture with two examples: the first is the rebellion of the *jagunços* in Canudos, in northeastern Brazil, which the incomparable Euclides da Cunha narrated so dramatically and passionately (2010 [1902]). The second example is how José Carlos Mariátegui, the great Peruvian thinker and essayist of the early twentieth century and the founder of Marxism in the Andes, discovered the indispensable role that Peruvian indigenismo played in the construction of Peru (1971 [1928]). At the end of the essay, I ask, but refrain from answering, some key questions raised by my reading of these two authors: How should "archaic" but contemporaneous ethnic groups be integrated into the modern nation? How should popular (folk, working-class) culture and society be addressed? As "the people," following Ernesto Laclau's analysis (2005)? Or perhaps as a "multitude," to appropriate the reflections of the recent theorists and critics of empire, Michael Hardt and Antonio Negri (2004), on this topic?

While my second essay dismantles the concept "nation," I devote the third and more complex essay, "'Now Time': Subaltern Pasts and Contested Historicism," to dissecting the concept "time." In this essay I ask how elements of the anachronistic and premodern past—in particular, the presence of supernatural beings and situations—can be translated and integrated into modern societies that have seen these archaicisms break through because of the direct action of indigenous people "on the move." In this essay, I offer, among other themes, a rereading of Marxist anthropologist Michael Taussig's work on the presence of the Devil in the tin mines of Bolivia (1980).

Won't the pursuit of integration in times of struggle and conflict be precarious and isolating? My fourth and final essay, titled "The Dimensions of the Nation and the Displacements of Social Metaphor in Bolivia," shows that the lack of connection between the "civic" and the "ethnic" continues to raise tension between time and space.

By discussing how social metaphors represent the evolution of the Bolivian nation-state throughout the twentieth century, this final essay revolves methodologically around the urgent need to reclaim, as part of the theme of ethnic nationalities, the subjectivities that are still being labeled "premodern" or "preexisting," which are prevented from participating in the production, distribution, and organization of knowledge, thus reinforcing the hierarchical structures of power. We can see how present-day indigenous movements are still hindered even by bureaucrats and administrators who critique the nation-state and aim to remake it, yet who still adopt positions that are problematic as concerns the spatial-temporal conflict. Are there alternatives that can overcome the temporal order of modernity? As opposed to modernizing efforts to marginalize national ethnicities, it seems to me that the most recent territorial conflicts in the Bolivian lowlands, particularly the claims to safeguard the TIPNIS (Territorios Indígenas del Parque Nacional Isiboro Sécure), would entail, among other things, the progressive decentering and displacement of capitalist economy, with a concomitant expansion of human and nature's rights tied to "postliberalism."

In short, the four essays in this book argue that ethnic movements—lately characterized as "societies on the move"—have introduced doubt into the rectilinear course of modernity. They have reopened the gap—the hiatus, Jacques Lacan would call it—between the symbolic and the real. The aim of *Embers of the Past* is to raise, but not to resolve, the conflict caused by this painful rupture. To that end, the decolonizing proposals in my essays insist that social demands that have never been fulfilled over the centuries should be brought back in the present (the past being a resource for our hardened present); that indigenous values should be accepted and integrated into society; and that a transformation of the self should take place, beginning by overcoming the egocentrism of modernity.

Chapter One

THE CHANGING FACES OF HISTORICAL TIME

It is time to go beyond elitist representations of mestizaje; beyond discursive modifications, made from the vantage point of power—as in Mexico and Bolivia, with their nationalist conceptions of mestizaje, which have turned it into a fixed, reality-homogenizing concept. Today, there is a need to complicate mestizaje with the shifting syntax of recent migrations, deepening the process of fragmentary multicultures. In what follows, I will explain this process through an important example from the modern Andes.

The Peruvian literary critic Antonio Cornejo Polar saw his fellow Peruvian, the indigenista writer José María Arguedas, as juggling mestizaje with transculturation. In his book *Los universos narrativos de José María Arguedas* (1997: 227–266), Cornejo Polar argues that in Arguedas's tragic posthumous novel, *El zorro de arriba y el zorro de abajo* (1973; translated as *The Fox from Up Above and the Fox from Down Below*, 2000), the character named Asto—a migrant from predominantly indigenous highland Peru to one of the country's booming coastal cities—never fully assimilates into modernity, nor does he comfortably adapt to the historical time of modernity.

A peripheral modern, the migrant Asto never entirely ceases to be a migrant, not even after he permanently settles in his new space and modifies it in his own image and likeness, because behind him, he always has the experience of his origins—not his recent past, but the more distant "ruins," which force him to see reality from a different perspective, in conflict with the forward-looking, rectilinear gaze of modernity.

Is the migrant's itinerant life a displacement, a spatial-temporal change that complicates the stability which narratives of identity grant to mestizaje? Cornejo Polar seems to think so. He relates itinerancy to the lack of a fixed center that is the hallmark of the mestizaje metaphor. According to Cornejo Polar, the migrant loses his totalizing sense, which, as a worldview, restrains mestizaje as an organic representation of reality.[1] When the migrant loses his roots through his itinerancy, his reality also suffers an enormous loss of coherence and organicity. Itinerancy elicits a hodgepodge of signs, which, hailing from ancient, ancestral times, invoke in their very confusion new situations of instability and disorder. Put another way: while the mestizo class in power strives to organize its complicated social and discursive order toward clear political ends, subjecting it to a search for an identity that is as homogeneous as it is brittle, the migrant seems to let his erratic behavior throw reality into disorder, contaminating everything.

This disorderly displacement explains the behavior of the outstanding examples of highland migrants in Arguedas's novel, which contrasts the alienation they encounter in the city with the authenticity of a past that stubbornly and violently refuses to disappear altogether. It isn't the immediate past, the so-called historical past, that we are called on here to recover, but rather the mythic past, which is rehabilitated by the complex and conflictive characters who inhabit this open and inconclusive novel. Their stories are multiple, told by multiple voices, among which the presence of myth and magic is fundamental. Indeed, the alternation between present and mythic past, the coming and going between randomly eventful modern life and the world of ancient memory, expresses the impossibility of moving ahead on one level without settling some scores on the other. And when two worlds of unequal power and prestige come into contact, a culture conflict takes place that is basic to an understanding of the narrative. Let's look at one revealing passage about this conflict, the spatial-temporal struggle that Cornejo Polar observes in this novel.

Asto, one of many highland migrants who go down to the coast en masse, arrives in the boom town of Chimbote dazzled by legends of its wealth. Chimbote is the reality with which Arguedas confronts him. Understanding it—a new and intricate city, a cutting-edge city—is a real challenge. He must become familiar with its disorder and diversity. Here, the immediate past, close to the migrant's recent history or memory, grows feeble and recedes when confronted with all the opportunities that the present offers him. Chimbote, a no-man's-land, a borderland city, a myth of the dispossessed, represents the possibility of radical change. This change is underwritten by the high wages that capitalist industry offers the migrant. But the city does not only enlighten and attract; it also burns and kills. Nothing is guaranteed. The only sure thing is that migrating means betting on change.

Adapting to the norms for behavior in this new sociocultural reality, Asto doesn't shrink before this challenge; on the contrary, he steps up to it and gets comfortable with the modern capitalist machinery of Chimbote. This machinery encompasses the need to set up a strategy for recapturing the money paid out as salaries by creating bars and brothels, which, incorporated into the least visible strata of the empire, entail the destruction of the wage-earners' moral strength. The story focuses on Asto when he first enters an elegant brothel and asks for a prostitute named "Argentina." Dazzled by the money and by the blond prostitute, the Indian denies his identity: "Me *criollo* . . . from the coast, goddamnit; me from Argentina, goddamnit. Who highlander now?" (2000: 42). This rejection of his past, this transformation from poor campesino into prosperous fisherman, allows Asto to leave his insecurity and fear behind. But his adventure, almost lost in the multiplicity of voices in the novel, acquires a new dimension only when it is suddenly displaced to another "history," which takes place "two thousand five hundred years ago" (2000: 53). Sustained by this system of brusque displacements, the correlations between the level of plot set in the present and the level of myth from the remote past cannot go unnoticed by the reader. Asto repeats acts carried out by Tutaykire ("Wound of the Night"), while Argentina becomes the "harlot virgin" of the legend, both tales ending with the alienation and annihilation of Asto (2000: 54). Myth is transformed and brought back to life, once more relevant, and the narrative becomes transcendent, profound, and amazingly powerful.

The presence of the mythic past in the present reveals the existence of a deep cultural conflict. Indeed, what Asto faces is not an individual conflict so much as an ethnic one, which rips to shreds the assumption that we belong to the national homogeneity that we had taken for granted until well into the last two decades of the twentieth century. Today, however, we have become conscious that, far from such reality-simplifying notions of homogeneity, ethnicity is a complex way to rework, to rethink, to reinvent culture, connecting the present with the ancestral past, the past of "ruins," so different from the recent past, the historical past. And this connection between present and remote past has its own tremendous ambiguities, which keep the cultural world from having clear and conclusive divisions. Therefore, ethnic groups occupy spaces with permeable boundaries, from which identity can be negotiated with great flexibility. Deep down, who is Asto? An Indian? A mestizo? In the cultural conflict brought about by his migration to Chimbote, Asto cannot be categorized as one or as the other: he has become both. So even the most "primitive" and most isolated people end up in contact with other societies, particularly with the dominant societies, from which coloniality is reinforced. In the same way, continuity and rupture are facets that can be found in the personality of the migrant, and they are tremendously important in the ideological construction of ethnic groups. In this sense, the memory of the past—the kind of memory that brings myth into the present—cannot be measured by the rationalistic criteria of whether particular events are true or false; the proper measure is how strong and convincing they are in the migrant's consciousness, how much they set him apart, and how much they disengage him from the homogenizing political arena. Thus, the migrant creates an ethno-national cultural conflict, not merely an ethnic conflict.

In the case of Arguedas's novel, the presence of the mythic past in the present complicates the already chaotic situation of Chimbote even further. One of the foxes, transformed into Don Ángel Rincón, cannot find the words in Spanish to express the chaos of Chimbote, and instead refers to it by the Quechua term *lloqlla*, meaning "an avalanche of water, earth, tree roots, dead dogs, and stones that come rumbling down on the bottom of the current when the rivers are loaded with the first rains in these beastly Andean foothills" (2000: 91). This "human lloqlla," the only way to describe Chimbote, is not a comparison but a crude metaphor—a catachresis—that apprehends and sheds light on its reality.

There is no doubt that the process of describing Chimbote as an avalanche is metaphorical. I would like to add, however, that migrating, as an individual process that is at the same time a collective one, means feeling a kind of homesickness in a present that should be full but that too often is frustrating; it means feeling nostalgic for a "back then" and an "over there" that you suddenly discover aren't from your experience of your immediate past, properly speaking, and discovering too that you cannot draw a straight line from this past to the future. This suddenly discovered "back then" and "over there," as in Asto's experience in the novel, are the "here" of sleepless but fragmentary memory and the "now" that runs forward but also delves down deep, vertically, into a thick time that accumulates but doesn't synthesize the experiences from some past of ruins, the product of a mythic time left behind long ago that continues to perturb the present angrily and violently.

I am speaking, then, of a sui generis present, of a "here" and a "now" that, in a way distantly reminiscent of the orgiastic chiliasm of the Anabaptists,[2] is now joining forces with the activist demands of the oppressed strata of society. As in present-day social movements, these demands are eventually transformed into activist movements of specific social strata. These postponed desires, buried in memory, suddenly gain social and political importance, thus giving rise to a subaltern consciousness that, unlike the "proletariat's consciousness of itself," becomes the point of departure for the historical earthquake we are currently living through. It is this incorporation of the remote past into the present, this use of the past as a resource for the present (Eller 1999), that gives the current movements their specific role in the dynamic development of society as a whole.

This present, which to me seems to govern the actualization of the past that is buried in memory, becomes an explosive agent in daily life. The "here and now" of thousands of migrants, who remodel the city, who impress a different rhythm on it and give it a different physiognomy, also creates a "proposal" that profoundly subverts the foundations of the hierarchical political/social order. Thus, the fact that they were constituted far from traditional social institutions shows that the movements resulting from indigenous migrations in the present entail setting in motion a new way of thinking that, quite unlike full modernity, is connected with eschatology (*pachakuti*, the world turned upside-down). And nothing would be more mistaken than to try to understand these movements exclusively from the point of view of modernity, seeking to frame them in a historical time that doesn't suit them and that today is in crisis. Modern and archaic at once—that is, half-modern, superficially imbued with the ideology that governs the teleologically oriented movement of a time that goes chasing after goals decided upon in advance—the indigenous migrant, the essential component of today's movements, bears a way of thinking that, in tension with the modernity that she also participates in, has roots in much more underground, vital, and elemental regions of her psyche.

This use of the experience of the past as a resource for the present is characterized by the kind of sudden displacement we noted in Arguedas's novel. For the Indian immigrant, the present becomes the breach through which what was once intimately his, what once resided in the deepest recesses of his psyche, such as myth, blossoms in a sudden outburst, takes over the outside world, and transforms it. Somewhat like the chiliasts of past centuries, he lives yearning for this change: his metaphors, such as the lloqlla that the migrant perceives in the city, or the pachakuti, which expresses the untimely overturning of reality, are psychological situations that cannot be conceived in terms of modernity. In this sense, his metaphors, his symbols cannot be made to fit the modern "history of ideas." These metaphors are not the jewels of national culture; they are crude symbols that the migrants spin from analogies with the sensations of everyday life. This aspiration to join the immediate present has little to do, as I have said, with optimistic hopes for the future or with the experience of the past that governs conservative thought. The attitudes of the migrants who make up social movements are characterized by tense expectations that define those attitudes as a need to revive the old "ruins" of the ancestral past—by using them in catachresis.

If the mythic past, as a resource for the present, abruptly transforms the outer world, catachresis is the rhetorical device that best describes its symbolic construction.[3] As with lloqlla, used to describe and explain Chimbote in Arguedas's novel, catachresis, the crude origin of metaphor, must rely on "what this means is" to translate the ancestral term into an exercise in mestizo language ("human avalanche"), thus giving rise to metaphor. Born from vernacular language, these metaphors are as unpoetic as they are rudely expressive, and they have both blinding limitations and enduring power.

The transformation of catachresis into metaphor comes at a high cost, however: to be established as a metaphor, the word *lloqlla* had to be torn from its rustic, catachrestic, mythic origins, because otherwise its laborious synonymy would have been shuttered. What I mean is that, for the fusion to be possible, one of the two terms has to yield, narrow its differences, leave the place that culturally belongs to it, in order to facilitate the production of the new meaning. Let's not forget, however, that we still have the hermeneutic option of revealing the warp and woof in this laborious process of enunciation, of allowing the subaltern catachresis to make a comeback, and of listening—as Arguedas does in his novel—to the interactions of the many disparate consciousnesses and languages to be found in its convoluted origin. For Cornejo Polar, this is the strategy that best illuminates the multicultural texture of language, as well as the deep political anxiety that we might take what is obviously varied, scattered, and heteroclite, and make it all uniform.

The past as a resource for the present—as what I call an "ember of the past"—governs my critical view of modernity. The past as resource—which I reinterpret as myth incorporated into the present as a "wager," not as a rational certainty—organizes my reading of every chapter in this book, which is dedicated to exploring the crisis of historical time.

The statement "the present is another time now," with its chiliastic overtones—Karl Mannheim said that "the only direct, identifying characteristic of Chiliastic experience is absolute presentness" (1997 [1936]: 195)—is the slogan that several insurrectionary movements in the Andes have used to express the feelings of indigenous consciousness at historical moments of insurgency.[4] I wonder, however, whether this "different time" evoked by indigenous consciousness is substantially distinct from historical time as perceived by revolutionary movements that grew from the middle classes. In other words, do indigenous people perceive the insurrectionary present differently than a middle-class urban revolutionary would? But even within the consciousness of the dominant culture, does the middle-class revolutionary have a vision of the past and future that differ from conservatives' perceptions of time?

Given that views of time depend on where the observing consciousness is located, they raise problems that are difficult to solve. I have no doubt that the indigenous insurrectional present is sui generis, but its subversive characteristics, and especially its place in the crisis of the dominant historical time of modernity, call for detailed examination. That is the purpose of this chapter. To that end, I will continue this analysis of the changing faces of historical time by contrasting the notions of tradition and revolution. This contrast—and current political science has appropriately resolved the conflict between tradition and revolution by conceiving tradition as something living, quite unlike traditionalism—will allow me first to differentiate between, and then (following the work of Reinhart Koselleck, 1985 and 2002) to connect, two complementary metahistorical categories: the "experience of the past" and "the horizon of expectations" (1985: 255–275). The former dominates the conservative mentality; the latter is closer to the revolutionary mentality, which since the French Revolution has played an important role in the historical construction of modernity.

After going over the constitutive elements of historical time, I will also debate the categories used by Koselleck. In this way, I will settle in the indigenous insurrectional present, in its particular relationship with the past and the future, from the here and now of the crisis of modernity. This will give rise to a reflection on the "absolute presentness" connected with the new representation (what I call the catachrestic representation) of reality, that is, a representation that requires the oppressed, the traditionally oppressed social sectors, to begin renaming reality, appropriating and rearticulating the well-worn metaphorical and symbolic constructions of nationality.

1. TRADITION AND REVOLUTION

Few concepts have been distorted, both deliberately and unintentionally, in as many ways as tradition has. It is sometimes seen as inert, stagnant, belonging to a dead past; at other times it is taken to be a dynamic means of understanding history. The latter was the case when Bolivian political scientists recently rethought the results of the 1952 revolution, recapturing for the present day such modernizing reforms as the incorporation of indigenous people as full citizens through universal suffrage. But in attempts to analyze the concepts of tradition and revolution, the resemblance between them has not always come across as natural.

This mismatched pair formerly seemed to be a genuine oxymoron: in Western culture, tradition and revolution are antinomies that, as we will see below, imply two opposite but complementary ways of conceiving history, the development of historical time. It should be added that the concept of historical time itself seems to be in jeopardy today as a result of the exhaustion of modernity. The social movements are what have put a check on the future utopia envisioned by modernity, resisting it with the absolute presentness of now, which is as distant from the conservative view of the past as from the liberal ideal of the modern state that political science protects at all costs.

Let us begin with tradition and revolution—concepts that, though usually antithetical, have adapted to the flow of historical time. Four decades ago, Bolivian historian Jorge Siles Salinas published his keen observations about tradition in his book *Ante la Historia* (1969). Relating tradition to ethics, Siles Salinas pointed out three categories that distinguish tradition from revolution and allow it to be experienced as a promise of continuity: faithfulness, admiration, and gratitude (1969: 37).

The triple ethical dimension on which tradition is based contrasts with the notion of revolution, which, in the case of Spanish America, derives from the revolutionary independence movements of the nineteenth century. Indeed, it is clear that, for the conservative mentality, the individualistic morality promoted by nineteenth-century liberal revolutionaries is alien to the ethics of faithfulness. This virtue, which undergirds all the others, is a categorical imperative incompatible with the individualistic motives promoted by a revolutionary mentality; it has the quasi-religious meaning of "dedication" or "devotion" to a divine cause, the only way by which individuals can fulfill their destiny as persons, overcoming the scattered focus brought about by the confused multiplicity of trends and aspirations that individualistic free will presumes. Faithfulness, in other words, is given to a higher cause that overcomes the fickleness of time.

If destroying the past with an eye to beginning a new life is the implicit program of every revolutionary movement, it could be said that, in contrast to the conservative viewpoint, hatred of the past and a consequent optimism about the future are basic to the revolutionary psychology, quite apart from the sort of program it espouses—that is, aside from whether it is liberal, nationalist, or socialist. Therefore, a fair portion of political reformers, the ones who are alienated from tradition, have always started from the belief that the past can be completely destroyed. As everyone knows, the nineteenth-century liberal revolutionaries themselves—most of them thinkers and men of letters imbued with ideas drawn from the European Enlightenment—built the "national cultures" of Spanish America through processes of political rationalization that took as their point of departure the conviction that history could be controlled and governed according to plans of progress that they had already laid out. Since then, revolution has meant nothing other than a proposal to overcome the past and to fulfill history through a utopian, ideal, teleologically organized scheme.

Since revolution implies the destruction of the past, it is also, from the conservative viewpoint, shockingly ungrateful. Hence the beneficiaries of the Revolution of Independence, like so many ungrateful new Adams, having created the nation-states of Spanish America, considered that their respective national histories had begun all of a sudden in 1809, the first year of their uprisings against Spain. And, in addition to being like Adam and dubbing themselves "new men," the revolutionaries of this historical moment stopped at nothing to achieve their central aim: overcoming and demonizing the Spanish past.

In order to delve a bit deeper into the contrasts between tradition and revolution, let me now return to two metahistorical categories mentioned above: the "space of experience" and the "horizon of expectations" (Koselleck 1985: 255–275).

2. THE EXPERIENCE OF THE PAST

I should make it clear that tradition and experience have no difficulty connecting with each other when change is slow and gradual. When that is the case, there is a bond between past and future that refutes the belief that tradition is opposed to progress (Calhoun 2007: 21). As a project, tradition does not only look to the past; it also projects itself into the future. Because of this, tradition has to be reconstructed, at times purified, at other times enlarged. I should also make it clear, however, that since the French Revolution modernity itself has taken on the task of separating the horizon of expectations from the experiences of the past. So, based on this typical modern orientation toward tradition, which modernity considers obsolete and backward, I have drawn a categorical distinction between the experience of the past and the horizon of expectations.

Frequently invoked by conservative thought, the space of experience is the past, which, incorporated into the present, keeps the memory of historic events from being lost. What we are dealing with is a continuity of the past in the present that allows no ruptures or breaks. On the other hand, the horizon of expectations is the future that connects with the present, pushing history forward, inviting us to participate in a utopia that is usually one of revolution and change. The future made present, the horizon of expectations leads us to the "not yet" of the unfulfilled, of the things we have yet to experience. So you can see that, even though both categories join in the present, the present itself loses its specific weight, as the "now" of concrete action is diluted in past experience or future expectations. Indeed, it is paradoxical that the present should become the future, or that it could also be the past: the present is the only time that exists and ceases to exist, disappearing as such to become the past, or because, in one more instant, it will be the future.

For European modernity, experience and expectations are not symmetrically complementary concepts. Quite the contrary: both are concepts that, when viewed from the vantage point of the modernizing European revolution, have become as opposed to one another as those of tradition and revolution. Let us look at some of these differences.

Revolutionary modernity perceives past experience as a completed whole, whereas future expectations are scattered through a temporal expanse that will be carried out in stages, bit by bit. Thus the specific weight of expectations gravitates in the orbit of "not yet," rather than in those of "yesterday" or of "now."

Modernity has its reasons for connecting tradition with experience. In both, the past has nothing in common with the teleological construction of the future. Both are as whole and complete as their occasions are over and done with. For both tradition and for experience, the past is organized as an entirety that could be divided only with difficulty into a before and after. More interested in the registers of memory than in chronology, both jump around in time, unconcerned with recording the continuity of events in an ordered way.

By contrast, revolution and future expectations correspond to a new space, which, like any other horizon, cannot be fully seen because it is still under construction. They are based on a future that cannot be read yet and can only be intuited according to the notions of prediction and of "perfectibility."

The opposing categories of experience and expectations are also complementary. Let us take a look at what unites and what separates them.

Experience and expectations are similar in that neither is tied to clock time; their chronology may coincide or not coincide with historical time. Both categories are situated in space and time, allowing us to think of them as the space of experience and the horizon of expectations, but the latter is more flexible, since it easily combines spatial dimensions with temporal projection. In other words, the space of experience is a good deal more rigid than the horizon of expectations, because the latter can include within the same chronological time situations that would be impossible if considered from the viewpoint of historical time. Here I am referring to "the contemporaneity of the noncontemporaneous" in civilizations that have undergone unequal "development" but are nonetheless situated within the same chronological time. In this sense, time has a heterogeneous dimension, which has been studied by Koselleck, whose analysis of these metahistorical categories I follow.

Given that it is neither a product of nature nor chronological, historical time is a human construct that makes the various spaces of experience coincide with the various perspectives of the future, including tensions and conflicts that both categories give rise to when they clash with one another. The difference that I have pointed out between chronological time and historical time does not mean, however, that chronological time has no influence over the organization of historical events. Mannheim has noted that the chronological order in which human events occur is connected to the horizon of expectations constituting the future utopia that molds the form in which we experience time (1997 [1936]: 189).

Experience of the past and expectations of the future are not natural categories; instead, they are related to social and political events, to the concrete actions of human beings, their institutions and organizations. All of these actions have well-defined forms of internalizing conduct that imprint their particular temporal rhythms on events and make them historical.

Another thing that experience and expectations have in common is that they occupy the past and the future from the viewpoint of a present that is rather inactive and significantly impoverished. Indeed, every horizon of expectations, every future utopia, has to assume a series of temporal continuities that start from a chaotic, impoverished present that we are called on to reform. The teleological argument of modernity insists on a criterion of credibility that can pull us out of the stagnation we are living through in the present by projecting for us a promising future that we must construct. From present chaos to future cosmos, this teleological movement is in a sense a way of making up for the miseries of the present by means of social, political, moral, even literary support, as we will see when we look at the revolutionary nationalist thought of Carlos Montenegro. Our revolutionarism, steeped in literature since the Romantic liberalism of the nineteenth century, seems never to have parted from its European Enlightenment origins.

So what connections can be drawn between the present and the experience of the past? Based on tradition, history has another exclusive form of being, which is being "from" the past. As Jorge Siles Salinas has observed, "The past that we are presents itself to us under the extremely peculiar form of having been" (1969: 9). As may be apparent, the present is much more passive in the conservative mentality. Intangible because it has no form of "real existence," the past makes the present possible: that is, it is a "having been" that retains an unimpeachable presence in the formation of both the present and the future. Note, then, that experience reaffirms our condition as "heirs," as legatees of the past, not as fevered "citizens" building the future from nothing, a view that fits the revolutionary expectations of development and progress. The latter start out from a sort of "year zero," the year of great revolutionary deeds, an experience quite distinct from the one that has been accumulated by tradition.

Therefore, countering the progressive view of events, and in frank opposition to Carlos Montenegro's historical view in *Nacionalismo y coloniaje* (1994 [1943]), an essay written a good quarter of a century earlier, Siles Salinas presents the conservative thought in *Ante la historia* (1969) that heirs were not the first people ever to live, nor do they transform life through their labor: they merely continue it. It is from their past living that human beings set out on their own personal destinies.

And because the present does not belong to the feverish labor that constructs the future, we can say that, according to the experience of the past, the present should be understood from a different posture. Indeed, the present is linked to an experience that always anticipates the end of history. Bound to the evolution of Christianity, the conservative present, which is the product of past experience, is also heir to a way of seeing things that until well into the sixteenth century based its expectations on the double game of constantly anticipating the end of the world, then deferring that end yet one more time. In other words, the space of experience always held the anticipated presence of the end of history; the future was always placed as an immovable milestone, set at the end of the road of empirical histories. To this way of thinking, which refuses to recognize any prognosis projected onto the future, it is impossible to disentangle the experience of the past from the Judeo-Christian *ordo temporum* and the doctrine of salvation. Thus, when historians and theologians "spoke of *profectus*, less often of *progressus*," they "referred to the soul's salvation" and its upward movement, "ascending from the visible to the invisible" (Koselleck 2002: 223). Alien to progress and to *perfectio*, this profectus spoke of the Kingdom of God, which must not be confused with the limitations of the temporal kingdom, the kingdom of this world. It was thus no mere coincidence that profectus linked the misery of this world to the approaching salvation of the elect.[5] In other words, the future was not the horizon of worldly expectations connected to progress; quite the contrary: it was an anticipated revelation that illuminated the present from the past.

Set apart from progress and from "perfectibility," there is nothing utopian about this experience of the past. As Mannheim astutely observed, this mentality "lacks all those reflections and illuminations of the historical process which come from a progressive impulse" (1997 [1936]: 206). Therefore, it cannot give rise to "the ideal of the modern state which aspires not merely to be a political state (*Machstaat*), but also a cultural state" (207). Unconcerned with building a new social and political project, and uninterested in the ideal of progress, the conservative mentality left it up to its liberal opponent to, so to speak, force it into the arena of ideological conflict. It is instructive to note, as Mannheim does, that conservative oligarchies, which acquired their social stability from their ownership of the land, never elaborated a theoretical interpretation of the present, of their own position in the world, the discovery of conservatism being subsequent to the economic and social events that gave birth to it.

As for the conservative form of experiencing time, once again, in opposition to the progressivism of liberal thought, for the experience of the past everything that exists has a nominal value that has reached the point it has in the present due to the slow, gradual, continual process of time. For this conception, history cannot be thought of as the "arrow of time"[6] moving inexorably forward into the future; rather, it must be viewed as a collection of events that experience the past as a virtual presence. Lacking change and historical breaks, this conservative form also should not be confused with the insurrectional conception of the absolute present, that is, the "now" preached by social movements today.

3. THE HORIZON OF EXPECTATIONS

I think it is clear that revolution was the event that decisively separated the horizon of expectations from past tradition. Indeed, following the French Revolution other phenomena emerged—in particular, acceleration and progress—that lent their own rhythm to modernity. Acceleration and progress replaced the immutable historical milestone of the Final Judgment with an empirical world that grew in complexity day after day. This "brave new world," as Aldous Huxley dubbed it, came together as a *plurale tantum*, accelerating time and shortening distances in such a way that human events began to change, becoming interdependent and intersubjective. It was precisely this movement that allowed the German language to distinguish between *Historie* pure and simple, as the totalizing occurrence of the past, and the evolutionary process of particular histories, which received the name of *Geschichte*. It is this selfsame movement that today brings us the paradox of a historical process so accelerated that it has left us without the time to have time.

It was as a result of the events of 1789 that revolution acquired the metahistorical character that made it responsible for putting convulsive everyday events into historical order. In other words, since then revolution has gained vital importance because it has become the regulating principle of knowledge about the actions that it has caused. So from 1789 on, the revolutionary process has been twinned with the consciousness that conditions and affects it.

As revolution slowly erodes and secularizes the eschatological expectations of conservative thought, it also transforms the Final Judgment into an intrahuman political objective of social emancipation that gives it new spatial and temporal characteristics: the revolution becomes "worldwide" and "permanent." And if the world must change completely, naturally the revolution must last until that goal is met, a fact that reinforces its permanent character.

In short, the history of the future ended up becoming the history of the revolution. For this reason I conclude that, as a metahistorical category, the French Revolution was the model of this accelerated change, of this movement toward the future that takes no account of past tradition. The movement also implied that the weight of experience should give way to the expectations of a new world and should lose its right to guide human life. With the "chains of the past" broken—a recurrent image that the national anthems of Spanish America repeat ad nauseam—the way was paved in the nineteenth century for building the republic, a goal glimpsed on the horizon of revolutionary expectations. Put another way, republicanism and nation building became the two aspirations of the revolutionary movement that sought to achieve for political action what progress endeavored to gain for history in general.

Republicanism and revolution, then, were the concepts "on the move" that opened up the new future. Both enlarged the gap between experience and expectations; both reorganized politics to admit the presence of new social actors.

Over the course of the past two centuries, and from different places and positions, conservatives have harshly criticized the accelerated movement toward the future that began with the French Revolution. Thinking about Bolivia, for example, Siles Salinas refers to the revolutionary spirit as the loss of historical consciousness (1969: 88) and states that "the insignificant peoples are the ones that always claim to start over fresh and that live in a perpetual state of reformism, radicalism, or revolutionarism" (88). He later reaffirms that "the Revolution presents itself as a negation of the past, as one of the typical manifestations of the antihistorical spirit" (91). Republicanism and revolution also go hand in hand in Siles Salinas's critique; he notes that "the idolatry of the French Revolution has deep roots in our Spanish American countries. Undoubtedly its high water mark was Romanticism, with the indelible Francophilia that the nineteenth century left behind in our culture" (94).

As might have been expected, this experience of the past could not adapt to the expectations put forward by the revolutionary projects of nation-state building. Among the essays written in Bolivia, Montenegro's work *Nacionalismo y coloniaje*, which established the ideology of "revolutionary nationalism," contains a look at history that has little in common with the history proposed by Siles Salinas.

Nacionalismo y coloniaje turns to a number of literary genres (epic, drama, comedy, tragedy, and novel) to organize and give prospective meaning to the various stages in Bolivia's republican history. In the essay, Montenegro immediately notes the insistence of ideology on opening a new horizon of expectations for the Bolivian people, a horizon that, by smashing the limitations of the oligarchic past, would link up with the spatial-temporal coordinates of Europe, which, by privileging the novel, the bourgeois genre par excellence, sought to separate itself from the prerevolutionary experiences of the past, which Montenegro considered constitutive of the colonialist thinking of the "anti-nation." (1994 [1943]: 107–10).

In the early 1940s, Montenegro sought "the truth of Bolivia's future" (1994 [1943]: 13), distancing himself from the "anti-Bolivianist" ideas of official historiography, which, by interpreting reality from the "retrograde" viewpoint of the oligarchy, had forgotten that the people are the source of Bolivian nationality. Thus, if the oligarchic criollo class—the antination—could not overcome colonialism but only reproduce it, it was time to forge a new social construct, one that would be teleological and forward-looking, able to represent the interests of the popular sectors: that is, the nation. In this process, it is instructive to observe how far Montenegro was in 1943 from analyzing the nation from a dependency theory point of view. Nevertheless, and bearing in mind that Montenegro's thinking was the result of a populist moment in which the geopolitical theorization of the Third World had not yet been developed, it seems to me that one of the most attractive aspects of his essay is precisely this interest in creating a horizon of expectations that, by breaking with the experience of the past, opened itself up to the future of nation building, thus anticipating the National Revolution of 1952.

If we catalogue the most important aspects of the historical time proposed under the horizon of expectations created by *Nacionalismo y coloniaje*, what immediately jumps out is the opposition between nation and antination. This resulted from Montenegro's need to contrast the chaotic present of liberal oligarchy with a promising future of popular democracy. This future expectation was therefore a bridge that Montenegro, as ideologue, built between the utopian ideal and a degraded reality. The bridge itself was the notion of progress.

As Mannheim (1997 [1936]: 198–200) noted, the concept of progress—the primary characteristic of the horizon of expectations that was brought into play by the historical time of modernity—derived from the peculiar way that capitalism developed. Given the unequal development of capitalism, advanced in some regions of the planet and held back in others, it was judged prudent to reconcile the utopian world of norms and the belief that reality could be transformed and gradually, through its continuous upward movement, made rational. Around 1800, the notion of progress was already linked to the existence of "noncontemporary" realities that conflicted with the nature of chronological time.

As knowledge of the world was expanded by frequent scientific expeditions, the analysis of the territories inhabited by human beings at different and very unequal levels of cultural "development" also grew more complicated. The science of the time first had to compare them synchronically, but later it began to place the data in a diachronic order. In this comparative process, European science, the science of d'Orbigny and von Humboldt, was called on to measure the degree of development in "barbarous" America and to interpret it in terms of progress, comparing the continent with other, more "advanced" civilizing processes. Thus, since the early nineteenth century, the notion of progress has also rested on the concepts of acceleration and development, building the temporal structure that Petrarch had longed for centuries earlier when he expressed his wish that he had been born in some other era (*Nam fuit et fortassis erit felicius evum*, "There has been and perhaps will be a happier age"), and which d'Alembert and Diderot had made reality when they constructed history according to a varied spectrum of immanent temporal rhythms. In this way, as we well know in Latin America, this pair, "enlightened" by civilization, set itself the task of putting pedagogical policies into practice, following the project of the *Encyclopédie* as the only historical possibility for constructing the future. Both d'Alembert and Diderot rushed to construct this future, even if their haste might lead to catastrophe, and so they established the "before" and "after" that the experience of the past had never registered.

Since this notion of progress was opening the way for the temporalization of history, it is worth noting that, in the case of Bolivia, the relationship that Montenegro established between history and literary genres also allowed for temporalization and prognosis to be set in motion in the text of *Nacionalismo y coloniaje*. Thus, the national epic of the early nineteenth century yielded to the drama and comedy of the governments whose grotesque military caudillo politics twisted and distorted the possibility of constructing a national identity. The only possibility for regaining rational action came at the moment when the original epic was connected to "the vitalist impulse, which is none other than that of the novel" (Montenegro 1994: 241).

Bound up with the historical time of modernity, the novel was thus intrinsically connected to the construction of the nation-state. Since Montenegro observed the reality of the Andes from the vantage point of the bourgeois novel, later we will see how the proposals in his essay raise some serious epistemological questions.

Beyond the novel as a literary form linked to social change, we find that revolution itself, a concept "on the move" so dear to the temporalization of history, has lost its horizon of expectations and, so to speak, has become too narrow. Perhaps this is why, in Bolivia, some current political scientists look back longingly at the old times of the National Revolution and clothe them in the vestments of tradition. This narrowing of the horizon of expectations, which liberalism has also experienced recently, now affects representative democracy. We can see this in the course that our experiments in constituent assemblies have been taking, as they have found it so difficult to establish the democratic and reasoned dialogue that was supposed to be created by the opening up of "public spheres," which elsewhere have facilitated nation building on a base of relatively homogenous horizons of expectations. So we might say that our most recent attempts to modify the political and social organization of our conflict-ridden countries reveal that we are living through a profound crisis in the temporalization of history.

4. THE RESOURCE OF THE "OTHER"

Let's go back to that declaration "The present is another time now." This statement reveals the crisis of the project put forward by modernity and its temporalization of history; it also represents the crisis of the model developed by Koselleck, which was based on two categories: the space of experience and the horizon of expectations. These categories now must be reinterpreted with the gaze of the "Other" in mind.

With claims to universality, Koselleck studies both categories from the viewpoint of Eurocentric modernity; that is, he presupposes not only that his categories are applicable to the French and German historical experiences, but that they are equally applicable to the experiences of "noncontemporary" regions such as those in the Third World, which have entered modernity on an unequal footing (Mignolo 2007). I doubt greatly whether much of Koselleck's model could be reproduced without major corrections, particularly when it comes to explaining the historical actions of insurrectional movements currently taking place in geographic regions that are physically and conceptually far from the West, such as the Andean region.

Throughout this chapter, you may have noticed that in his temporal explanation of modernity, Koselleck grants the greatest importance to the horizon of expectations, which is basically the notion of progress. While noting the growing difference that accelerated progress is introducing into both metahistorical categories, Koselleck observes that the horizon of expectations moves further every day from the experiences of the past. I should point out, however, that this relative distancing from the past does not have the same characteristics for the insurrectional movements of today, given that they are not unthinkingly following the Western way of seeing things. Since the modernity put forward by the West has not turned out to be truly universal and homogeneous for all, it seems to me that we are obliged to rethink historical temporality based on the crisis in the project of modernity.

Over the past two and a half centuries, the constant indigenous insurgencies in the Andean region have been marked by a very particular consciousness of awaiting the catastrophic overturning of the colonizer's historical time. This new perception of time—the untimely overturning that would produce the "here and now"—means that the present must connect in a different way to past and future. We are not talking, then, about a past that has anything to do with tradition, the dimension on which conservative thought is based, or about a transitory present that, like the arrow of time, only sees the future as the fulfillment of development and progress. On the contrary, this is the time of the "other," which, as we might note in the novels of José María Arguedas, bears those embers of the past that may hypothetically serve to give the future a very different meaning. With this change, the other has glimpsed a profound transformation in social relations, and a more fundamental shift in the relations of power.

The crisis I am speaking of resulted from the profound discrepancy that has arisen between the historical time of the dominant culture and that of the dominated culture, with regard to both the space of experience and the horizon of expectations. In other words, if these cultures in conflict seem to blend together under the rituals and representations of the dominant hegemony's imagined community, in practice the dominated culture takes a very different approach to time, leading not to a history governed by the homogeneous time of modernity but rather to the presence of intertwined and permanently clashing histories (Gilly 2003: 28). Thus, the subaltern movements of the present insist, in the face of the frequently homogenizing forces of political science, on the presence of diverse, interwoven histories, despite the nationalist illusion that claims, in the fulfillment of its political project, to have absorbed the representation and the organization of the aspirations of all subaltern classes. So the homogenization to which the nationalism of the dominant sectors leads is a distortion of our complex reality.

The crisis I am speaking of has two special characteristics: first, it marks the moment of transition, the "threshold of an era," when otherness, the gaze of the other, was introduced into our uncertain future; second, and closely related to this threshold of an era, this was also when the past was introduced into the present as the resource of the other. These two characteristics have augmented the role that the contemporaneity of the noncontemporaneous plays in the construction of a new politics of culture, now termed "plurinational." The crisis has given rise to a diverse gaze, decentered from the logos of modernity, which assesses historical knowledge in a different way; it has also produced the knowledge that we are living through a transitional period in which it is hard to reconcile the traditions established by the dominant culture with the innovations of the present; and finally, the noncontemporaneous can also produce accelerated rhythms, which come from social demands that surpass the limits of modernity (see chapter 4).

In addition to these characteristics, the crisis also relates to the fact that a whole range of conflicts remain unresolved; in the case of Bolivia, widespread demands (Ernesto Laclau would call them "equivalential demands" [2005: 171]) have brought down the institutional system of "democracy by pact" that had been established by agreement among the political parties over the past few decades. Given the severe institutional crisis that Bolivia, a veritable laboratory of new social movements, is going through, it is no longer possible to hold on to a single, universal, and homogeneous interpretation of historical time; now it is necessary to work from "isolated constants" that swing from ancient to modern and are situated in "particular historical articulations" (Koselleck 2002: 242) that do not partake exclusively of the homogeneous time of European modernity.

The preceding observations, which were formulated about the crisis of the historical time of modernity, are useful because they bring me back to the revolutionary nationalist model proposed in Montenegro's essay. Indeed, they allow me to question, using the gaze of the other, which I now invoke, the horizon of expectations of *Nacionalismo y coloniaje*.

At the end of Montenegro's book, he reconciles the epic and the novel in a harmonious Hegelian synthesis that turns the history of Bolivia into a tragicomic interval, situated between the loss of epic values during the caudillo governments of the nineteenth century and their recapture in the novel as a literary genre. I have the impression that Montenegro took the Hegelian category of Totality as his starting point for coming up with a utopian resolution to the historical fissures produced by the tragicomic drama of an oligarchic class—the antination—that was incapable of paying proper attention to the details of concrete reality. However, while trying to overcome this obstacle, *Nacionalismo y coloniaje* falls into the trap of its own utopian prognosis. In other words, Montenegro jumped the gun when he celebrated the end of Bolivian history on the advent of revolutionary nationalism. Indeed, the social movements of the present teach us that history cannot be the abstract ideal of a preestablished narrative plot. Its plural, conflictive, and unpredictable nature, alien to any sort of totalizing temporality, forces us to look at history with other eyes, from outside the lettered orthodoxy of nationalism.

I may be criticized for analyzing Montenegro's book, written in the 1940s, with observations based on historical events taking place in the present. But although I am aware of this possibility, I still insist on making my critique from this "now" and not, for example, from a proletarian perspective of the 1950s, because proletarians and middle-class revolutionaries were following the "forward-flying arrow" of modernity, blind to the theoretical earthquakes that have been occurring in the Andes since the 1920s.

Given that Montenegro's book established the novel as the literary genre through which the future should be observed, his critical gaze continued, in my opinion, along the same direction that European Marxist aesthetics, especially of the Lukácsian-Hegelian variety, imposed on history. Along this direction, given over to the construction of future expectations, Montenegro complained that the backwardness of its oligarchic antination had kept Bolivia from constructing a national culture on a par with that of Argentina or Chile, as witnessed by the fact that we had no intellectuals of the same caliber as Juan Bautista Alberdi, José Victorino Lastarria, or Domingo Faustino Sarmiento. In the process, Montenegro did not take a good look at indigenous culture. Even though Indians were not political subjects with full rights at the time, they had still produced, in the judgment of some well-known Andean intellectuals, important works that were truly decolonizing. Montenegro should have taken them into consideration, especially if he really wished to investigate *coloniaje*, the colonial system, as the title of his essay would indicate. So it seems to me that if his goal was a proper appreciation of coloniaje, he should have passed the novel, as literary form, through the filter of Andean reality, rather than forcing Andean reality through the filter of the European novel, with its roots in Greek epic poetry.

Let me turn now to two examples of Andean writers who were already carrying out a radical critique of the colonial system when Montenegro was writing his essay, and were using this corrected gaze to observe reality as it should be seen: José Carlos Mariátegui and José María Arguedas.

For both Peruvian writers, modernity and its historical time had to pass through the filter of Andean reality, not the other way around. In the case of Mariátegui, what was revolutionary in his theoretical thinking— the Peruvian case is peculiar, in that Peruvians dominate the field of theory, but not the field of revolutionary action, in which thinking is put into practice—was its consistent allusion to the Indians' responsibility for solving their own "problem." In 1924, 1926, and 1928, when he published his famous *Seven Interpretive Essays on Peruvian Reality*, Mariátegui repeated the statement which no one in the Andean world, steeped in revolutionary thought, could dodge any longer, and which a few years later José María Arguedas made his own: the Indians were the only ones who could confront their own colonial condition. Of course, Mariátegui later toned down the radicalism of his thought, based on the critiques he received from the Third International, particularly from Argentine trade unionists, who forced him to modify his socialist strategy, asserting that the workers' vanguard had at their disposal activists of the Indian race who had contacted their unions and political movements. Mariátegui ended up accepting that it was the urban "historical agents" who were destined to put the Indian point of view into practice.

In 1941, two years before Montenegro published *Nacionalismo y colo-*

niaje, José María Arguedas refuted Mariátegui's urban solution to the Indian problem with his novel *Yawar fiesta*. Profoundly decolonizing, *Yawar fiesta* does precisely what Montenegro neglected to do: it puts the novel through the filter of reality—not only Andean reality but the complex dynamic, covered earlier by Mariátegui, between the highlands and the coast. At this moment, Arguedas was already refuting Mariátegui and discrediting the legitimacy of the urban trade union sectors for mediating in the solution to the Indian problem. In other words, Arguedas denied that indigenous communities had to follow the ideological route of unionist and urban proletariat modernity. The complexity of this argument surpassed by a wide margin the vision of Montenegro, who was unable to produce the type of decolonizing thought that could already be found in the Andes at the moment he wrote his *Nacionalismo y coloniaje*.

Let me conclude these reflections on Montenegro's essay with one last observation regarding mimesis. In Montenegro's work, the "historical future," the horizon of expectations, took on the temporal linearity of the European model that served him as his analytical tool; as a result, his book turned mimesis into mimicry.[7] Mimicry is copying the outward appearances of something without observing the intricate twists and turns of reality; that is, seeing the same through a "pre-text"—in Montenegro's case, the educated Western model of observing reality—that smoothes over differences because it imposes a "before" that presupposes the meaning and dangerously simplifies the reading of reality. Thus, *Nacionalismo y coloniaje* superimposes on reality the reading of a model that, as I have said, is now being seriously called into question by emerging positions that reclaim the right to exist from the vantage point of the new debates on epistemology, politics, and ethics. These debates, which cannot be reduced to abstract universals such as the Hegelian category of Totality, now adopt the perspective of social movements, which, ever since this rearticulating present began to use the past as a resource, has resisted being explained in terms of the uniform principles of the philosophies of history.

I think these observations on Montenegro and the crisis of historical time should begin to clarify the need to know whether the gaze of a middle-class urban revolutionary is or is not equal to that of an insurgent from the countryside.

Molded by a reading of the same European thought that was decisive in constructing the ideology of revolution, a local activist from the middle class will observe the process from "inside" modernity, from the horizon of expectations that doesn't question the rhetoric of progress or the triumphant linear path of revolution. In other words, a revolutionary will continue to frame his thought in universals that will determine a priori how reality should be observed. In the end, for him the revolution will continue to be a worldwide act, a universal act, laid down by the historical route of the West.

By clear contrast, a subaltern from the countryside will question that gaze, countering it with one of another sort, the product of her conflicted positioning in the structure of modernity, a gaze that is completely sensitive to the fact that modernity overshadows that other side of things called "the colonial difference," that is, the production of situations of colonial subjugations founded on odious racial distinctions that the subaltern has to put up with almost all the time, as they are constantly reproduced in everyday interactions. In other words, European thought, no matter how revolutionary it might be, neither sees nor feels coloniality, the local gaze of the other, of the oppressed, a gaze that, with the arrival of the current insurgent movements, is now there to correct and modify the injustices that the National Revolution itself completely overlooked.

Thinking and feeling from this colonial difference also meant that they would have to modify the spatial-temporal coordinates from which the thought of modernity was organized; that is, the notions of the space of experience and the horizon of expectations would have to undergo fundamental changes so that they could continue to serve in a world where the historical time of modernity is in crisis.

How does this new twist in the space of experience come about? The dominant culture introduced a clear difference between conservative tradition and the progressivism supported by the revolution. Coming from the West, the dominant culture separated tradition from revolution, but today, subaltern culture is busy bringing them together in a way that is a little strange and rather novel. The tradition in question is the insurrectional tradition of the multitude, a new historical phenomenon, in conflict with Western modernity, which is uniting the various popular sectors in mass mobilizations that bring the embers of the distant past into the present. This past, overshadowed by the dominant culture, had little visibility until very recently (Hylton et al. 2003: 16). I am speaking of an insurrectional tradition, which, by recalling its own history—one of constant insurrections throughout the long centuries of subjugation—can feel no gratitude toward the other past that the conservative mentality venerates and insurgent thought denounces as colonialist.

For its part, the horizon of expectations for the dominant culture is one of progress and development. Looking at it from the point of view of the insurgent movements, from the gaze of the indigenous peoples, this homogeneous time conflicts with the contemporaneity of the noncontemporaneous, which questions modernity from its own arcane view of things, thus creating worlds in conflict. Actually, it could be said that the horizon of expectations of Western thought has been called into question and conflicted by a plurinationality that for all its difference remains part of the universal project of nation building. This also means that the national project cannot remain in the hands of a dominant sector; it must be opened up to intercultural dialogue. In other words, this isn't a matter of going back to the old national project, looking at it now "from the bottom up." Rather, it demands the fashioning of a new project, one that, seen from its new and balanced spatial-temporal coordinates, will encompass the lineal time of modernity and the other time, "different in its human densities, its moments of condensation and its keys of meaning" (Gilly 2003: 27). Thus, history will become the object of a construction that, by overcoming homogeneous Western time, will fill up with the "time of the now" that Walter Benjamin called for in his "Theses" (1968 [1940]: 263). This is the past in the present, the resource of the "other," which I will now describe.

Busy reinventing the past, the "now" is the trimmed and shortened version of the future: it includes the desires of that great subaltern sector that was formerly denied entry to the banquet of modernity and that is impatient now to exchange its misery for an earthly paradise. It is from this present that the past is to be rethought; from this present we can perceive phenomena that have always been available to us but that we have not always sufficiently appreciated. With the crisis of the dominant power, with the gradual strengthening of social movements, with the subaltern insurgencies, these phenomena from the past reappear in the present as genuine "ruins" accumulated in the subsoil of memory.

As a semantic model of the crisis, the present, which expresses the time pressure that is felt for changing reality, also expresses the active demands of the oppressed strata of society. This is a utopian mentality, in conflict with the future expectations of modernity. So the present interweaves contrasting histories in search of a new order that won't be another vertical ordering, "from above," but instead will stick to obtaining, in a much more harmonious way, a worldly spiritual goal of political and social transformation.

Much like Mannheim, who delved into the utopian mentality that arose in the oppressed strata of postmedieval European society, or Mariátegui, who sought in the values of the indigenous community the possibility of giving a mystical meaning to the conflictive modernity of the Andes, in the present-day indigenous movements I see flashes of the past interweaving with our current world, as these movements eagerly strive to have their rights, lost in the past, restored to them. This is the spiritual ferment of the social sectors that demand to have their land returned to them and to be allowed to govern their own territory autonomously. And these are movements that are robustly material, aware of their historical claims, but also subject to a strongly utopian platform that would unite, from the present, the past and future.

The past as resource is remote from the liberal ideal of the modern state. Nothing would be more mistaken, from the point of view of the gaze of the other, than to try understanding the present from the conservative tradition or from the Enlightenment idea of revolution. Therefore, the past can also be used to reconsider the movement of literary tropes under which the Eurocentric culture of our peoples was organized and anchored in the metaphoric construction of national identity. Consequently, and with the aim of complicating the metaphorical-symbolic construction of the nation, it seems necessary to me to look into the rural, peasant origins of metaphor, above and beyond its decorative stability. It is the crude, primitive origin of catachresis that helps us study, like the ember of the past that it also is, the present of social movements. Indeed, if the historical time of modernity is being questioned now over the actions of social movements, so is the rhetorical model on which it is based and from which the nation-state is organized. If the state is founded on a tropological movement that gives pride of place to the totalizing metaphor, today its influence is yielding to the force of synecdoche, whose preference for the part over the whole sets the decadence and dissolution of the constituted order in motion, as Hayden White saw (1978), while also marking the inadequacies of the totalizing concepts on which the nation-state was founded.

Parting ways with the dominant system of thought, subaltern rhetoric walks back the dominant culture and questions its forms of knowledge, including the metaphors that organize its discourse. Undermining the foundations of patriarchal, criollo-mestizo metaphor, vernacular language —as in the case of the human lloqlla that Arguedas describes—somehow manages to dismantle the symbolic-metaphoric level on which the dominant culture is based, particularly historical time, the great metaphor that constitutes modernity.

Regarding this difficult, complex topic, here we should add, very briefly, in connection with the past as resource for reviving its embers in the present, that spatial-temporal rhetoric also complicates the homogenizing category of "nation-state," a totalization built by the elitist privilege of naming and representing. Thus, the ability of language itself to subvert the model of modernization relates to the fact that the dark side of reason escapes the dominion of metaphor through the *abusio* of vernacular language, a kind of linguistic return of the repressed, of the past that isn't dead, just silenced, penned in by the rhetoric of the dominant strata.

Bearing these embers of the past very much in mind, let me conclude this chapter by indicating that the decolonial perspective guiding my reflections is particularly sensitive to the analysis of the topics neglected by the thinking of modernity. I take decoloniality to be the concept that explains the need to criticize the rhetoric of modernity that would deny difference, that would exclude the other. Protected by the logic of modern European rationality, this rhetoric silences the histories of others, represses their subjectivities, and subalternizes their knowledge and their languages. Given that European modernity as practiced in Germany, France, and England constructed its narratives of salvation, emancipation, and progress by subjugating other peoples, from the profound colonization of the concepts of time and space,[8] it seems to me that the decolonial idea should deal with the urgent need to complicate historical time—the way the other is always situated "behind" dominant modernity—while recognizing that spatial-temporal differences were and are interwoven with what Aníbal Quijano has called "the colonial matrix of power" (2001). Therefore, to decolonize means to unveil the hidden complicity between the rhetoric of modernity and the logic of coloniality. This implies incorporating into the analysis of modernity this contemporaneity of the noncontemporaneous, which has traditionally been taken as a sign of "backwardness" on the temporal scale, and of "primitivity" and "barbarity" on the spatial scale.

Finally, I think there is no guarantee that the subaltern effort at decolonization will succeed, that it will effectively manage to escape the politics of the marketplace, and that it will be able to remove itself from the framework of capitalist "totality" and globalization. It seems to me that only by reclaiming the "outsiderness" of subaltern subjectivities will it be possible to overcome spatial-temporal frames, like those raised by Koselleck, that belong to a modernity that constantly reproduces coloniality because it refuses to recognize the dark side of its own being. Indeed, so long as the logics that govern our societies continue to be silenced by the rhetoric of progress and development, they will be unable to rid themselves of the logic of power, the practice of oppression, and the concentration of knowledge in the dominant groups that organize learning. However, I think that now, no longer deceived by power, we see something happening that has never taken place before in our multiple nations: the arrival of "societies on the move" (Zibechi 2006), of multiple singularities that can put an unexpected twist on this controversial modernity and speed up human events, using pluralism as a factor of innovation. We are living, then, in superimposed times, incomplete times, partial times, which keep us from living under the unitary logic of modernity, constantly reminding us that if we can't erase the traces of colonialism, we will remain separated from our longed-for integration.

Chapter Two
IS THE NATION AN IMAGINED COMMUNITY?

Rereading the classics in the social sciences, one begins to notice that even authors who analyze social reality from the perspective of class struggle tend to interpret societies as organic wholes, subject to rules of analysis that reinforce the criteria of unity and homogeneity through which human events are usually evaluated. The same is true when, as often occurs in the study of postcolonial societies, a historical analysis ignores the deep ethnic and racial divisions that mark political life in those nations. Similarly, concepts as important to the study of social organization as "national culture" are based on a straightforward assumption of a supposed national cohesiveness that simply does not correspond to reality. Thus, the triad of lettered culture (literature plus journalism), nation-state building, and the organization of culture is based on a debatable model, one that places its hopes on the rational and teleological organization of a social utopia. As I noted in the previous chapter with regard to the metahistorical category of future expectations, this is a Hegelian-style European model proclaiming the lineal, enlightened construction of modernity, which, after overcoming all the obstacles that present-day reality has strewn in its path, will necessarily lead to the future social utopia, be it capitalist or socialist. This inalterable course of historical events, this rectilinear path to seizing control of the state, is based on a profound conviction that the crises of the various historical and economic cycles will follow, one after another, without ever casting doubt on the lineal and progressive character of History.

As I look into the discourse surrounding the nation—which, because it deals with the collective organization of the people, is the most important discourse in the enlightened construction of modernity—I will emphasize that when critics talk about imagining the nation, they rarely take the complex relationship between nation and ethnicity into account as they should. In other words, this chapter asks whether an explanation of the nation also calls for an ethnic component, or whether the nation itself, unmoored from any situation predating its own organization, is the sole source of nationalism. To my way of understanding, the nation can only be theorized in strict relationship with the theme of ethnicity, which is linked to profound cultural conflicts that influential modern essays have ignored. For Benedict Anderson (1983), the origin of the nation lies in a "print-capitalist" nationalism that emerged from the sphere of the educated elite. This nationalism swallows up ethnic differences with a Eurocentric vision that overlooks or minimizes local conflicts. To counteract this view of things, in this chapter I will examine the writers Euclides da Cunha of Brazil and José Carlos Mariátegui of Peru, superlative intellectuals and analysts of Latin American culture. Neither could separate the study of modernity from the cultural conflict generated by ethnic identities that, given their archaic character, obstructed and called into question the forward progress of the official nation.

The "persistence of 'then' within 'now,'" Ernst Bloch's simultaneous presence of the nonmodern in the historical time of modernity (1991 [1935]), can be seen in the stubborn presence of ethnic identities as described in the essays of da Cunha and Mariátegui from the early twentieth century. These identities, uncomfortably grafted onto the project of Latin American nation building, reveal notable exceptions among intellectuals—writers who took a critical view of the triumphal liberal perspective on history, who were more cautious than most in fathoming the perilous formation of our nations.

Wishing to update the social criticism of Mariátegui and da Cunha, another aim of this chapter is to bring both writers into the present. Thus, I analyze how each linked the theme of ethnicity to the concepts of "multitude subalternity" and "the people." I feel that Mariátegui and da Cunha can help us reflect on themes that form part of the discussion about the nature and composition of the most recent social movements.

1. NATIONALISM, NATION, AND ETHNICITY

As the rhetoric that created the nation, there is no doubt that nationalism has been the most important discourse developed by modernity. Its origins are hazy, but they include the seventeenth-century English rebellions against the monarchy, the struggles initiated by eighteenth-century Spanish American elites against Spanish colonial rule, the French Revolution of 1789, and the reaction to that revolution in the late nineteenth-century German intellectual world (Calhoun 2007: 52).

Since its early modern origins, the discourse of the nation has been the way that people have been organized collectively. Thus, nationalism created the theory of administrative legitimacy, which states that ethnic borders should never cross or contradict political borders. The discourse of the nation also stressed that ethnic boundaries should not allow for divisions between ruling powers and the ruled. This discourse took up the question of ethnicity so that those who held power could not set themselves apart from the mass of civil society for other reasons. Having overcome the fragmentation of the nation into multiple ethnicities, nationalism successfully spread its three main ideas: that humanity naturally divides into nations; that these nations can be recognized by certain local characteristics, which call for being researched; and that the only legitimate form of government is one that has been self-determined by the nation (Kedourie 1993: 9).

Now, it wasn't easy for nationalism to encompass ethnicity, which was and remains a complex, slippery, and highly subjective phenomenon. That is true even though ethnic groups are said to have objective historical and cultural characteristics. For some writers, ethnicity is the symbolic use of some relevant aspect of culture to differentiate a given group from others (Eller 1999: 8). The slippery nature of ethnicity comes up when each ethnic group chooses the aspects of culture that are supposed to represent it and set it apart, including religious and linguistic elements. Thus, every ethnic group claims real or supposed common ancestors, a shared memory of a given historical past, and one or more symbols that lend coherence to its behavior. Given that ethnic groups frequently address the dominant culture, their demands for cultural recognition transform public space and engineer new relations of domination and exclusion (Wieviorka 2001).

An ethnic group's "cultural difference" may be real or subjective, but that has little bearing on the importance of its group identity. Its identity exists as a memory of the group's origins, whatever the actual case may be. Origins and lineages are often invoked as distinguishing elements.

They can turn into a genuine ideology of continuity with the past that the group promotes. It scarcely matters whether the group's memory of the past is true or demonstrable. The bottom line is that every ethnic group bases its behavior on its consciousness and self-perception of difference, scarcely bothering to explore how "objective" it may be.

It is in the dialectical relationship between the self-perceptions that ethnic groups have of themselves and the perceptions others have of them that diversity is gradually homogenized by dominant groups, which frame and use ethnic divisions in their symbolic and imagined construction of reality. This homogenizing process is facilitated by the fact that identities tend to be flexible and negotiable. Indeed, ethnic groups are flagrantly mobile, able to change by assimilating other identity and cultural patterns, even as they keep their self-determination and their status. That is why Frederick Barth (1969) thought of them as shifting groups that can give rise to active political movements.

Though the discourse of nationalism promotes the incorporation of all ethnic groups, the strengthening of institutions, and, through the creation of the nation-state, the standardization of the national language and forced acculturation, it is obvious that few states can really be classified as mononational. This fact forces nationalism to open up over the course of time and entertain the demands of ethnic groups that refuse to give up their self-determination.

Though nationalism became the preferred discursive form for social demands for political autonomy and self-determination, this accomplishment was not easily achieved. Indeed, the meaning of nationalism had to be constantly renegotiated. Proof of this lies in the new nationalisms that proliferate today in the West, as well as in the new nationalist attempts to decolonize the state. This is particularly true in postcolonial societies where ethnically based social movements are strong. We see, then, that nationalism—that constantly changing notion—is not an artifact of the past, but rather a living presence that has incorporated preexisting ethnicities into its rhetoric.[1]

As all of this shows, the relationship between nation and ethnicity is complicated. In academic terms, the fact that scholars cannot agree on the nature of that relationship means that, for some, the prior existence of ethnic difference cannot explain the nation, while for others, ethnic difference is the source of nationalism. Understanding the importance of this problem, Eric Hobsbawm (1990) stated that the basic characteristic of the modern nation is precisely its modernity. The noun cannot be understood apart from its defining adjective; that is, *modern* nations have nothing to do with ethnic identities, which are fundamentally archaic in nature. As we will see, Benedict Anderson argues his influential essay on the nation as an imagined community along the interpretive lines set out by Hobsbawm.

For other writers, such as Anthony Smith, the prior existence of ethnicity is the basic source of the nation (Smith 1981). For them, belonging to the nation is always a product of prior ethnic mobilizations (Calhoun 2007: 67). This interpretation runs counter to Hobsbawm's, but as we will see, it accords with the analysis of Indian historian Ranajit Guha, one of the main theorizers of subalternity, who also disagrees with Hobsbawm and Anderson on the subject of nationalism.

According to Hobsbawm's and Anderson's interpretation, the discourse of the nation swallows up ethnic difference in the same way that the translation of ethnicity into nationalism is, in part, a conversion of traditional cultures and ways of life into more specific historical demands. Ernest Gellner (1983) suggests that this transformation takes place due to the development of an educated "high culture," which extends the human interactions that once took place only face-to-face. Benedict Anderson develops this notion when he accentuates the role of print capitalism and its mass marketing of newspapers and novels in the constitution of the nation as an imagined community. I will return to this point later when I discuss the theme of educated culture.

Craig Calhoun notes the emphasis that Herder and Fichte placed on the "originality" of the German language in the formation of German national character; thus, Fichte "claimed a supra-historical status for German nationality. . . . This does not mean that Fichte and others of similar orientation saw glory only in the past. On the contrary, they envisaged a dramatic break with many aspects of the past," and therefore saw the need to construct a new history that would correct the lack of a consciousness that reflected the self-construction of the German nation-state (Calhoun 2007: 64). In consequence of this aim, the metaphor of "awakening" began to represent the entire German rhetorical effort to give the nation a new identity. This effort also required that political demands take precedence over ethnic claims.

In criticizing this focus, we therefore cannot lose sight of the role of language, of "high culture," in nation building. At issue is the homogenizing language, which, in casting aside vernacular languages, adopts the paternal language of the dominant elites. It is through the intermediary role of this dominant language that the nation is imagined and created.

Hence the homogenizing language of the elites appears in two guises: (a) formulating a civic model that swallows up ethnic difference; and (b) marking a superiority derived from the colonial structure of knowledge and opposed to linguistic variation.

In sum, the civic model—the continuity of ethnic difference within the modern nation—depends, as Anthony Smith (1981, 1986) has noted, on the process of social construction established by the discourse of nationalism. Given that ethnicity changes slowly, Smith suggests that it is possible to trace a "genealogy of nations" in which the structural variables of culture and society testify to the transformation of ethnic into national difference. The crucial moment in this genealogy occurs when the members of a given ethnic group become citizens and are thereby assimilated into the national project imposed by modernity.

By giving value to gradual change over historical time, the ideologues of nationality imposed the unity of the nation under the prevailing logocentric perspective of modernity. One of the most important theorists of this conservative tradition is Benedict Anderson.

2. THE NATION: A CONTESTED CONCEPT

Setting nationalism apart from "conscious political ideologies" such as liberalism and fascism, Anderson introduces an interesting take on the topic: he suggests that we should relate nationalism to the "great cultural systems" that preceded it, such as dynastic succession and the religious community. Wishing to study nationality, "nation-ness," and nationalism as "cultural artifacts of a particular kind" (Anderson 1983: 21), that is, as historical forces that could be transplanted to a wide variety of social situations, including the realm of other political ideologies, Anderson proposes that the nation should be understood as

> an imagined political community. . . . It is imagined because the members of even the smallest nation will never know most of their fellow-members, meet them, or even hear of them, yet in the minds of each lives the image of their communion. . . The nation is imagined as limited because even the largest of them, encompassing perhaps a billion living human beings, has finite, if elastic, boundaries, beyond which lie other nations. . . . It is imagined as sovereign because the concept was born in an age in which Enlightenment and Revolution were destroying the legitimacy of the

divinely-ordained, hierarchical dynastic realm.... Finally, it is imagined as a community, because, regardless of the actual inequality and exploitation that may prevail in each, the nation is always conceived as a deep, horizontal comradeship. (1993: 23–25)

Critics frequently overlook the fact that Anderson takes language to be the most important cultural condition for the nation. His "imagined community" privileges the language promoted by the "high culture" of local elites who subsume different dialects into their discourse. This language of "high culture" derives from the colonial powers, which, over the course of historical time (defined by Benjamin [1968 (1940): 261] as "homogeneous, empty time"), coincided with the print technology developed by the capitalist system. As Gellner observes, print allowed "high culture" to permeate every civic space, making it the secret to the success of capitalism. Thus, everyone read the same products of lettered culture (novels and newspapers), creating a fraternal, horizontal imaginary community, living in the same time, ruled by the same temporal moment, which synchronized the human events that are, in the final analysis, subject to the linear development of historical time. With the growth of citizenship, the people, who could no longer interact with one another face-to-face, consumed these technological advancements that were produced by the relations of capitalist production.

This fundamental contribution of Anderson's text—that the forms of communication produced by capitalism are basic to understanding the identity of the imagined community—has drawn the critical attention of three important cultural critics.

Mexican sociologist Claudio Lomnitz raises doubts about the reality of the imagined community as a "horizontal link based on fraternity" (Lomnitz 2001: 335). For Lomnitz, this description of the community obscures and distorts the concrete experience of Latin America, where different sectors of society and ethnic groups have always been linked by "vertical ties of loyalty" and dependency, not exactly ties of "camaraderie" (335). Indeed, Anderson seems to forget that Latin America has always been the scene of a struggle between a "strong" form of citizenship and another "weak" form, subjugated and dependent, composed basically of the ethnic majorities. Given that "cultural difference" has profoundly marked the heterogeneous nature of our reality, it is difficult to agree that the power of nationalism originated in these ties of fraternity, which to this day are instilled in future citizens in our grade school classrooms. In reality, the "strong" citizens, the first-class citizens, were those who could use their communication capabilities, both oral and written, to address all other citizens through their cultural products: journalism and literature.

For her part, the cultural critic Mary Louise Pratt has grave doubts about the communicative power created by bourgeois nation-building projects and generated through print capitalism. For Pratt, there is an enormous "distance between the homogeneity of the imagined community and the fractured reality of linguistic experience in modern stratified societies" (Pratt 1987: 51). Pratt also expresses doubt about the fraternal and horizontal nature of that community. On the one hand, Anderson's concept is distressingly androcentric; on the other hand, it neglects to question the fact that "high culture" creates the national ideal not in the image and likeness of the dominant class that forges it, but rather in that of the other, their subordinates. Pratt questions the naming power of grammar and insists on supporting heterogeneity, vernacular languages, and autochthonous ways of life, which are what represent cultural difference.

But the most troublesome limitation of Anderson's theory is that he does not incorporate the interactions of the extremely unequal interpretive communities that live within nations into his concept of the imagined community. Pratt considers Anderson an inadequate observer of the phenomenon of multiculturality. For her, the imagined community is a utopian construction of the nation, one that clashes with the dystopian communities that do not fit comfortably in the unifying language of nationhood. Pratt's critique (1987) goes on to postulate "contact zones" and the struggle for interpretive power by the fragmented subjectivities of multiple cultures. In this way, the subaltern sectors of society would simultaneously need to identify with and dissociate from the dominant group.

These "contact zones"—linguist Roman Jakobson (1976) used the term "contact" to refer to speech events that questioned the language code itself—help not only to differentiate among the interactions of different classes, races, genders, and ages, but also to relate them to each other, taking care that their interpretations do not imply nonexistent harmony or dystopian relations based on the bad faith of the actors.

In other words, Pratt criticizes Anderson's neglect of social heterogeneity, which, as far removed as they are from the academy and the lettered elites, have to be conceptualized differently, distinctly from the sovereign, horizontal, and fraternal community. Anderson's notion is dominated by the linguistics of a community whose perception of language is based on the norms of a modern vision of a unified, homogeneous social world.

Forged from the point of view of the lettered elites, this imaginary community comes under harsh criticism in a brief review by subalternist historian Guha (1985). The validity of the Anderson thesis is based, as I have indicated, on a foundation of print capitalism, which from Guha's point of view carries a problematic colonialist slant. If we were to overlook the fact that the spread of Western liberal ideas organized the political nationalism of the colonized peoples, Guha argues, we would fall into the error of ignoring the stubborn nationalism of the masses. Indeed, Guha points out that Anderson's imagined community is a failure because Anderson doesn't realize that the discourse on nationality, forged in the interaction between local elites and the colonizer, clashed constantly with the other, popular sort of nationalism, which was rejected by "high culture" but was just as interested in power. In the case of India (poorly described by Anderson, according to Guha), the nation and nationalist discourse were forged in the parallel and relatively autonomous political worlds of elites and subalterns.

According to Guha, in preindustrial societies, where the peasantry is a major social force and with unmistakable politics, traditional values that clash with liberal culturalist ideas and with the political aspirations of the bourgeoisies are often set aside and given no importance. Omitting this working-class experience of nationalism makes it impossible for Anderson to set out a more balanced explanation of the "origins" of the nation. For Guha, it would also be necessary to keep in mind that official and popular nationalism run alongside each other, in parallel. Anticipating Pratt's critique, Guha declares that reducing language to an expression of print capitalism is problematic for two reasons: first, because it ignores the diverse uses of everyday spoken language; second, because it uncritically accepts the discourse about modernity and the historical time that establishes it.

Guha's argument against basing the discourse of the nation exclusively on linear time is convincing. For Guha, there are moments in national history when the community's self-image ceases to line up with the horizon of expectations in modernity. These are moments when the community returns to itself and follows a cyclical time, quite unlike the time of the flow of history. In other words, the homogeneous and empty time of modernity—homogeneous because, independently of any particular episodes, it takes place "in" time; empty, because it is like a bottomless bag that can contain countless events—cannot explain the shortcuts that take place over the course of history. Historical time has its setbacks, its lapses, which participate in aspects of millenarianism, of utopianism, and which function as "resources of the present" that call the triumphal march of history into question. This movement dominates the course of Spanish American history from the nineteenth century through the early twentieth.

3. LETTERED CULTURE

The modernizing perspective on building the Latin American future was based on a totalizing view of reality that grew from the important foundational essays of nation building, such as Domingo Faustino Sarmiento's *Facundo*, a book that created the paradigm of civilization and barbarism in the mid-nineteenth century.

If the *letrado*, the educated or lettered member of the elite, is the type of intellectual who is able to represent public life, Sarmiento is a clear case of the Latin American writer who has a vocation of representing the nation, who publicly recognizes that representing it means accepting that one has an obligation to society. It also means that there is a risk that the letrado will ultimately be dogged by the ideas he presents in his works. Thus, we give the name "lettered culture" (*cultura letrada*) to the representation of modern public life in the different literary genres. Dedicated to the art of representation, the letrados were not sociologists or social scientists, properly speaking, but "men of letters" who, since the nineteenth century, have been "in symbolic relationship with their time" (Said 1994: 13).

Luiz Costa-Lima (1992: 152–154) argues that Sarmiento's work is the most important of the Romantic liberal period. Around the middle of the nineteenth century, Romanticism created a close relationship in Latin America between politics and literary creativity. A hybrid text that incorporates biography, essay, history, and narrative imagination, *Facundo* (1845) was originally published in a series of pamphlets that circulated among the opponents of Argentine dictator Juan Manuel de Rosas. A biography of a minor regional strongman, Facundo Quiroga, who was allegedly assassinated by Rosas, *Facundo* presents a general, pessimistic diagnosis of the Argentine society of the time.[2] Indeed, *Facundo* is based on evidence of the backwardness of life in the provinces, the flagrant contrast between the rural towns and the "lettered cities."[3] Sarmiento drew a contrast between the urban centers and the rural hinterlands of our countries. This contrast came about because the main cities and ports of Latin America displayed the same civilized modernity that was to be found in the European centers of power, with which they had close commercial ties. The "logic" of diffusionism therefore demanded that the cultural models imported from the international centers of economic power should be held in the highest regard and transmitted to the hinterlands of our societies, where they would replace homegrown cultural forms, in keeping with the totalizing vision of their "civilizing" point of view.

Beginning with works such as Sarmiento's, these rationalizing discourses that were at work in organizing the national states of Latin America, particularly the positivist discourses of progressivism and the irreversible movement of history that dominated the second half of the nineteenth century, were based on the premise that Latin American unity had practically already been achieved. Thus, writers emphasized education, a fact that reinforced one of the most important characteristics of their ennobling, altruistic view of history: the good intentions of the educators (journalists and men of letters) who, trained in Enlightenment doctrine, sought to have our countries join the community of learned nations. Joining that community would parallel the close link between raw natural materials and the dynamics of the world economy. In this way, the rationalizing model of these letrados was ultimately consistent with the project of spreading the ideals of the rising bourgeoisie. In the countries where the liberal project of the nineteenth century succeeded, it drew in the most traditional sectors of the old oligarchy and established a foundation for organizing the liberal-oligarchic state.

Still, it must be acknowledged that the struggle between liberals and conservatives was more fiction than reality. Recall that both liberals and conservatives belonged to the same oligarchy, making it difficult to distinguish between them as two sharply antagonistic social sectors. In general, neither of the two factions had any interest in responding to the pressing demands of the people. Nevertheless, it is also true that liberals and conservatives had their differences with regard to the question of social demands. The antiliberalism of Paraguayan dictator José Gaspar de Francia and Argentine dictator Manuel de Rosas became so authoritarian that neither of them ever hesitated to eliminate their rivals in the most violent ways imaginable. Moreover, their antiliberalism closed the borders of their countries to foreign investment. Liberal governments, by contrast, opened their countries up to European economic and cultural penetration. Liberalism developed public education and adopted the lifestyle of Western democracies.

It is worth noting that neither liberals nor conservatives did away with the colonial order of things. The cases of two letrados—Francisco Bilbao of Chile, the leading light of liberalism, and Francisco García Calderón of Peru, conservative par excellence—prove that no insurmountable political gulf separated the two doctrines. Implicitly or explicitly, both agreed that no popular mass could uphold a claim to rights of their own. Thus, despite their critiques of social reality, they put forward no concrete political alternatives, because they fundamentally did not disagree with the positions taken by the dominant oligarchies. The same was true in Bolivia, where, despite the competing positions taken by Alcides Arguedas and Franz Tamayo, the concept of race remained the determining factor in building the nation, both Tamayo and Arguedas being linked to the colonial structures of power.

Despite the unsullied liberal, progressive view of history, which made the lettered city the one true seat of civilization, reality continued to demonstrate that this utopia only concealed the fractured, "backward" face of society. This was the result of the failure of the urban bourgeoisie, which led the old-style great landowning families to ally themselves with the military. The rise of the dictator Rosas was a clear example.

We should point out, however, that the situation in Brazil was different, which also helps explain why Euclides da Cunha had a clearer view of the contradictions generated by modernity. We cannot speak of the failure of the urban bourgeoisie in Brazil, where the bourgeoisie did not play a determining role in politics until well into the twentieth century. The old landowning class kept control of the country throughout the Brazilian Empire period (1822–1889), refusing to share power with the military. Only after the Brazilian Republic was declared in the late nineteenth century did army officers appear on the political scene, where they took power alongside the export-oriented agricultural bourgeoisie. Actually, this bourgeoisie lost power after 1930, when the military elite established a new social pact that placed them at the apex of the country.

Brazil was also an exception in European colonial history. Portuguese colonial administrators did not exercise power in so harsh and vexatious a way as the Spanish; instead, they tolerated local powers and avoided the regionalization found in the Spanish empire. Another major difference was the fact that the Portuguese monarchy itself moved to the Americas to escape the 1808 Napoleonic occupation of Lisbon. As a result, Brazil never had a true independence movement or popular uprising. Despite the crises of the monarchy (Emperor Pedro I abdicated in 1831 in order to deal with pressing affairs in Portugal, and the Regency period for his young son, the five-year-old Pedro II, lasted until 1840), the empire held on for half a century, giving Brazil a level of stability scarcely to be found in Spanish America during those decades. The Brazilian army remained in the background: military officers took power only after the advent of the Republic, when they became powerful agents for the oligarchs. The doctrines of positivism and Social Darwinism were centered in the military academy (the Escola Militar), from which they spread throughout society, giving the military the intellectual tools they needed to impose their will on the civilian sectors of society (Costa Lima 1992: 155).

4. THE BRAZIL OF EUCLIDES DA CUNHA

Despite the well-known cases of writers openly committed to the liberal civilizing project—Sarmiento in Argentina; Francisco Bilbao and José Victorino Lastarria in Chile—there were also notable exceptions, lettered elites who took a critical view of the triumphal liberal perspective on history. These were writers who began to express doubts, in works written early in the twentieth century, about the limitless bounty of modernity, writers who took greater care in exploring the formation of our nations. One such work was *Os sertões: Campanha de Canudos* (2010 [1902]), a remarkably critical nonfiction book by Euclides da Cunha, written during the period when Brazil was consolidating its First Republic. That era, with its positivist prism for observing reality, had completely superseded the long stage of institutional monarchy in Brazil that had begun in 1808. Nevertheless, as da Cunha's book testifies, the Republic had not been created without spilling some blood, nor could its liberal politics, fraught with Social Darwinism, survive before being tested by the violent opposition of rebel and millenarian movements. The millenarian movement based in Canudos, in the northeastern state of Bahia, fiercely resisted assimilation by the modernity that the republic was enforcing with bloody military repression. It is worth taking a good look at Brazil as an example of the crisis of modernity before we examine da Cunha's impressive book.

During the first decade of the twentieth century, Latin America reacted against the positivist ideas that had held sway there since the 1850s. This reaction led some writers to look at liberalism with critical eyes. Certain historical events, such as the 1898 war, which spelled the end of the Spanish

Empire in the Americas, and the 1896 Canudos War in Brazil, prompted this reaction (Williamson 1992: 304–306). Indeed, the humiliation experienced by Spain at the hands of the United States increased the fear in Latin America of an imminent Anglo-Saxon danger that could spell the end for the values of the Spanish-speaking world. That military event gave rise to a revaluation of our spiritual traditions and led to calls for curbing the modernizing materialism that was pouring out of the United States. Uruguayan writer José Enrique Rodó's influential essay *Ariel* (1900) joined the intellectual production of other great modernist writers, such as Rubén Darío of Nicaragua and José Martí of Cuba, to give us clear proof of the intellectual disdain that was felt at the time for the United States.

After the long constitutional monarchy period in Brazil, the 1896 rebellion of Canudos demonstrated the failings of the liberal republic that had only recently been established there. Mario Vargas Llosa used this historic (and literary) event as a background for imagining his novel *The War of the End of the World* (*La guerra del fin del mundo*, 1988). My interpretation of the rebellion differs somewhat from Vargas Llosa's. Where Vargas Llosa tends to see the federal state of Brazil as undeniably superior, depicting the "tragic necessity" of exterminating the uncouth jagunços (the pejorative term applied to the rebels of Canudos) in the name of modernity, da Cunha's treatment of the same war is an impressive narrative of the confusion caused by the presence of modernity in a Latin America still weighed down by colonial social and economic structures.

Euclides da Cunha, a prominent journalist, engineer, and positivist sociologist, was sent as a correspondent for a Rio de Janeiro newspaper to cover the third rebellion of Canudos, an event that shook the civic consciousness of Brazil in the early twentieth century. The product of his observation of that terrible rebellion is the book *Os sertões*.

Os sertões is, among other things, the story of the successive military campaigns, each fiercer than the last, that the Brazilian federal army carried out against the people of Canudos between 1896 and 1897. A veritable "bandits' cave," in the words of one of the expeditionary officers, Canudos was located in the heart of the *sertão* (backlands) of Bahia and was defended tenaciously and quite successfully by the jagunços under the millenarian leadership of their prophet, Antonio Conselheiro ("Antonio the Counselor"). The four military campaigns against Canudos ended with the defeat of the jagunços and the deaths of thousands of Brazilians on both sides, including, ultimately, Conselheiro himself. *Os sertões*, a true epic of social disaster, could be considered a sui generis foundational essay of the Brazilian nation, its origins in the raw violence accompanying the rise of the military to power rather than the tinsel display of romantic love found in the novels of the era. *Os sertões* seeks to reveal the causes for the rise of this millenarian movement, a kind of anachronistic pietism, a veritable "ruin" of the past that sought refuge in an isolated and forbidding landscape, stubbornly refusing to participate in the progress of history, the "arrow of time" that had sailed forth from the positivist bow of the military.

Os sertões is also an exposé of the holocaust produced by an army trained in European war techniques, a modern army that eradicated a poor town in the sertão from the face of the earth. Their bloody campaign served as proof that Brazil was not the romanticized vision found in so many other works that observed and documented Latin America. Quite the contrary: da Cunha puts Brazil on view with all its radical inequality, its tragically divided national geography. The country was so divided that when the federal soldiers marched against Canudos, they did not conceive of their job as a crusade to recover the most profound aspects of their national heritage; rather, they were undertaking a war whose goal was to conquer a "foreign land," one cut off from the principles that "scientifically" governed the construction of modernity.

As a witness to the heroic defense that the fierce jagunços put up against the brutal assault by Republican troops, da Cunha felt that his ideas were called seriously into question. He therefore balanced his "civilized" inclination toward liberal positivism, which would have him believe in the innate inferiority of local culture, against the compassionate respect that his writing gradually acquired toward the inhabitants of Canudos. These were the true "wretched of the earth," who, quite strictly speaking, had no other alternative but to be rejected and classified as a group of social degenerates. Put another way: da Cunha's consciousness was at odds with his positivist observation and documentation of reality. The journalist realized that the rebellion of Canudos was not the blindly capricious effort on the part of the jagunços to return to traditional constitutional monarchy that he had been led to expect, but rather a newly emerging religious vision, anchored in ancestral myths that were seemingly out of place in the modern world. The tragedy of this unresolved and contradictory situation, brought about by the opposing forces that kept Brazil from becoming a single, uniform territory, gave *Os sertões* its tremendous emotional force and made da Cunha's book an excellent study of the way racial determinism crumbles in the face of the rebels' humanity. It allows us to see the hidden face of a reality that resisted, and still resists, being studied as a homogeneous totality in which modernity overcomes the alleged backwardness and degeneracy of those who are denied access to the banquet of Western civilization.

Based on *Os sertões* we can state that da Cunha never renounced progress; on the other hand, he was aware that the fruits of progress shouldn't be for the exclusive enjoyment of the elites. What's more, because of his tragic view of the events at Canudos, da Cunha was tormented by his difficulty in explaining how the people there could be prepared for joining modernity without having their identity destroyed. In his mind, the construction of the longed-for Brazilian nationality remained in doubt. And isn't the search for identity still as much a burning issue, just as problematic, in the first decades of the twenty-first century as it was one hundred years ago?

The background to these questions, one that explains the fragility of "national culture," is the presence of unequal cultures that have not fused together and given way to a new civilizing project and that do not live together in harmony. So can we still affirm the existence of the imagined community as theorized by Anderson? The example of Canudos, where ethnic relations demonstrate the inadequacy of civic culture, reveals the contrary. In Brazil there has never been a convergence between the ancestral cultures and the successive models of Western civilization that have become hegemonic among the dominant groups, only opposition, for one reason: the social groups that have held power (political, economic, ideological) since the arrival of the Europeans, members by inheritance or by circumstances of Western civilization, have supported historical projects that leave no room for local cultures to thrive. The dominant position of these groups, including the presence of their modernizing armies, with their origins in the stratified class structure of colonial society, was expressed in an ideology that could conceive the future (development, progress, advancement, even revolution) only according to terms set by Western civilization. Cultural difference, and specifically the presence of multiple local cultures, was always understood as an obstacle along the only path toward the one valid goal. The colonial structures of power and of knowledge, expressions of a mentality inherited from the Iberian conquerors, did not let them see or imagine any other way forward: local cultures, such as the culture of the sertão in northeastern Brazil, simply had to disappear. These cultures were inarguably inferior from the colonizer's point of view, and unacceptable for the construction of the future.

But Euclides da Cunha, who also considered the mestizo of the sertão to be "an unbalanced hysteric" (2010 [1902]: 97), must have nonetheless understood that the peasants' stubborn defense of their customs cast doubt on the scientific method of observing reality; that the Social Darwinism of the era was inadequate, too limited, for judging events.[4] Indeed, how was it possible (from a positivist point of view) for a corrupt, degenerate ethnic group to stand up so successfully to a modern army, trained in the most advanced European fighting techniques?

Within *Os sertões*, the tragic, mystical figure of Antonio Conselheiro—that "great man gone wrong" (142), that "pietist who longed for the Kingdom of God" (139), that fearsome jagunço who "reproduced the mysticism of the past" (137)—tragically shattered da Cunha's evolutionary attitudes. Indeed, it was not *kronos*, lineal and progressive historical time, that blazed the trail that Conselheiro and his sertão rebels took; it was instead the *kairos* of a time fraught with the deep crisis generated by a painful truth: that there were two Brazils, two nations divided by the struggle between the opposing forces of modernity and coloniality. Indeed, Conselheiro's behavior was the product of a struggle between two different historical projects. It wasn't a simple matter of formulating alternative projects within the framework of one common civilization—projects that could hypothetically change the reality of the moment without questioning the deepest values of that civilizing project.[5] Rather, it was a matter of understanding that these were two different projects, based on distinct views of the world, nature, and society; that each posited different value hierarchies; that they did not share the same aspirations or understand in the same way what it meant to be fully human. They were projects that expressed two different concepts of social organization. For all these reasons, projects of social unification proposed that unity should be achieved by eliminating the people of the sertão. Regarding this eclipse of local culture for the benefit of foreign, imported culture, da Cunha wrote:

> Having lived for four hundred years on a vast coastal plain, in a pallid reflection of civilized life, we suddenly found ourselves with an unlooked-for inheritance: the Republic. We ascended abruptly, swept up in a torrential flood of modern ideas, and leaving, in the heart of our country, a third of our people languishing in age-old darkness. Deluded by a secondhand civilization, blindly copying down what we had best left in the organic codes of other nations, while utterly ignoring the needs of our own nation, in our revolu-

tionary zeal we only deepened the contrast between our way of life and that of our rude native sons, more foreign in this land than immigrants from Europe. For what separated us from them was not an ocean; what separated us was three centuries. (160; my translation)

As mentioned above, da Cunha discovered that the Canudos rebellion was not aimed at restoring the constitutional monarchy, as the supporters of liberal republicanism believed; instead, the rebels sought a resurgence of a "diffuse and incongruous religiosity" (161) that was incompatible with modernity. The Canudos rebellion gives us a chance to read Anderson's theory against the grain.[6] Indeed, da Cunha's book introduces doubts about the possibility of achieving the oft-mentioned unity of the nation, that "fraternal, horizontal community" which Anderson (1983) theorized as "imagined."

5. MARIÁTEGUI AND THE CASE OF PERU

Unlike Brazil, nineteenth-century Spanish America was unable to unite as a single political entity. Brazil's ability to carry out the construction of one homogeneous and relatively efficient nation-state contrasts with the fragmentation of Spanish America. In the case of the Andes, states were built before any true nations had been organized (Favre 1998). Compared with the independence movement that took place in Mexico, Peru became independent in 1821 with insufficient support from the masses. Nor did it have enough support to settle accounts with its colonial past. On top of this frustration, some years later there came Peru's military defeat in 1879, the occupation of a portion of its national territory by Chile, and economic collapse. With all this background, it is clear that Peru was not a nation and that the project of building a republic had failed. At the close of the nineteenth century, according to historian and essayist Alberto Flores Galindo (1989: 5), there was no telling what the social reality of Peru was. Indeed, after a full century, Peru had still not been able to resolve the cultural conflict between elites and the popular classes, and the differences that the colonial structure had established in politics, religion, ethnicity, and gender had only grown more profound. In broad outline, Peruvian society was divided between a rich and privileged dominant class of European origin and a broad, poor popular sector composed of indigenous people, the descendants of enslaved Africans who had been brought from West Africa to Peru in the seventeenth century, and Chinese laborers who worked in the nineteenth-century guano mines. An intellectual precursor of José Carlos Mariátegui, the anarchist Manuel González Prada, called nineteenth-century Peru a country "of gentlemen and of servants."

In the nineteenth century, Peru increased trade with the imperial powers of Europe, especially the British, forging tight bonds with the world economy. The Europeans and Peru's coastal oligarchs united to exploit the mineral riches of the Andes, build railroads, and establish great cotton and sugar plantations. This economic expansion was based on the poorly paid labor of indigenous, black, and Chinese workers. Profits filled the bank accounts of British and German companies and also financed the magnificent haciendas of the Peruvian criollo elites as well as their frequent trips to civilized Europe. Within Peru, these criollo oligarchs established a strict hierarchy that intertwined class and caste domination, thus creating a pseudo-bourgeoisie that set up the ideological foundations of a country where the vast majority were denied political representation and economic rights, excluding them from the imagined community of those who could claim national citizenship (Starn, Degregori, and Kirk 1995: 164–165).

Under these conditions of dependency, the War of the Pacific between Peru, Bolivia, and Chile (1879–1883) was a hard blow, because it increased awareness that the country had not managed to become a true nation. In the most favorable scenario conceivable, the war might possibly have led to a transformation of Peruvian society; as things turned out, however, all it did was to further fragment the social whole. Recent studies, such as Florencia Mallon's on the Comas region (Starn, Degregori, and Kirk 1995: 168–186), show that the war with Chile gave rise to a deep cultural division in which the nationalism forged "from above" became completely divorced from the nationalism "from below" developed by the peasantry. Mallon notes that the Chilean invasion of Peru's central plateau set off a complex political game carried out by the local indigenous peasants, whose properties were directly threatened by the invading army, with the encouragement of merchants, priests, and other local authorities. It was a fierce guerrilla campaign against the aggressors. Events such as this one, detailed in Mallon's interesting study, together with subalternist analyses such as Guha's on the prose of peasant insurgencies (1983), prove that indigenous Peruvians had developed a basic sense of nationalism—we could call it an "alternative nationalism" or an "other nationalism"— rooted in their love for the land and the stubborn sense of territoriality that held them together as a separate ethnic group, apart from the official nationalism. Indeed, as Mallon notes, from this conflict on, the highland indigenous peasantry developed their understanding of national politics as well as their own concept of nationalism based not on a symbolic sense of nationhood but on their love of the land. In this way, Chileans were their enemies not because they were Chilean but because they had invaded and destroyed the land, their means of subsistence and making a living. Instead of an abstract analysis of the nation, they grasped the concrete reality of what political debates meant for life in the indigenous community.

This was the sort of conflict that Peruvian lettered culture not only discounted but even concealed when the educated elites sought to organize the modern nation under the "democratic authoritarianism" (*cesarismo democrático*) of the early twentieth century. Thus, letrados such as the prototypical traditional intellectuals Víctor Andrés Belaúnde and Francisco García Calderón Rey presented their own social class, the early twentieth-century Peruvian oligarchy, with a vision of the country that lacked any kind of collective project.

Writing from Paris, Francisco García Calderón replicated the theoretician's practice of separating ideas from their historical context. Thus, his writing bore the same anti-Yankee stamp that Uruguayan writer José Enrique Rodó had displayed in his critique of North American imperialism, written in 1900, when the North had just begun to encroach on Latin America. Rodó's "Arielismo," whose sphere of influence included García Calderón, formed part of that long letrado tradition that I have described above, in which writers from El Inca Garcilaso de la Vega through Sarmiento and beyond forged a "national culture," which, when combined with the Arielismo of the late nineteenth century, became a critique of capitalist materialism. These critiques, which never completely broke with the Romantic liberalism of that era, were contradicted by a group of Peruvian writers, and particularly by the ideas of José Carlos Mariátegui.

Unlike García Calderón, Mariátegui reflected on society not "from" Paris but "from" Lima. The place where Mariátegui elaborated and enunciated his ideas was not simply coincidental; it was, to the contrary, consubstantial with the Peruvian Marxist's two reasons for parting ways with Arielismo, a philosophy rooted in an exclusively culturalist analysis of the problems of Spanish America and of Peru in particular.

In the first place, Mariátegui's thinking was no longer just an imitation of European views. By thinking about the reality of Peru from within the very heart of the colonial structure, Mariátegui could see the colonial condition from "outside" the ways of thinking cultivated in Europe and the United States, though he later said he had received his best intellectual training in Europe. One result of his geopolitical location was an insistence that any analysis of reality had to be grounded in the material and political economic history of the moment, quite apart from all philosophical abstractions. When he thus revealed the economic basis for neocolonialism, he put his finger right on the problem—and doing that touched a raw nerve: Peru was not, and would never become, a modern European society, because the very root of its modernity was burdened with a different sort of colonial structure, with a socioeconomic structure that exhibited the "persistence of 'then' within 'now'" that called into question the linear and teleological flow of history.[7]

Thinking against the grain about the meaning of history was the basic change that Mariátegui introduced into his reading of the realities of Latin America. The evolutionary meaning of history that Hegel had set out—the notion that the world is all governed by the same historical time, with Europe at the center of the movement of history—had a powerful influence on European Marxism. In contrast, the school of progressive and "organic" intellectuals from the South—Antonio Gramsci is their most important thinker—creatively questioned Hegel's logocentrism. This was the transformative school of Marxism to which Mariátegui belonged. He began the new Latin American tradition of complementing a reading of reality in the old class-structure terms (aristocracy, bourgeoisie, proletariat) with a novel understanding of material inequalities, contextualized in space and time.

Second, his work helped put an end to the culture fetishism into which Eurocentric theoreticians had largely fallen in Peru. By turning their full attention to cultural matters, they had forgotten the socioeconomic basics that should condition any reading of reality. A heterodox Marxist in the fullest sense of the term, Mariátegui was the first to undertake a rigorous analysis of Latin American society. In the 1920s, when Mariátegui was elaborating his thesis about Marxism as a myth for our times, the Mexican thinker José Vasconcelos, along with other important Latin American intellectuals, was using the concept of *indigenismo* to explain the future of Latin America. Vasconcelos and the others did this based on understandings that had little to do with the actual cultural conflicts in which our countries were immersed. It was different with Mariátegui. His *Siete ensayos de interpretación de la realidad peruana* (1928; trans., *Seven Interpretive Essays on Peruvian Reality*, 1971) gave an illuminating perspective on the situation of indigenous people in the real economic, political, and historical context of the Andes.

Other factors made Mariátegui's thinking even more relevant, especially his plan of applying the principles of historical materialism flexibly so that they could take root in the socioeconomics of history and culture without falling into economistic determinism.

Two currents of revolutionary thought from the early 1900s help explain Mariátegui's heterodox Marxism: first, Italian Marxism, to which he had been exposed during his years in Italy through his relationship with the Communist Party and its newspaper, *L'Ordine Nuovo*; second, the ideas of Georges Sorel (1907), which deeply influenced him. In the confluence of these two European currents of thought, Mariátegui created his own messianic views, uniting rationality and myth.

Mariátegui ended up in Italy from 1920 to 1923 after being sent into exile by the Augusto Leguía dictatorship. While writing a column, "Letters from Italy," for the Lima newspaper *El Tiempo* during these years, he attended the famous 1921 Livorno Congress of the Italian Socialist Party, which led to the founding of the Communist Party of Italy under Antonio Gramsci, a founding editor of *L'Ordine Nuovo*. There is no indication, however, that Mariátegui came into contact with Gramsci's thinking during his relatively long stay in Italy. Though it is generally assumed that Mariátegui had access to Gramsci's ideas when he undertook his analysis of Peruvian reality, nothing in the records can prove a direct influence of Gramsci on him. It seems he was slightly acquainted with Gramsci, but he does not cite him—unlike other Italian writers, especially Benedetto Croce and Piero Gobetti, whom he does quote regularly.

The links between Mariátegui and Gramsci are undeniable. Indeed, Gramsci's new approaches to Marx were in the air of Italian culture, and Mariátegui probably discovered them through the works of Gobetti, who analyzed the function of the economy in the creation of a new political order. But his assimilation of Gobetti's historical criticism should not make us lose sight of the fact that Mariátegui always thought "from" Peru. Thus, by connecting the indigenous problem with the problem of land and the contemporaneity of distinct cultures, Mariátegui's criticism discovered in the agrarian structure of Peru the roots of the nation's backwardness and the reasons that the indigenous masses were excluded from political and cultural life. Hence his understanding that, by identifying the Indian question with the land question, he had discovered the crux of a problem that only a socialist revolution could resolve. However, the fact that both linked Mariátegui to the *indigenista* movement and distanced him from Marxist orthodoxy was his political (rather than doctrinaire) perspective on the confluence between the "modern" workers' movement and the peasantry. Simultaneously with Gramsci, Mariátegui understood that the peasant question was, above all, an indigenous question (Aricó 1980: xi–lvi). He was greatly helped in this by his knowledge of and interest in other Peruvian writers who were dedicated to the analysis of indigenismo. It was during his research, mediated by his reading of the works of Castro Pozo, Uriel García, and most importantly Luis E. Valcárcel, that Mariátegui got into the rural world of Peru. As a good organic intellectual, Mariátegui connected his reading with his publication of *Amauta*, a journal that helped link the intellectuals of coastal Peru, influenced by the urban workers' movement, Marxist socialism, and other European currents of thought, with the intellectuals of Cusco, who represented the indigenista movement.

It is worth looking more deeply into the similarities between Gramsci and Mariátegui, particularly in regard to the spatial nature of their thought. On the level of methodology, both differed from other letrados in that they insisted on taking political economy into account while being careful not to fall into orthodox Marxist determinism, with its rigid separation between "base" and "superstructure." Both Gramsci's essay "Some Aspects of the Southern Question" and Mariátegui's *Siete ensayos* emphasized space, and especially the political and economic inequalities generated by geographic differences—between northern and southern Italy, in the case of Gramsci, and between coastal and highland Peru, in the case of Mariátegui. While Gramsci emphasized spatial inequalities, Mariátegui read them historically, over time, as the results of colonialism and imperialism (Aboul-Ela 2007: 31). Likewise, while the central issue for Gramsci was the gap that had opened up between the proletariat of the North and the peasantry of the South, Mariátegui only mentions the proletariat sporadically, as an important phenomenon in the growth of Peru's cities. Mariátegui was clearly conscious of the role that class analysis played in European Marxism; its sporadic, ever-changing character was one of the aspects that he underlined.

One of the most salient characteristics of this interpretation of Latin American reality was Mariátegui's analysis of the cause of the spatial inequalities that colonial rule created. In the chapter on Peru's economic evolution in *Siete ensayos*, Mariátegui makes clear that the attainment of national independence (across Latin America generally, and in Peru in particular) did nothing to free the region from economic dependency, which was only consolidated when trade and financial exchange between the new nations and the new empire grew in the nineteenth century. Here, Mariátegui had done an in-depth analysis of the intrusion of North American hegemony at a time when other writers, especially the "Arielistas," perceived only a vague, abstract, spiritual threat from the North and never approached to the socioeconomic heart of the problem.

The other fundamental aspect of Mariátegui's thought is his critique of lineal, teleological time, which he declared inappropriate for explaining Peru's complex situation. He intensified this critique when he had the unprecedented idea of creating a "cultural field" where rationality and myth might meet. This came from the impact of Sorel—or rather, the myth of Sorel—on Mariátegui's thought.[8] Introducing Sorel in one of his key essays, "El hombre y el mito" (2011 [1925]: 387), as "one of the highest representatives of French thought of the twentieth century," Mariátegui counted him as a critic of Marx on the path toward parliamentary social democracy. Indeed, Sorel's influence was important because his ideas took the place of Marxist orthodoxy in Mariátegui's analysis of the process of industrial civilization. This important change, which can also be seen in the work of Gobetti (Paris 1980: 127), is fundamental to an understanding of "Man and Myth," the essay in which Mariátegui explains "the Sorelian theory of myth."

Criticizing the exclusively rational nature of the perception of historical time, Mariátegui (2011: 384) justified "the urgent need for myth" as a vacuum—infinite space, in Pascal's terms—that opposed and even dissolved "the idea of Reason" on the plane of life experiences. Insisting that man is "a metaphysical animal" and that "without myth, the history of humanity has no sense of history" (2011: 384), Mariátegui, influenced by Sorelians such as Édouard Berth, emphasized the role of myth in the explanation of human events. Robert Paris argued, quite accurately, that "Pascal's wager," which oriented the Sorelian concept of myth, had no place whatsoever in any individualist philosophy that was divorced from community (Paris 1980: 137). Thus, myth, the irrational or mystical element inherited from Sorel, appears in Mariátegui's works as the instrument of a dialectic that seeks to bring the values of the past into the present. In this return of the past, one cannot help noticing a metahistorical paradox similar to the one St. Paul enunciated when he spoke of values that are of the world but that do not reside in the world. In other words, the sphere of myth cannot be that of modern reason, and in the final analysis rational, lineal, teleological discourse is also incapable of explaining the intricacies of the complex realities of Latin America.

When he returned from Europe, Mariátegui was faced with a great agrarian convulsion, which, as in 1915, affected every local jurisdiction in the southern Andes. The structural tension between peasant and landowning economies, the preaching of the indigenistas, the conflicts between midsized merchants and regional bosses—these realities brought out for Mariátegui the messianic, nativist stamp of this stubborn past, which refused to disappear, which indeed was very much present in every uprising that took place, always preceded by the rebirth of indigenous culture.

6. THE PERSISTENCE OF "THEN" WITHIN "NOW"

Mariátegui's thinking grew out of his consciousness that Peru was immersed in a very different reality from Western societies, so he was particularly sensitive to the fact that Peruvian reality combined different times, superimposing disparate stages of history in a single territory, from the primitive to the modern industrial economy. For Mariátegui, this motley Peru called not for a modernized theory but for a collective myth, which, as a true "wager," would fight to realize its values, even without a guarantee of success. There was, then, an undercurrent of spontaneous enthusiasm in his thought. We can see it in the relationship he established between "the mystical wager," indigenous communities, and the past as resource for the present. How can we explain this wager, which brought the indigenous community and its constitutive values closer to the present?

When he compared the Peruvian and European experiences, Mariátegui observed that the criollo class of large landowners wanted to skip a basic stage in capitalist development: they wanted to become entrepreneurs without first undergoing the necessary dissolution of feudalism. In his judgment, this was an unrealizable dream; the landowners were behaving like feudal lords and rentiers and were unable to transform their class character into that of a genuine bourgeoisie. What path, then, did the country need to follow? Should the great landowners disappear? Be forced, perhaps, to learn in the hard school of small-scale farming? Such a solution would have led Mariátegui to back the standard liberal ideal of creating a numerous agrarian petite bourgeoisie. Perfectly aware of this liberal solution, Mariátegui radically distanced himself from it, proposing instead a utopian solution whose protagonist and agent would not be the criollo or mestizo small landowner living from his rents, but the indigenous peasant.

The indigenous people, then, with their social and cultural forms from the pre-Hispanic past, would provide the necessary elements for solving the land problem that had been created first by Spanish colonial rule and then by liberalism. We can now glimpse the ways in which, for Mariátegui, the situation of Peru had modified the traditional Marxist schema: first, its bourgeoisie was not a true bourgeoisie but merely a group of aristocratic liberals or liberal oligarchs, incapable of creating the conditions for the rise of capitalism; second, the protagonists of its socialist revolution would have to be a proletariat expanded to include the indigenous peasantry.

Mariátegui's point of departure was an idea developed by Manuel González Prada, a Peruvian anarchist who deeply influenced the country's Left in that era: the indigenous question was a problem not of philosophy or culture, but primarily of economics and agriculture; it was a question of distributing land to benefit the country's masses, four-fifths of whom were indigenous and peasants. Of course Mariátegui was well aware of the vast differences between modern communism and the communism of the Inca era, systems that were only comparable in "their essential and incorporeal likeness, within the essential and material difference of time and space" (Mariátegui 1971 [1928]: 74). Here we see the modification wrought by Andean space on the lineal concept of time in European Marxism. If socialism had to be imported, it would have to be by discovering the proper soil, the exact geocultural conditions, that would allow it to flourish: it couldn't be thought of as a mere blueprint. It was a new European creation, and it demanded a precise knowledge of the terrain.

Having described the problem, Mariátegui, like his contemporary Luis E. Valcárcel (1927), found that he had to rethink the *ayllu*, the indigenous Andean community structure, not as an analogue to modern socialist structures, but as something distinct, something that could only be understood if one started from a meticulous analysis of the local space within which it existed, that is, an analysis of Peru's agrarian history. Nevertheless, and despite the need to undertake a detailed analysis of how the indigenous community—the nonmodern structure of modernity—should be incorporated into the nation, Mariátegui expressed his conviction that an indigenous resurgence would come about not through a process of material "Westernization" of the Quechua lands, but through myth.

This surprising conclusion led Mariátegui's critics to accuse him of being inconsistent. In effect, Mariátegui argued that the great landowners were incapable of "skipping ahead" and becoming capitalist entrepreneurs without first going through the stage of the dissolution of feudalism, yet at the same time he was arguing that the marginal, exploited indigenous peasantry could go straight from their serflike condition to socialist organization. That is, in one case he believed in the necessity of a Westernizing, feudal-dissolution / capitalism-building process, while in the other case he felt that indigenous peasants could skip all that and achieve socialism directly. Is there really a contradiction between these two arguments? I think not. With his conceptualization of the indigenous community, Mariátegui was simply arguing that the mobilizing power of myth transcended that of liberalism and that in so doing it became one with the power of the indigenous masses. But there was still a need to organize a working-class protagonist who could carry out the socialist revolution. It wasn't that the indigenous people should take the role of the proletariat; it was that the proletariat should expand and become much more inclusive. In other words, if his wager on mysticism went beyond individualist liberalism and connected Mariátegui with the indigenous masses, his Marxism forced him to rethink who the protagonists of revolution would be and to assign a key role to the peasantry. But this did not mean that his would be a Marxism only for the peasants and would exclude the industrial proletariat. Quite the contrary: Mariátegui insisted on the importance of the proletariat and spoke of a class-based party, a workers' party that would include both industrial workers and peasants.

In sum, Mariátegui called for total revolution in Peru. To achieve this goal, he called on the strength and influence of messianic sentiments and argued that it was imperative to incorporate them into his revolutionary project. Aware that Marxism would have a chance for success in Peru only if it first joined together with Andean culture, Mariátegui introduced the mystical wager of the indigenous community into his thinking. Indeed, the defense of community strengthened their rejection of capitalism. Due to the persistence of "then" in this structural "now," Peru could follow a different historical evolution from that of Europe. In reality, as Cornejo Polar argues, Mariátegui looked at the course of Peruvian history as a "process of conflicts imbricated in a future in which certain alternatives are hegemonic in each moment, while under the surface, subordinate options constantly arise that could become salient and then hegemonic at some future period"; he goes on to point out that "what once was hegemonic can subsist residually for greater or lesser amount of time" (Cornejo Polar 1993: 60–61). Mariátegui located himself in the tension between these opposing contemporaneities, according to Cornejo Polar, on a radical terrain of analysis and reflection: the problem was neither to develop capitalism nor to recapitulate the history of Europe in Latin America; it was to construct Peru's own way forward. Thus, it could be said that the essential trait of his thought was the rejection of progress and the lineal, Eurocentric image of world history.

7. ON NEGATIVITY: "MULTITUDE," "SUBALTERNITY," AND "PUEBLO"

How should we understand the ethnic problematics of da Cunha's and Mariátegui's texts today? Should we look at it strictly in terms of the view of lineal history associated with modernity?—perhaps be amazed by the obstinacy with which ethnicity has refused to disappear, and then admit that it had to exist in order for us to attain our longed-for social cohesion? I think there is no clear answer to these questions, because, as I have been arguing throughout this chapter, the key to solving the problem of ethnicity cannot be history if history is conceived as unidirectional progress toward a final, universal, and totalizing goal. Letting go of notions of teleologically predetermined progress, we can understand the history of people in the sertão of northeastern Brazil or in the highlands of Peru only if we view it as a discontinuous series of hegemonic formations that cannot be placed in proper order within a framework of universal narratives that transcend contingent historicity. In this sense, the notions of "the multitude," of "subalternity"—a name given to subordination, whether expressed in terms of class, caste, gender, age, or any other condition (Guha 1983)—and of "the people" refer only to real social formations that resist being encapsulated within a Hegelian teleology.

Before examining these ideas, seeing how they can help us understand today the works under discussion here, there are two points to briefly clarify. First, the unity of social actors—whether designated by the concept of "the multitude," of "subalternity," or of "the people"—is not the result of some prior logical connection that can subsume all subjective positions under a single, predetermined conceptual category. "The people" is always a contingent moment, a "floating signifier" (Laclau 2005: 129) that "fills up" with a plurality of social demands through "equivalential (metonymic) relations of contiguity" (227). Having no a priori constitutive role, these demands are permanently in flux.

Second, the passage from one configuration of "the people" to another involves a radical break, not a chain of events located in logical order, and so the temporal causality of such events is fragmented. This doesn't mean that the elements of the emerging formation must be totally new; rather, it means that the point of articulation—the partial object around which hegemonic formations are constructed as new wholes—does not arise from any sort of logic related to the historical time of modernity. In this way, what is decisive in the emergence of "the people" as a new historical actor is that they should be able to articulate popular demands, not that there be any prior logic to coordinate those demands. Ernesto Laclau explains that speaking of the people means referring to a "constitutive and not derivative" configuration; that is, "it constitutes an *act* in the strict sense, for it does not have its source in anything external to itself. The emergence of the 'people' as a historical actor is thus always transgressive *vis-à-vis* the situation preceding it. This transgression is the emergence of a new order" (Laclau 2005: 228).

Having no prior logical connections and no teleological conditions to fix their order, the concepts of "multitude," "subalternity," and "people" lack a transcendental ontological principle to make them possible. There is a certain seeming analogy between "multitude," as Hardt and Negri imagine the concept in *Empire* (2000) and *Multitude* (2004), and what Laclau terms the "people," in *On Populist Reason* (2005). But the similarities are superficial.

The point of departure for "multitude" is the Deleuzian/Nietzschean notion of immanence. Hardt and Negri relate it to the process of secularization that takes place in modernity. Given that this process requires a historical actor to bring it about, Hardt and Negri conceive of the multitude as a "spontaneously and radically immanent" actor (2000: 47) that today has reached its greatest visibility with the construction of the empire, a "deterritorialized" and limitless entity, which, unlike earlier imperialisms, "has no center" (299).

Note, then, that the multitude is an emancipatory subject that is constructed spontaneously, not politically. It is distinguished by "being contrary" to any form of social organization that is subject to the rational principles promoted by modernity. Given that its aim is universal desertion, it identifies with the nomadic, rhizomatic movements of people who cross borders and voluntarily cease to belong to a fixed territory. Having decided for rebellion in a natural way, the concept of "multitude" needs no political construction of the subject, a fact that sets it apart from the concept of "the people." In this regard, I find some similarity between "multitude" and "deterritorialization." The latter is promoted by the resistance of the colonized subject, who emerges, according to Homi Bhabha, regardless of identity and at a moment of catachresis (which I will discuss later). Hybrid in its articulation of cultural difference, for Bhabha as well as for feminist critic Gayatri Spivak (1988), subalternity cannot be represented hierarchically and stands apart from any binary structuring of social antagonism.

"Deconstructive" in the fullest sense of the term, the concepts of "multitude," as elaborated by Hardt and Negri, and "subalternity," as theorized by Spivak and others, have in common the fact that they are always "contrary" (this is their negativity) toward every elitist project for constructing society. Indeed, subalternity is "strategic" in the sense in which Spivak understands it, because, having no constructive function, it exists only to render obsolete any attempt of the dominant culture and way of knowledge to reestablish their authority over the social whole. Given that its "being contrary" is also a way of opposing the "narrative mode of production" of classical Marxism, the subaltern is the "absolute limit" imposed on any narrative that would construct the nation. This means, as John Beverley saw with regard to Spivak (Beverley 1999: 85–113), that the subaltern in the colonial and postcolonial world must necessarily be distinct from the notion of "the people," resisting any sort of totalizing suggestive of the Gramscian equation of "nation" and "people," and so denying any possibility of constructing a single concept that would encompass both. For Spivak, the subaltern is that which resists signifying. Therefore, like "being abject," "being contrary" has negative repercussions in the symbolic order, in the representation of the social.

The alterity of the subaltern disturbs the elitist presumption of believing that the educated sectors of society are the ones that construct the meaning of history. Likewise, the "deconstructive" nature of subalternity has no pretensions of becoming a political project or of transforming the subaltern into the subject of history. In this way, the meaning that Spivak gives to subalternity—I examine Guha's divergent opinion below—explicitly connects subaltern politics with "deconstruction." Thus, for Spivak, catachresis means the collapse of all pretense of meaning and a rejection of the metaphorical / symbolic order related to the return of the repressed, of the social surplus that figures out a way to subvert the rationalizing model, the model viewed "from above" as the promoter and organizer of national culture.

The reader may recall that I referred to catachresis in the introduction as a literary trope distinct from metaphor. Taking catachresis to be *abusio* and metaphor to be *traslatio*, catachresis is using a word to mean something other than what it usually means, for lack of a literal term that gets the idea across: the *arms* of a chair; the *wing* of a roof; a *leaf* of a book, and so on. Metaphor, on the other hand, transfers the meaning of one word to another, not out of necessity or because of some urgent need to do so, but from a desire to create a new mental image: the *light* of science. The difference between needing a term because one has no other means of expressing an idea, and transferring meaning to another term with the aim of creating a new and much richer image, nevertheless became diluted over time, so that Cicero already thought of catachresis as the use of an inappropriate term instead of some other, more precise and more appropriate term. In this way, catachresis became an "audacious and abusive" rhetorical figure, fraught with clearly pejorative meaning (Parker 1990).

This identification of catachresis with the abuse (*abusio*) of metaphorical transfer (*traslatio*), especially in the case of efforts to build "wild analogies," remained an irritant throughout the centuries. Thus, catachresis, taken to mean an extravagant, forced metaphor, reappears in important twentieth-century critical texts (for example, Northrop Frye's *Anatomy of Criticism* [1957]) as a violent, unexpected metaphor. It seems to me that using this rhetorical figure in the "deconstructive" analysis of subalternity follows the route that connects catachresis with the "improper use" of metaphor, because, leaving aside the questions of good taste and moderation derived from the bourgeois social order, catachresis ultimately reinforces the opposite semantic field—the field of mysterious, illogical apparitions repressed by the human mind, of subaltern sensibilities that emerge at moments when the symbolic / metaphoric construction of the social is worn out and in crisis. Indeed, Patricia Parker notes that the violent and impertinent "intrusions of catachresis" subvert, often without meaning to do so, "the very model" of control created by the measured and well-administered use of social metaphor. When the latter is replaced by the abusive use of catachresis, there is "a potential linguistic return of the repressed," of what has been asleep and has now suddenly roared back to life (Parker 1990: 73).

Neither the notion of "multitude" nor the "deconstructive" analysis of subalternity has much in common with the notion of "the people" as used by Laclau, or with the "politics of the people" imagined by Guha. While "multitude" is the spontaneous negation of domination, "the people" is a political construction. It is a negativity that willfully splinters the social base. "The people" is a political articulation of "heterogeneity," which, according to Laclau, "presupposes the establishment of equivalential logics and the production of empty signifiers" (2005: 241). Thus, "the people" has nothing to do with our natural tendency to struggle against oppression, because the *populus* is never "contrary" about everything; it is against certain things and in favor of others. Likewise, the construction of a broader "contrariness"—a comprehensive popular identity—calls for a long period of trench warfare, more binary than hybrid. Nor is it realistic to imagine an imperial whole which lacks a center and from which the internal poles that face off against power have disappeared.

Corresponding to the concept of "the people," Guha's idea of subaltern negativity involves the positionality of a stable subject, so that the terms "people" and "subaltern classes" become interchangeable (Beverley 1999: 87). As we know, nationalist discourse, with its anti-imperialist character, centers the category of "the people" around a narrative that will stabilize its meaning metaphorically and metonymically, attributing interests, duties, and common sacrifices to the *populus*, though different social groups and classes don't share equally in those interests. In this sense, and keeping the dominant nationalist discourse in mind, Guha devotes himself to the task of setting the boundaries of what the subaltern should impose on this hegemonic representation. For Spivak, the subaltern cannot be the same as her notion of "the people," because its "deconstructive" nature means that an "absolute limit" must be imposed on any narrative that could organize social life around nationalism and the nation. In contrast, Guha argues that the subaltern contains not only the working class and the peasantry, but also the middle-class strata that are not accorded the label of social classes in the Marxist sense of the term. Broadening the Gramscian notion of the subaltern—"subalternity" was a euphemism Gramsci used for the proletariat and peasantry—Guha champions an even broader and more inclusive meaning for subaltern identity, but he never abandons the idea of binary antagonism as its articulatory principle. For Guha, the struggle is still national, a struggle to seize power. Therefore, subalternity, unrelated to the "top-down imagined community," is, according to Guha, the "politics of the people," a new way to think of hegemony "from the bottom up."

How, then, is this "bottom-up" view revealed in the works of da Cunha and Mariátegui? Did they both see the ungovernable outburst of ethnicity, or, to the contrary, did they see the ability of different indigenous peoples to create a new social articulation that would renew the meaning of the nation?

In *Os sertões*, we see the tragic, filthy jagunços awaiting the promised miracle of Conselheiro's return:

> Some of the sick fell after only a few steps and were carried away, four soldiers to each, held dangling by arms and legs. They didn't writhe, didn't groan; just passed by, motionless and mute, their eyes wide open, staring, as if dead. . . .
>
> A horrible hag, a repulsive and skinny witch—perhaps the foulest old woman in the backlands—was the only one who raised her head, pelting onlookers with threatening stares, like sparks; restless and trembling, agile in spite of her age, . . . she carried a small girl in her arms. . . . And that girl was a terrifying sight. Her left cheek had been torn away, some time ago, by a grenade fragment, so that her jawbones stood out, white as snow, between the scarlet edges of the wound, which had healed over. The right side of her face was smiling. And it was appalling to see that incomplete, painful smile, lighting up half her face and suddenly blinking out on the other side, into the emptiness of a scar.
>
> This old woman was carrying the most monstrous product of the whole campaign. There she went, with her trembling gait, following the long line of wretches. (Da Cunha 2010 [1902]: 472–473; my translation)

Who were these unruly and macabre jagunços? Were they a multitude? Perhaps a people without a nation? Along with Beverley (1999), I am inclined to define them, taking into account the ideas of "multitude" and "subalternity," as the "poor in spirit" mentioned in the Sermon on the Mount. Nevertheless, there is another important distinction between the two notions: the multitude, according to the theory of Hardt and Negri (2000, 2004), is like a hydra's head with no face, or with many faces—that is, a collective subject arising from globalization and cultural "deterritorialization"—while subalternity, by contrast, expresses a class, gender, and occupation, that is, a specific identity, with flesh and bone, that loves, suffers, and dies.

For Machiavelli, the first modern thinker to look at national liberation movements, the idea of national unity was fundamental. In all his writings, the notion of a "people without a nation" constituted the heterogeneous, the servile. This notion, which could also be assimilated to that of the multitude, meant a way of doing politics beyond the limits of the nation and of representation, traditionally related to the idea of hegemony. Therefore the multitude, a notion far from that of national unity, came to mean an amorphous social subject, created on the outskirts of global capitalism, far from the borders between nations.[9] This notion of multitude, which has now become useful for defining social movements, gives rise to one of the possible explanations of the nature of the jagunços described above. Let me analyze it in the light of a recent interpretation of da Cunha's work.

In his book *Nightmares of the Lettered City* (2007: 215–228), Juan Pablo Dabove sees these jagunços as a violent "constituent power," whose origin is distinct from the violence exercised by the "constituted power" of the state. Dabove offers an excellent analysis of the paradox that nationhood is constructed through the careful control of memory (the violence with which power disciplines *los de abajo*, "those on the bottom," must be forgotten or imaginatively concealed) in order to impose on the actual participants in the violent events a national dimension that they have never known. But the past forgotten by official history—a sort of "ruin," despised by the dominant culture—contrives to "bewitch" the present so forcefully that it cannot function without recognizing and integrating that past. So for Dabove, this violence of the dispossessed is an excess—a "lack of balance (*desequilibrio*)," as he notes that da Cunha put it. We should look at this excess in greater detail.

For Dabove, the diabolical power of the jagunços flowed from the multitude and caused the nation to regress to being a nomadic horde, so that the civic nation—that is, the construction of the nation—was left completely overthrown and meaningless. Dabove notes that, as a "multitude"—he follows Hardt and Negri's analysis here—the "constituent power" lacks the capacity to "territorialize," that is, to intervene in the reorganization of the state. The violence of the jagunços, then, was an example of how the dispossessed acted in a way that kept them from incorporating their own past into present-day societal organization.

I see two possible interpretations of the function that the "constituent power" of subalternity can play. On the one hand, there is Dabove's interpretation in his apposite observations on the defeat of Canudos. He explains the excesses according to a "deterritorialized" logic that situates the jagunços as primitive, archaic, prepolitical, destined to disappear. In this sense, his interpretation sees the jagunços' actions as destructive of the dominant culture, as a radical means of dismantling the symbolic level of reality. Like Spivak, whose take on this places subalternity "beyond the state," Dabove also interprets the violence of the "constituent power" as an act that spoils the constituted state and that rejects any subaltern participation in its future reconstruction.

Dabove's reading emphasizes the colonial structure of power, which in the case of Brazil did not disappear with the nineteenth-century construction of the state. Indeed, elitist attempts to build the nation-state and control power, while insisting on the inevitable course of modernity, justified violence as a primary activity for the state to use against human groups that refused to be compulsorily incorporated into a state formation that did not represent them.

Banditry was the result of a poorly formed nation-state. It posed a challenge to the metaphoric-symbolic organization of the state. *Os sertões* calls into question not only the legal framework that allows the state to violate the lives of the jagunços, but also the place of enunciation from which its violent incursion into the backlands gains support. In this sense, da Cunha's book questions the law, the judge who sentenced these jagunços to death, and the legislator who drew up the law that characterized the way of life in the sertão as criminal.

The trope of banditry is constructed as a catachresis, that is, as an excess that overflows the metaphorical construction of the nation-state. Like true absurdities left in the wake of violence, the jagunços, with Conselheiro at their head, are the excess that negates love—the balanced, harmonious relation between heart and head, the relationship that "heals" racial differences, disparities between social classes, and language and legal divergences in nineteenth-century novels.

The catastrophic excesses described in *Os sertões* destroy any possibility of constructing balanced metaphors that could be used to organize society. Da Cunha's text emphasizes all that is absurd and unbalanced, a fact that, when viewed through a positivist gaze with an early twentieth-century tinge of Social Darwinism, affects both the territory of Canudos and the human beings who live there. In reality, everything in *Os sertões* is unbalanced: the land suffers a "cruel oscillation" between the extremes of heat and cold, between flooding and drought, between barbaric sterility and marvelous exuberance. It is as if nature found satisfaction in creating this perverse "game of antitheses." The logic of excess also encompasses a series of internal contradictions: torrential rains that destroy the land with their "corrosive acidity" instead of improving it; rivers that reverse course; landscapes that are the opposite of what they appear to be; the glare of the midday sun making a desert look like a glacier. As a place of extremes, the sertão is an empty, barren land—the image with which the narrative opens and closes. Inaccessible, unknown, it is full of forces beyond control: torrential rains, heat extreme enough to make rocks crack, droughts that erode the soil. Those who live in this territory bear similar characteristics: the *sertanejos* can be horrifying and beautiful, barbarously cruel and extremely devout, "distorted by fanaticism" and "transfigured by religious faith." All of these contrasts are crowned by the fact that Canudos, as a social organization, is nothing but "organized banditry."

Overturning every organizing principle of the lettered city, Canudos is the "monstrous *urbs*," a "deterritorialized" city, because it doesn't display the order with which the disciplined construction of the modern, civilized city is conceived. If the imaginary of the nation-state entails the homogeneity of its inhabitants, as citizens with equal rights and duties, Canudos achieves equality in the barbarous wild, where being a jagunço represents the monstrous state of mestizaje, a prime metaphor for nation building. In *Os sertões*, the metaphor grows exhausted and unbalanced. In this way, the jagunços seem like a uniform, homogeneous mass of unconscious brutes, of unbalanced hybrids. Canudos is thus not a civilized community but a monstrous "human polyp."

This reading sets Canudos apart from the idea of "the people." In this sense, Dabove notes that the violent movement in the sertão and Conselheiro's pietism made it impossible to construct a genuine "popular subject." The jagunços were thus an excess that modernity could not control. On the other hand, and in contrast to this "deconstructivist" reading of da Cunha's book, would it be possible to argue the opposite—that is, that the Canudos movement contained the germ of a rebellion opposed precisely to the existence of the elitist republic, of the nation imagined "from above," from the spheres of power? In other words, would it be possible to carry out a different reading of the culture conflict, pointing out that the movement detailed in *Os sertões* entailed a narrative of peasant insurgency, in the terms that Guha uses to approach this problem? Though Ariana Johnson's study of this theme (2005) tells us that the answer is yes, it is hard to maintain that da Cunha's work itself considers the rebels of the sertão to be a "people" asserting their identity.

The "politics of the people" are much more visible in Mariátegui's analysis of Peruvian reality. His version of socialism called for building new social relations and a new state that would overcome the limitations of the parliamentary system and bourgeois democracy. His increased understanding of peasant rebellions in the Andes, and the debate on indigenismo that he helped start, show that Mariátegui was aware of another possible way of situating socialism, far removed from orthodox Marxism. Revolutionary but nondogmatic, Mariátegui counterposed heterodoxy against revolution. Indeed, his Gramscian notion of the "popular/national" was closely linked to the limited size of the Peruvian working class. It caused him to pay close attention to other social groups that were also being exploited. The small number of industrial workers could be supplemented by joining forces with peasants, sugar and cotton plantation laborers, and artisans.

Mariátegui supported the role of the peasantry because he was one of the first to think about them from the perspective of their unusual condition as both a class and an ethnic group. They were peasants, but they were also Indians, that is, human beings who stubbornly held on to their own culture despite Spanish colonial domination and the persistence of feudalism after independence. Mariátegui saw quite clearly that if indigenous culture had managed to keep its own languages and customs, that was because the material bases of the culture had also been consistently maintained. In this way, as Paris has noted (1980: 119–144), Mariátegui's Peruvian socialism had room for both workers and peasants, encompassing both within its view of "the proletariat."

By incorporating the indigenous into his view of the new popular subject, Mariátegui linked artisans to poor peasants, plantation and industrial workers, and middle-class intellectuals. He clearly contrasted his socialism with the construction of the democratic subject as imagined by the dominant sectors. Thus, in his popular politics the vanguard of the proletariat would be the miners, with their double status as both workers and peasants. Therefore Mariátegui, far from conceiving of an authoritarian party, opted for a socialism that intended not to solve every possible conflict, but rather to unite the masses and offer them an identity. The construction of the popular subject was, then, a serious attempt to raise once more the subject of revolution, assigning the peasantry a key role in it. This does not mean that Mariátegui denied the importance of the working class, only that he strove to build a class-based party that would include both workers and peasants.

Another important aspect of this "politics of the people" was that Mariátegui's heterodox Marxism succeeded by recognizing Andean culture: the collective farming of indigenous Andean communities was what set the agrarian structure of Peru apart from that of any European country. Consequently, the approach of importing and mechanically replicating revolutionary arguments from abroad was a nonstarter. The revolution was impossible without the peasants; they would more than make up for the numerical weakness of the workers, but in order to count on their participation the revolution would have to guarantee a better life for the countryside. Unlike capitalism, socialism would not mean the destruction of the indigenous community. The country could not be built at the expense of its broad peasant and indigenous sector.

Since defending the indigenous community would strengthen the peasantry's rejection of capitalism and the construction of the popular subject, Peru could not follow the same historical path as Europe. That was why Mariátegui based his analyses and reflections on radically different terrain than that of Western Marxists. Had he avoided contact with organic intellectuals—indigenista poets and essayists—his Marxism would have lacked what became its most essential feature: his concept of the past as a resource for the present, and his rejection of the linear, Eurocentric image of world history. Indeed, the most important conclusion to be drawn from Mariátegui's socialism is its break with the image of history that Europeans have imposed on underdeveloped countries, an image that classic Marxism continues to use unquestioningly. A diverse, heterogeneous country, the product of a historical evolution that did not follow the classic model, called for a different interpretation that would stress the specificity of the past and its continued vitality in the present and that would seek to articulate a different popular subject from within Andean history.

In short, Mariátegui's book reconceptualized the nation from the perspective of "those at the bottom," which has little to do with the fraternal imagined community of "those at the top." This reconceptualization, drawn from an analysis of Andean space, the locus of the profound temporal differences of Peru's incipient modernity, was closely tied to subaltern theories of the popular. Put differently, "the people" is the concept that comes closest to recognizing the temporal differences that separate the hegemonic sectors from the subaltern sectors. In this connection, Dipesh Chakrabarty states:

> Subaltern studies, as I think of it, can only situate itself theoretically at the juncture where we give up neither Marx nor "difference," for, as I have said, the resistance it speaks of is something that can happen only *within* the time horizon of capital, and yet it has to be thought of as something that disrupts the unity of that time. (2000: 95)

Indeed, this quotation from Chakrabarty helps us see that if equating the nation-state with modernity is a result of a historical moment when "the people" is equated with a modernized citizenry, then subalternity breaks that temporal unity and, in pushing for the opposite, settles into the concept of "ungovernability." This concept expresses the difference between the "radical heterogeneity" of the subaltern and the homogenizing rationality of the state. Ungovernability is precisely the space of resentment, of disobedience, of marginality, of insurgency. To this way of thinking, it is pure fantasy to suppose that the "return of the plebeian" (Gutiérrez, García Linera and Tapia 2000) could come about in the modernizing form of "civil society." In its normal meaning, Hegel's civil society (*bürgerliche Gesellschaft*), which is linked to linear time and to development, requires formal education, technical and scientific knowledge, the nuclear family, political parties, business, and private property, and these criteria exclude the huge sectors of the population that find it very difficult to achieve full citizenship. This exclusion, this limitation, is, precisely, subalternity.

What, then, can replace the concept of "civil society"? Could it be "hybridity," as Hardt and Negri imagine? Could the concept of hybridity sidestep the danger of becoming submissively subjugated to the marketplace and to globalization? Given that subalternity struggles to keep from being crushed by the weight of reality, we have to say, by way of conclusion, that the crisis of the nation as imagined community, together with the politics of the multitude under the condition of globalization, which has weakened the state, must continue to be thought through with the same dedication Rabasa shows in his recent book. This project will have to incorporate the concepts of identity, citizenship, and democracy. The notion of "multitude" is an important and significant step in this innovative theoretical endeavor. However, it will be important to continue drawing finer distinctions about subalternity as a distinct form of historical agency. In the final analysis, reconceptualizing the nation will be possible only if we situate ourselves at the outer boundaries of Western historical temporality. As da Cunha saw in the early twentieth century, the unresolved struggle between modernity and coloniality creates hard-to-control "excesses" that go unnoticed if one uncritically adopts points of view, like those of Anderson's imagined community, that can only see the situation through Western rationality and that forget to size it up and contrast it with the subversive qualities of the local.

Chapter Three
"NOW TIME": SUBALTERN PASTS AND CONTESTED HISTORICISM

How can the histories of excluded social sectors be included in the narrative of the nation? Or, to put it differently: how can the subaltern pasts that resist interpretation in terms of the seemingly unobjectionable progressive course of modernity be reconstructed? These questions are related to the cultural conflict created by the view of history as thought from Western rationality; they concern the existence of "minor histories," histories that do not always prepare, as one might hope, for the exercise of democracy or for citizenship practices based on the spread of reason in the public sphere. Considered strange, ex-centric, by the rational thought that dominates the sciences, these histories read the lettered project of the nation against the grain, and they adopt, implicitly or explicitly, a critical outlook on the identity narratives I referred to in the previous chapter.

In refusing to represent the achievement of a totalizing view of reality, which absolutely is the goal of every higher narrative, there are pasts that resist being historicized—in other words, being explained rationally. In the central part of this chapter, after looking at themes related to the time of the now and the subaltern past as a resource for the present, I will deal with some examples of those pasts that are not strictly historical, that are guided instead by the "agency of the supernatural." That is, they are not governed by linear time but are rather "enchanted" facts, belonging to the "time of the gods," alien to the way of life of those who observe and study them. When researchers try to "explain" such enchanted events, fruitlessly invoking skills acquired in the study of science to understand the supernatural, those events appear to them as stubborn knots, as knotted cords, disturbing the smooth surface of historical events.

Why should we bother with these subaltern pasts? The answer is simple: because they exist, independently of whether we believe in them or not. Not only do they exist; they take place as figures—"allegories," Walter Benjamin called them—that "illuminate" the present, modifying it with a presence that resists being historicized. Hence we understand that by breaking the linear flow of history and its cause-and-effect relations, these "events" manage to insert themselves into the present. Writing history, then, is not the same thing as making these subaltern pasts a resource for the present. I am speaking of the "resources of the other," which, cut off from the possibility of thinking from modernity, also must be taken into account—that is, incorporated into historical practice. As modern and secular as we may seem, we inhabit enchanted fragments that force us to see history in two ways. In the first, as modern subjects, we perceive these "enchanted" pasts as mere objects of observation and study. In the second, we meet "illuminations" that change and modify the present; that impose limits on historical interpretation; that oppose it with their stubborn resistance to "historicizing everything," to translate the enchanted into a narrative of modernity that ignores these conflicts and paradoxes.

1. THE HIDDEN FACE OF MODERNITY

I argued in chapter 2 that what Dipesh Chakrabarty calls "political modernity," which fundamentally consists of the handling of public affairs (the *res publica*) through the modern institutions of the state and administrative bureaucracy, cannot be thought of without using categories and concepts rooted in the Western intellectual tradition. As Chakrabarty notes:

> Concepts such as citizenship, the state, civil society, public sphere, human rights, equality before the law, the individual, . . . democracy, popular sovereignty, . . . and so on bear the burden of European thought and history. One simply cannot think of political modernity without these and other related concepts that found a climactic form in the course of the European Enlightenment and the nineteenth century. (Chakrabarty 2000: 4)

Considered universal, the ideas that arose from the Enlightenment implied a secular view of human development, which colonialist thought inculcated in the colonizing elites. Thus the secular view, which had a powerful effect on these elites, was imbricated with the formation of a

Latin American modernity that adopted the form of modernity imposed from Europe as its own.

Our difficult task of state building emerged from the fact that soon after independence was achieved, the supposedly "universal" concepts of modernization ran up against societies that remained colonial. Therefore, in Latin America, postcoloniality—more properly, postcolonial studies— means becoming conscious that one cannot speak of the "colonial period" as a synonym of "coloniality." The latter did not disappear at independence; it kept going through the period of nation-state building, which in many cases has still not concluded even today. We can speak of independent states created in the nineteenth century that continued to be colonial because they were founded without being able to overcome the influence of the colonial structure that Aníbal Quijano (2001) has called "the coloniality of power."

At the moment of independence, the countries belonging to the Viceroyalty of Peru had an indigenous population who, while not entirely reduced to servitude, were unable to exercise self-determination, unable to govern their own affairs. Socially marginalized, these people were denied the possibility of participating in the consolidation of the new independent national states. In countries whose diverse populations included blacks, mestizos, and Indians, those populations were invisible to the states as they revolved in the orbit of coloniality. For example, Mexico, whose early twentieth-century revolution allowed an important portion of its population to participate in the administration of the state, also let coloniality persist until the present. Even in the south of the continent, Uruguay and Chile—especially Chile—had an opportunity to build solid national states, but the successive crises of the twentieth century, which reinforced the authoritarian tradition, camouflaged as democracy, hindered the state's full modernization.[1]

In the case of countries with large indigenous populations, it is clear that if the state had actually been modern, there would have been no reason for the so-called indigenous movements to take place. Given that there was always an aim of working with a double politics of including the indigenous populations in an abstract sense (under the concepts of citizenship and legal equality) while excluding any actual indigenous people in practice (under an active, constant discrimination that persists to this day), the existence of the indigenous movements is tangible proof that the state in Latin America never became fully national, which means that our modernity had enormous problems with taking shape in practice.

Latin American modernization got its start at an unprecedented historical turning point: the formulation of a new system of social domination based on the concept of race. Quijano correctly asserts that the category of "race," the first truly modern category, created the idea of a biological structure that established inequalities and hierarchies among people and that explained the limitations of the "lower" populations for creating valid historical and cultural artifacts.[2]

The first victims of this category were indigenous people. From the moment the indigenous population were first called "Indians," Europeans established a basic universal classification of all members of the human species. Locating Indians and blacks on the lower rungs of the human ladder, this system of social domination was also associated with a new system of social exploitation, composed of the well-known forms of labor exploitation (slavery, servitude, small-scale commercial production, reciprocity, and capital), incorporated into a unique system of producing export goods for the world market. This pattern of power meant that Europe would control knowledge and use historicism as a category of domination.

The idea of social equality is one of the paradoxes that Europe created in its zeal to consolidate modernity. I call it a paradox because Europeans did not produce an idea of equality that could be applied to all of humanity, that was truly universal, because they conceptualized the equality of all human beings while displacing the Americas, Asia, and Africa, thus racializing their populations and therefore situating them on a lower level. If the ideas of individual freedom and citizenship arose from the idea of equality, it then follows that, as limited by European thought, the peoples classified as racially inferior could not attain the same citizenship, nor could their institutional framework build what we call the modern nation-state. I therefore insist that the paradox of modernity, its fundamental contradiction, was rooted in the fact that it generated inequality between citizens who had been granted legal and political equality only nominally—a situation that has not yet been overcome even today.

What can be said about the historicism on which states are seemingly founded? It seems to me that the historical time of our modernity has run into huge piles of rubble, powerful ruins of the past, unanticipated by the Weberian process of the "disenchantment of the world." Therefore re-enchanting it is the goal of my insistence on covering topics from the world of hidden mysteries, such as the resource of the past, that can help us understand the cultural conflict created by the mismatch between worlds with unequal power and prestige. The return of the repressed is related to the "here and now" that questions development and progress, both of which are tied to the rectilinear time heading toward the future. The "here and now," by contrast, shortens the future; it allows us to think of a qualitative spatial-temporal differentiation unconnected to historical time, theorized by Koselleck as the "horizon of expectations." This differentiation is tied to the ecstatic, redemptive experience of the unforeseeable overturning of the world. Thus modernity will never accept the existence of times pregnant with meaning that do not correspond to a rational explanation of history. Because of this, the use of the past as a resource anticipates the realization of the future at some point of ecstasy that lies beyond history, that assumes it from the here and now of everyday events that do not correspond to the prognosis—which is to say, that have not been planned in advance.

The "here and now," the moment and place that mark the appearance of the "Angel of History," Benjamin's ever-approaching image, is the present that bears those embers of the past that have not yet been resolved. "Here and now" is a subjective reconstruction of the past, alien to the "objectivity" that dominates the analysis of historical facts. This reconstruction, which can be thought of as the "Angel of History," as a renewed image of Benjamin's messianism, performs two functions. The first is to reclaim from the past the cultural or historic symbol that best displays the fissure, the gaping wound, opened by the colonial past: it is this irresolute fact that forges an image or symbol that gives the past its mythical character of resistance, which the other projects onto the present. The "here and now" thus performs this ethnogenetic function of absolute creativity.

Its second function is to see to it that past, present, and future relate to each other, but that they not be confused with the linear character of the historical time of modernity. In this sense, the "not yet" that projects us into the future is countered by a present that Mannheim called "absolute," which I prefer to explain as the resource of the other that the past brings with the finality of obtaining justice and achieving self-determination. These are demands of the present—sometimes violent, not devoid of an impatient machismo—that have their instrumental value. The violent, impatient *Now, damn it!* thus serves as a tool for struggle and for communication, that is, as a resource that subalternity finds in the economic, political, and social struggles of the present. In this way, the cultural conflict—we define it as an ethno-national conflict—only makes sense if it is studied in the context of these struggles, these challenges, and the circumstances that give rise to them.

It is important to bear in mind that "here and now" is a resource that the other "invents" to bring the mysterious, the mythic, into the present. One of the great errors made in interpreting the statement "The present is another time now" is taking it as a mere survival of the past, and thus distorting it by understanding it as a need for returning to ancient times. It isn't about returning to the past in order to stay there; it is about transporting that past into the present, for clear social and political ends. Subaltern pasts remind us and demonstrate to us that the nonmodern and the modern are contemporaneous; they share a "now" that is expressed on the historical level but actually has a prior ontological character. This ontological "now" preceded the historical vacuum that the historical method assumes there exists between "there and then" and "here and now." In reality, we approach the "time of the gods" because it is not alien to us, because it somehow lives in us: the gods are signs that meddle in historical time, that contradict it and make it incongruent with itself.

Our "entry" to the banquet of modernity may have followed the rhythm of historical time as woven by philosophers and social theorists (Hobbes, Jacques-Bénigne Bossuet, Jacques Turgot, Condorcet, Kant, and Hegel)—a time that had the virtue of measuring a society's progress through various "stages" of improvement until it finally "came of age," just like modern European societies. But it turns out that as they followed the stages of historicism, our letrados had no chance of comparing their understandings with the social reality in which they lived, nor of seeing how they measured up, dazzled as they were by the Enlightenment, against the discoveries of important ex-centric authors. Indeed, it was only later, reading Benjamin, that we understood this historical paradox of modernity, which resides in the fact that the more we insist on the linearity of progress, the more we run into the "enchanted spaces" that show us the other face of the project of modernity. Thus, the invisibility of these spaces in Latin America has constituted one of the clearest signs of the difficulties modernity has run into; of the conceptual limitations that constrain its historicism, which cannot make sense of that other face of modernity.

2. THE NEED TO "PROVINCIALIZE" EUROPE

In his revealing study *Provincializing Europe: Postcolonial Thought and Historical Difference* (2000), Chakrabarty asserts that the critique of colonialism would be impossible if we did not bear in mind the way dissident sectors have appropriated the Enlightenment. Thus, for example, Frantz Fanon held on to the Enlightenment idea of individualism in his decolonial writing (1963 [1961]), "even when he knew that European imperialism had reduced that idea to the figure of the settler-colonial white man" (Chakrabarty 2000: 5). Similarly, in this chapter I again insist on the analysis of "historical time," on the fact that it is indispensable but also that it is insufficient for dealing with the study of the new political forms taking place in fragmented societies.

Trying better to understand ex-centric thought and its relation to the "here and now," I insist on the need to listen to the voices of certain thinkers who have been marginalized by history, for with their decentered viewpoints, distanced from the logos of modernity, they questioned two supposed conceptual gifts of the twentieth century, both tightly linked to the notion of modernity: first, historicism, the idea that all human events must be studied as a unity in linear dialectic development; second, the notion of the political itself, tied to the development of liberalism and attached to the concepts that arose in the Enlightenment. By "ex-centric thought," I am referring to the work of intellectuals who have been undervalued by the geopolitics of knowledge, subject as it is to the parameters established by Hegelian and Kantian logic, and who have critiqued the centrality and universality of European high modernity; they confronted it with an alternative way of thought that emerged from marginal, peripheral experiences, both in the Americas and in Europe itself, leaving us a legacy of indisputable worth in their theorizing.[3]

This alternative thought cannot be forgotten or avoided in moments of profound social fragmentation such as these, when we are obliged to rethink the traditional concepts of nation and state. Here I refer to the case of original thinkers who did not have the fortune of being properly appreciated during their lifetimes by academic institutions, but whose very current thought will allow me to question political modernity. I speak of the philosophers Walter Benjamin and Charles Sanders Peirce. Both were thinkers and activists with completely metropolitan intellectual roots, but their work provided an alternative consciousness to the orthodox historicist school of thought that still prevails even today in Europe and the United States. As we will see, it could be said that neither thinker's work abandoned the discursive universe of Western culture, yet each of them participated in a great liberatory movement.

In the Germany of the 1920s, Walter Benjamin, Franz Rosenzweig, and Gershom Scholem imagined a new vision of history that, with the proper adjustments, can still be useful for analyzing the most recent indigenous rebellions as critiques of modernity (Mosès 2009).[4] Indeed, in contrast to the optimistic vision of history, conceived as a permanent march toward the final realization of humanity, a vision seemingly straight out of Hegelian idealism, Benjamin proposed the idea of a discontinuous history in which disruptions are more meaningful than seeming homogeneity. In his "Theses on the Philosophy of History" (1968 [1940]), the product of the final stage of his thinking, Benjamin based his reflections about history on his direct experience of the great upheavals that marked history in the twentieth century.[5] But paradoxically, Benjamin's thought also recovered hope from the rubbish heap of historical reason. Indeed, with his categories of "rememorization" and "redemption," Benjamin took up utopia from a distant past that had awaited its sudden and unexpected fulfillment. Though Talmudic legend assigns a specific angel to each moment in time, the Jewish messianic hope that Benjamin allegorized in the figure of the Angel of History does not follow the stages of history, conceived as a logical concatenation of events; on the contrary, it emphasizes the disruptions of history that lay bare the thousands of loose ends that, like arcane hieroglyphs, form its warp and woof. Benjamin's work shows a certain hermeneutic penchant, arising from the ocularcentric crisis of modernity (Jay 1993), for overturning the historicist standards of unity and identity. In their place, there would be only interpretive communities that approach events according to their own norms for judgment, without having to account for the intrinsic and supposedly "objective" qualities of historical facts.

Similarly, Benjamin introduced his critique of the philosophical notion of speculation, whose sources date back to the ancient Greeks, contrasting it with the perspective of those who conceive of it more along the lines of the Jewish notion of contemplation. The word "speculation" is, as Martin Jay notes, a Latin version of the Greek *theoria* and "is rooted in the word *specio*, to look or behold. In more modern philosophy, the primary example of specularity can be found in the Idealist philosophers of identity, most obviously Hegel. Here the ultimate dialectical unity of Subject and Object is rooted in the *speculum* of the Absolute Spirit" (Jay 1993: 106–107). So it is that, in the fevered intellectual work of modern philosophy, alienated from the notion of contemplation, vision has been understood since seventeenth-century Cartesian rationalism "not in terms of an eye seeing an object exterior to itself but of the eye seeing itself in an infinite reflection" (107). Jay further asserts that the problematic implications of speculation were no less evident to other critics of ocularcentric historicism, among whom I would place the North American analytic philosopher Charles Sanders Peirce (1839–1914). In a sense, speculation evokes all the dangers of narcissism, with their solipsistic results. Indeed, Peirce felt that the excessive subjective self-absorption into which individualism degenerated was problematic. Medieval moralists warned that looking too often at the mirror would lead to the mortal sin of pride—a sin that grew more pernicious in modern times with the perversion of the prudent rule "Know thyself"; Peirce added to the perverse effects of narcissism his own observations about greed.

An indisputable precursor of the modern theory of semiotics, Peirce was the author of a monumental and intellectually rigorous body of work in highly diverse fields: mathematics, logic, physics, chemistry, and philosophy. He was also a heavy drinker, and the extravagances of his personality cost him his academic career. Yet he was an extraordinarily deep thinker, as Terry Cochran has argued:

> In fact, without the slightest hint of irony, one could affirm that the most coldly analytical response to today's historical disjunction was written by the American philosopher Charles Sanders Peirce. Peirce's aggressive essay on historical agency, published in 1893 under the title "Evolutionary Love," is the fifth and final installment in a series of essays in which he attempted to construct the backbone of his entire philosophy. (Cochran 2001: 78)

In this exploration of historical agency—that is, the search for a subject that sets history in motion, whether an individual or a collective in the form of state or nation—Peirce introduced the concept of "agapism," the doctrine that the law of love is the only truly operative law in the world. Peirce argued here that, of the three types of evolution—chance variation, mechanical necessity, and creative love—the third is the most fundamental.

Taking hate not as the opposite of love but as an imperfect state of it, Peirce rebutted the "Gospel of Greed" and lamented the fact that sentimentalism seemed no longer fundamental to human behavior. Peirce defined sentimentalism as "the doctrine that great respect should be paid to the natural judgments of the sensible heart," and he "entreat[ed] the reader to consider whether to contemn it is not of all blasphemies the most degrading" (1935 [1893]: 205). Comparing his position with the points of view expressed by Christianity, he concluded his essay with an analysis of the continuity of mind and a warning of the dangers of individualism. The economistic history of the second half of the nineteenth century and the first decades of the twentieth apparently did not take this warning into consideration.

As can be seen, Peirce's approach to the evolutionary meaning of history has nothing in common with those of other late nineteenth-century evolutionary theorists, especially not those influenced by political economy and by the theory of the evolution of species.

Peirce ironically summed up political economy as the assertion that "intelligence in the service of greed ensures the justest prices, the fairest contracts, the most enlightened conduct of all the dealings between men" (1935 [1893]: 207) and argued that it exaggerated "the beneficial effects of greed and ... the unfortunate results of sentiment" (210). Therefore, "ever since the French Revolution," he concluded, "it has been the tradition to picture sentimentalists as persons incapable of logical thought and unwilling to look facts in the eyes," with the result that the law of love has not found fertile ground to bloom as it should.

Though Peirce attacked the greater weight given to political economy in contrast to moral economy, he was hardly a defender of idealism, either in his capitalist analysis of society or in his harsh criticism of Marxism. Anticipating the late writings of Benjamin, Peirce tied history to the form of negative redemption that said that society cannot transcend its own historical moment, which was marked by the greed of capitalism. Linking historical agency to individual interest trivialized any attempt to explain historical change through moral improvement.

Here I would like to hypothesize that if "Evolutionary Love" had been widely read by Spanish American thinkers of the late nineteenth and early twentieth centuries, Peirce's ideas would have helped them to reflect in different ways on the social organization of our nations. His ideas on evolutionary love would have forced us to think critically about the historical interests involved in building nation-states subjected to evolutionist logics, which, being founded on greed, extended observations of plant and animal life to political economic views of progress. The most noted evolutionists of the era fell into this way of thinking. Darwin, for example, saw mechanical individualism as reinforced by the lawless greed of animals. Peirce wrote that Darwin should have added, as a motto for *Origin of*

Species, "Every individual for himself, and the Devil take the hindmost!"—the opposite of the message Jesus expressed in the Sermon on the Mount (200). Thus, Peirce harshly criticized Darwin's theory of evolution and, according to Cochran, "synthesize[d] his critical judgment in one brief sentence: 'Natural selection, as conceived by Darwin, is a mode of evolution in which the only positive agent of change in the whole passage from moner to man is fortuitous variation.' Darwin's notion of 'fortuitous variation,' change without causality and without any theological plan, stands in opposition to Peirce's strong sense of developmental history, of history that proceeds from worse to better by means of a universal, nonhistorical idea"—the idea of love (Cochran 2001: 80–81).

3. THE "TIME OF THE NOW": MESSIANISM AND REDEMPTION

A historical fact characteristic of Latin America is that nationalisms here have produced local versions of a stubborn European narrative structure demanding that every nation form its own "image of its future." Such an image is nothing but the historical form, dressed up as progress, that as Chakrabarty notes follows "this 'first in Europe, then elsewhere' structure of global historical time," which Third World nationalisms have copied, substituting for "Europe" some other locally constructed center (Chakrabarty 2000: 7). In this way, historicism has made historical time the measure of the cultural distance that, according to enlightened opinion, separates Europe from the countries of the Third World.

It is indisputable that Benjamin's thought clashed with this way of understanding the world, tied as it is to ascendant historical progress and molded by European modernist thinking. Opposed to such unilateral progressive ways of looking at human events, Benjamin introduced instability into every concept based on the ideas of the "future" and historical continuity. In his 1940 essay "Theses on the Philosophy of History," Benjamin rejected historical processes in their diachronic evolution and concentrated on the synchronic articulations of the present. In distancing himself from the concept of the historical time of modernity, the historian's task was to link to the present everything about the past that raised questions and proved troubling. In these theses, Benjamin contrasted the "image of the future" to the "presence of the now" (Benjamin 1968 [1940]: 261), which was based on the double model—both theological and political—of messianism and revolution. As Theodor Adorno has noted, Benjamin, who lucidly critiqued the center from the periphery of its own Western thought, refused to analyze the documents of culture from the historicist viewpoint that accumulates events as if they were commodities (Adorno 1991: 12); on the other hand, Benjamin, who nearly shared Peirce's thinking on this point, perceived from his critical position the decadence of industrialized society, which turned cultural values into market goods.

In "Theses on the Philosophy of History," the emergence of a political model of history did not presuppose the annulment of aesthetics, much less of theology. The aim of this essay was to radically purge history of any "image of the future" and to substitute for it a new image: that of "awakening the dead" (Benjamin 1968 [1940]: thesis 9, 257).

Illumination and awakening mean that what has been and the present "now" meet each other, for the first and only time, as if in a flash of lightning, both ready to build the new constellation. Note that the relation between what has been and "the now" is figurative—in Peirce's terms, "indexical"—a "blind impulse" (1935 [1893]: 201) causing an epistemological impact that does not have to mean anything, yet also not demanding that we relate it causally to the agents who produce it. It is as if Benjamin had translated Peirce's "index" into his own version of history (such as "blind impulse"). In his fourth thesis, on the concept of history, the secret reunion between past and present takes place in figures that are historical, but not temporal. In other words, redemption is simply the opportunity of the present to "index" the past in such a way that it can demand the future. This past, marked or "indexed" by the historian, is a conflictive, disruptive apparition, which the historian uses to construct a new figure. All this happens in a "time of the now," which has nothing to do with the temporality of representational history. Indeed, "reality" is present in symbolic form, not representational or conceptual form. The Angel presents reality in its sacred density; it is not a cognitive "re-presentation" but a "living presence" that occurs in symbolic form. Looking at Benjamin's Angel from a Eurocentric viewpoint, it is stuck in a "magical," "numinous," "pre-conceptual" (i.e., "primitive") viewpoint. But Western philosophy, being tied to graphic linguistic structures, only accepts the supremacy of the Word (*Verbum, logos*). Consequently, reality is "represented" through the linguistic code, by means of the logical "text," which must be interpreted, deciphered. Thus, reality is not only "logical" and intelligible but also linguistic and legible.

But the reality of the time of the now that characterizes this Angel of History, as of the symbols produced by other ways of knowing such as those from the Andes, is not logical and linguistic, but symbolic and figurative. Thus the Angel, and land for the Indian, are not objective reality, inert material farmed by the campesino; they are living symbols of life, of the cosmic and ethical order. The Angel of History does not "represent" the world; on the contrary, the Angel presents the world symbolically and knows it vitally. And this is a source of conflict, because the concept of history that Benjamin puts forward with his Angel is not subject to epistemological verification. Its indexical nature forces the historian, the "translator," merely to read the figure, which indexes history in being read. So the Angel of History, a powerful figure that has been interpreted in many ways, turns its back on the future, on the goal created by the structure of temporality. The Angel looks fixedly at historical time in its singularity and reminds us that we must not confuse the temporal with the historical. As Cohran indicates, "The temporal lends itself to narrative; the historical, only to figuration" (Cochran 2001: 38).

Historicism is measured in linear and homogeneous time. This is the "homogeneous, empty time" of modernity, which, as explained in the previous chapter, allowed Benedict Anderson to carry out his study on imagined communities. This causal time, waiting to be filled with a series of ordered events that go together with historical agency, was the butt of Benjamin's harshest critiques. To be precise, the linear time that has been so essential for progress-based European nation building is an open temporality that corresponds to the direction humanity must take in quest of its infinite perfectibility.

Now, as assimilated by "Latin American thought," this homogeneous time backed up the historical agency of the local bourgeoisies as they carried out their longed-for, and still incomplete, projects of creating "national cultures." An ingenuous notion—even ahistorical, if we observe it through Benjamin's eyes—time nonetheless provides a stable narrative structure for a historical understanding of modernity: the present is fleetingly situated between the past and the future that will replace it.

Historical materialism did not try to move past this idea of progress, which animates Western thought. On the contrary, its primary axioms are the unidirectionality and progressiveness of the dialectical process. The inversion or reversibility of this dynamic—a theme that I explored in the introduction when I referred to Adorno and his "negative dialectic"—is practically impossible because it would entail the *Aufhebung*, the ideal utopian state that is the goal of social and material development. In opposition to this dialectical process, Benjamin was not wrong to reject the idea of progress, which, from the viewpoint of Marxist orthodoxy, asserted that the proletariat, embodied in the vanguard party, would exercise its collective will at the moment when it attained its self-consciousness as agent of historical changes. This idea of progress, which articulates the agency in the materialist theory of history, also seemed false to Benjamin, because it remained stuck in an uncontrollable apparatus that has distorted the faith the masses have placed in it. Benjamin objected to these two aspects of the notion of progress—its domesticating effect and the ideal future it promised—based on his different understanding of historical agency, the refoundation of politics.

Historicism robs action in the present of its own presumed agency, because it perpetually postpones its meaning. Connected to this postponement of modernity—today modernity is spoken of as an incomplete project—is the idea of "not yet," which Chakrabarty's study delves into with relation to historical difference. For Chakrabarty, historicism is nothing other than the dominant sector's persistent habit of postponing the aspirations of the dominated sector of society (Chakrabarty 2000: 8).

As we can see in the "civilizing" essays by so many Latin American essayists writing about the nation, some historical time had to pass, basically for pedagogical reasons, before the dominated Indians and blacks could be considered citizens. The historicist argument deferred, and continues to defer, the rights of the great mass of people, relegating them to the "waiting room of history" (Chakrabarty 2000: 8) until the subjugated could acquire "historical consciousness" and become civilized. What's interesting here is that this "not yet" has now run into the anticolonial counterdemand of "the now," which marks the actions of the popular sectors once rejected and relegated by the civilizing state.

A certain expression used by postcolonial subaltern classes—"Now, damn it!"—casts doubt on the political construction of modernity. We are thus experiencing the time of the now as the consciousness of the unfulfilled nature of the historical time of modernity. The time of the now is clearly political, because it marks the violent, impatient form in which the suffering and humiliated masses enter history. The time of the now reads in our present day the traces of the forgotten, repressed past. In this sense, it revives a moment of the past, gives it new life, tries to realize today what was lacking yesterday. As "the now," which I define as a resource, Benjamin's time of the now implies no accumulative process, because it does not try to recover the past; rather, it tries to save it from oblivion. As I noted in the case of Mariátegui's theorizing of the ayllu, the emphasis is on the fact that, by skipping over the continuum of history, the historian-translator saves the past in order to grant it new meaning in light of the present. The image that is rescued is what Benjamin called "the 'time of the now' which is shot through with chips of Messianic time" (1968 [1940]: thesis 18, 263).

Benjamin did not invoke the class struggle dialectic. Quite the contrary: from his point of view, history is not at all an irreversible movement of progress; it is now a struggle constantly beginning over again between the return of the Same and the appearance of something completely new: redemption. In this regard, Gershom Scholem said that, in contrast to progress, the dialectical leap into the void of history that Benjamin termed "a tiger's leap into the past" was the leap out of the "historical continuum into the 'time of now,' whether the latter is revolutionary or messianic" (Scholem 1991: 85). This view of history actualizes the conflict that recurs at every moment in time between the two principles of repetition and revolution, of continuity and rupture, of the immutable and the new. Thus, the rupture of historical temporality, the appearance of the unforeseeable, is given the name of "redemption."

In contrast to the quantitative and accumulative vision of historical time, here we find the idea of a utopia that emerges from the very heart of the present, from a hope that is being lived today. Instead of history judging people, as Hegel had it, we now find people judging history. A reactualization of the past in the experience of the present, the history of the oppressed is discontinuous, whereas continuity belongs to the oppressors. On taking up the history of the vanquished, the most specific traits of their traditions are assumed: their nonlinear character, their ruptures, their radical negativity. It is the Angel who interrupts history and who never appears at the end of an evolution by stages. If we want to relate the Angel to local Andean cultures, we wouldn't be far off by complementing it with a reference to the rich concept of *pacha*.

For Quechua and Aymara speakers, pacha is the time-space that is concretized as the here and now, but that is generalized to vaster eras and spaces, those that I call the "absolute present." Remote from Western concepts and mathematical quantification, time in the Andean experience is like the breath, like the heartbeat, like the ebb and flow of the tide, like the cycle of day and night. Pacha is the drawing of a relationship between a "before" and an "after" that are alien to the way the historical "past" and "future" are conceived. Pacha, the dense present, the expanding present, is the time of the now, the qualitative time of planting, of weeding, of harvest. Secular and "enchanted," supernatural, this relationship between time and space—lived in time as it is lived in space—cannot be rushed or pressured. The supposed "profits" of time, so celebrated by the Western tradition, are seen as unimportant by this present, because over the long run they are all lost. Anyone who visits the Andean world quickly notices that unpunctuality is ubiquitous. But "Andean time," in Peru or in Bolivia, is no reflection of mere laziness; it is a different way of measuring things, alien to the stopwatch. The hour is good if the moment is right; if not, we experience it as a bad time to do something—*la mala hora*, "the bad hour."

The triple partition of Western time into past, present, and future does not correspond to Andean experience. In Quechua, there is a single term for "future" and "past": *ñawpapacha*. To differentiate them, substitutes such as *hamuq* (what is coming), *qhepa* (after), *ñawpa* (before), or *qayna* (earlier) are used. The "present" is *kunan*, which simply means "now," and *kunan pacha*, or "now time" (Estermann 2009: 200).

Just as in Andean temporality, the past is present in current time, "now" is a moment experienced as a permanent reactualization of the past, as the constantly repeated attempt to return to life what in another time was spurned, humiliated, scoffed at. This movement of historical consciousness drags all utopian tensions toward the future; that is, it anticipates utopia in the very heart of the present. Its central category is "recollection," which shouldn't be confused with memory, because redemption is a conscious act. Recollection, more a political act than an aesthetic or religious one, is not satisfied with calling up the events of the past; it seeks to transform them, to reinterpret them in the present. As a tool of the present's retroactive efficacy over the past, historical time stops being irreversible. In this way, having the law of historical time confront physical time is a special feature of theology: its ability to change its past in retrospect. As Benjamin asserted, this concept of time is not "immediately theological" because it does not progress inexorably toward the final salvation; but it is theology (not teleology) because it reclaims the religious conception that history is reversible and that "the before" can be changed. "The now" aims a serious blow at the homogeneous, progressive time of modernity.

Over the rocky course of its search for modernity, Latin America twice rejected the "not yet" with which the Western powers set it down in the waiting room of history. First came the independence movements of the nineteenth century. These brought about a purely political decolonization, because with the exception of José Martí they gave rise to no anticolonialist thinking at all. This project was followed by another, also political in nature: the nationalist movements of the twentieth century, which remained interested in the building of modern states, rather than in the possibility of creating an "other" project that might force them to look critically at the alien modernity of the West, along with its linear time of evolution and progress. One gets the impression that both modernizing quests forgot that subaltern pasts that, like twists and turns in the road, burst in upon the present and force it to undergo a process of translation that obliges it to become conscious of the need to modify the very text history "reads": modernity itself. Let's take a close look at this process.

4. THE SECULAR AND THE SUPERNATURAL

A frequently ignored aspect of culture is the fact that secular histories are written without our noticing the existence of two systems for interpreting events. One, the "disenchanted" way of thinking, in which human beings alone are the historical agents who propel change, is basically "empty and homogeneous" historical thinking as Benjamin defined it, supposedly natural and immune to the vicissitudes that cultural differences introduce in history. The other system, which has fallen into disrepute as nonscientific, is the "enchanted" way of thinking that arises in the "time of the gods" who people the world.

For those secular histories that run into these enchanted worlds, the conflict between systems is resolved in such a way that the scientific, disenchanted thinking ends up translating the enchanted thought, incorporating it into its logic, explicating it rationally in accordance with a Newtonian principle that, while obsolete, nevertheless serves as a basis for the "transparency of translation." According to this principle, the language of mathematics and physics, considered the highest sciences, controls our understanding of other languages, classified as dependent and insufficiently rational. In the Newtonian universe, which regulated the historical imagination, scientific events were completely translatable, from the language of mathematics, Queen of the Sciences, into the prose of the other dominant language, and then from these to the languages held less important on the scale of knowledge. Something along the same lines occurred in the relation between Newtonian physics and the capitalist economy.[6] The capitalist economy regulated the lives of human beings through the impersonal controls that the laws of the market—another "solar system"—imposed on society. Newton's laws, which Adam Smith admired, were thus the most precise tool for measuring individual and social phenomena, and applicable not only to gravity and inert matter, but also to all the realities that were being explained from the centers that were diffusing knowledge. Profoundly logocentric, Newtonian physics was recognized as the science that regulated all other realms of human knowledge. Indeed, Newton insisted on the mechanical principle of the union and total harmony of the universe. Given that this universe had no room for reflection on the supernatural, Newtonian translation was strictly controlled by the visualizing faculties of the "human mind" and by the ideal of objectivity, which as I have said dictated that events must be translated into the various languages under the auspices of scientific language, which was deemed superior.[7] This scientific language was determinative in the construction of a history without gods, continuous, empty, and homogeneous, which was also closely related to the other social sciences and to modern political philosophy. There was a "sameness" among them all.

It is worth questioning this "transparency of translation," which reduces everything to rational, objective facts. In other words, if the positive sciences point to the sameness of knowledge about things, regulated by the superiority of the scientific, the "time of the gods" would have to be considered to be a matter of "difference" bursting into the rational order and so contradicting its objectivity. A serious cultural gap is thus created when the divine, the enchanted, turns into the here and now, questioning the process of secular history. However, for the questioning of the profane world to take place, the enchanted must be translated into a disenchanted prose that simplifies and more often than not distorts the essence of the supernatural.

More than twenty years ago, the anthropologist Michael Taussig wrote his polemical study *The Devil and Commodity Fetishism in South America* (1980), which sought to explain the meaning for the modern industrialized world of the exotic idea of the devil. Asking how it was possible, given the capitalist relations of production and exchange that surround our everyday world, that peasant consciousness could represent these relations in such a non-natural and even malicious way, Taussig used Benjamin's "Theses on the Philosophy of History" to approach the image of the devil. Indeed, viewing the Andean miner as a historical subject in the process of forming—he called the Andean miner a "neophyte proletarian"—situated in the "moment of danger" when his peasant consciousness is falling apart due to the transition from the peasant mode of production to the capitalist mode of production, Taussig centered his analysis of the supernatural on the figure of the "Tío," an evil deity that inhabits the depths of the mines.[8]

Following Benjamin's axiom that articulating the past historically does not mean knowing it "just as it truly happened," Taussig sees in the Tío of the mines an image of the subaltern past that can illuminate the present, that is, the moment of danger that threatens to bring down the old peasant tradition and to turn these neophyte proletarians into the new "tools of the ruling class." Interpreting the figure of the Tío as the fetishization of the perversity inherent in capitalism, Taussig turns the pact with the devil into a "proletarian pact" that stigmatizes the distortion of the traditional values of peasant economy (family control of production, exchange, reciprocity, use value ideology) when it comes into contact with capitalist relations of production and with the alienation of wage labor in the mines. Taussig denounces the economic system that forces these men to exchange their souls for the destructive powers of the market. So the association of the pact with the Tío must have arisen in that "moment of danger," the here and now that revealed the contradiction between the peasant mode of production and the capitalist mode of production in the mines (Absi 2005: 124).

Taussig's suggestive interpretation has attracted many criticisms. He has been reproached for the overly idealized, Manichaean economic reductionism underlying the dichotomy between the capitalist and precapitalist peasant modes of production, and for his ignorance of the mechanisms of commercial penetration in the Andes (Godoy 1984; Platt 1983). I will not repeat these criticisms here; instead I will concentrate on the topic of translation. Is it possible to avoid violating the supernature when we try to explain it in secular terms? How should we narrate a present into which some supernatural event has abruptly intruded?

Taussig clearly establishes that the goal of his interest in the world of Bolivian mining is to explain historically why certain malevolent deities inhabit the consciousness of the incipient proletarians who work there. He aims to translate the enchanted reality into disenchanted prose so that we who live in modernity can become aware that the deities exist there in response to what the miners conceive as a debased and destructive way of ordering economic life. The Tío is a collective representation of how life loses meaning; it is, then, a supernatural manifestation permeated with a historical sense, which, wrapped up in a symbol—Benjamin's allegory— explains what it means to lose control of the means of production, giving these means of production control over human life. This phenomenon of commodity fetishism, which we moderns are not consciously aware of, is clearly recorded in a historical context (the premodern) that immediately precedes our own, in which one mode of production and of life is being supplanted by another. In the premodern context, the destructive process of alienation is dramatically represented by the catachrestic figure of the devil.[9] In this process of degeneration, the devil represents not only the profound changes that are taking place in the conditions of material life, but also the change that we find in the notions of truth and falsity that guide the reason for existence of human beings habituated to concepts radically opposed to creation and to life, tied to material conditions and social relations that are alien to the capitalist mode of production. So the supernatural belief in the Tío allows Taussig to assert that the nascent proletarian culture of the mines was in many respects antagonistic to the process of commodity formation.

When he translates the supernatural into secular reasoning, Taussig elaborates his conception of the devil as a belief explaining the dynamics mediating opposites that have met at a particularly crucial moment of historical development. Regulated by the historical flow of modernity, Taussig allows the supernatural to be translated as the conflicted mediation between two opposing temporal forms of apprehending and evaluating the world of human beings and of things. Following Marx (1971), he calls these opposing forms of evaluating reality "use value" and "exchange value." His analysis of the distinct metaphysical and ontological connotations of each concept allows him to contrast precapitalist popular mysticism with the capitalist form of mystification that Marx termed "commodity fetishism."[10] Taussig's explanation, resisted and criticized by other Andeanists, still lies on the linear historical stream that situates supernatural belief as something intrinsic to the process of the proletarianization and commodification of the peasant world.

Another interesting facet of this translation of the supernatural into "disenchanted" prose is its cover-up of use value. If workers in the mines conceive of the supernatural as something diabolical due to the imposition on them of exchange values created under the capitalist mode of production, then we might wonder why we, who also live immersed in the capitalist mode of production, don't react in the same way and instead adopt the economic process that disguises and distorts use value as a normal and completely natural phenomenon. Why is it that, with the maturing of the capitalist system, our moral outrage at the exploitation of humans by humans has dissipated? Why have the laws of the market that regulate this exploitation become quasi-objective categories, part of the natural order, guaranteeing a surplus and the unequal distribution of the profits? In posing these questions, Taussig interprets the supernatural, the demoniacal, as an illumination,[11] as a resource from the precapitalist past, the subaltern past, expressing the magical reaction of the beginner proletarians to the distortion of values produced in society by commodity fetishism.

From this point of view, the devil, a deity related to the production of the magical in the present, is not a return to the past or a turn to some archaic utopia. To the contrary, the supernatural ceases to be a simple testimony to the power of tradition, an unchanging mythological ritual from the precapitalist past, and is transformed into a here and now that responds creatively to the conflict occasioned by the clash between use values and exchange values. Thus, the magic of the production of use value counters the practice of exchange value, held to be the most important form of interaction in capitalist society.

Describing the contrast and the dialectical interaction between supernatural precapitalism and secular capitalism is no longer a merely rhetorical matter in Taussig's analysis; it becomes the very core of the social division between the dominant and subordinate groups. This division cannot be understood if one is unaware of the differences that exist between the system of use values that underlies peasant economy and the capitalist market economy. Above all, it is essential to comprehend the ways in which the capitalist market system engenders the commercial mentality that makes human beings turn into commodities, and in turn makes commodities be seen as living things that dominate human beings.[12] This paradox results from capitalism's drive toward market-based mediation, unlike precapitalist forms of organization, in which human beings consume the products of their exchanges directly, the capitalist market comes between people and introduces abstract laws that oblige people not to form direct relationships with each other but to connect through the exchange value of commodities.

Now the peasant mode of production, which the neophyte proletarians of the tin mines could not have left behind entirely, differs from the capitalist mode in many aspects. With the sudden introduction of capitalism, the beginner proletarian forces began to lose control of the means of production that they would have enjoyed as a peasant workforce. If, as peasant producers, these proletarians had lived in a system whose goal was to satisfy a number of qualitative needs, now as mine workers the new system forced them to carry out the goals of unlimited capitalist accumulation. Entering this system could not but produce chaos in the consciousness of these peasants in their process of becoming a proletarian workforce. It was this consciousness that perceived the change magically and that "illuminated," with its supernatural perception of this event, something that the modern mentality, immersed in the capitalist mode of production, has lost: the consciousness of the profound affective shock caused by the loss of peasant values and the adoption of the debased values of the capitalist market.

According to Taussig, the emotional blow suffered by the new proletarians was even greater because the organic conception of society that they held began to fall apart as a result of their entry into the new system of exploitation. Communalism and solidarity, the supreme values of the precapitalist system, gave way to greed, personalized self-interest, and the commodified world, which began to dominate social relations, devaluing the function of human beings. Interpersonal social relations thus began to be hidden in the guise of mere relations between things. From this point on, the lives of these proletarians would depend on relationships established by commodities, and the market would become the only guarantor of their spiritual coherence.

5. ON COMPLEMENTARITY AND RECIPROCITY

Let's take a closer look at the loss of use values, something that happens, according to Marxist theory, in the process of transformation from a precapitalist society to a system centered on abstract market laws that debase human relationships. As Taussig explains in his book, the transition from one system to the other is marked here by the presence of the Tío in the proletarian consciousness, not as something from the past or as a primitive superstition, but as an allegorical supernatural occurrence that illuminates the inadequacies of the secular present. Taussig, who translates the supernatural into a rational, secular explanation of why such an occurrence had and continues to have a place in proletarian consciousness, sticks to the linear trajectory of events, guided by the explanation of the theory of value from European Marxism, which is subject to the progressive sense of historical time. But as I will show, this explanation, interesting as it is, has shortcomings that raise doubts about the veracity of translations that ignore the ins and outs of the local, preferring to explain reality from imported models, imagined from the viewpoint of European historiography. So Taussig's argument contains errors which, in observing insufficiently the miners' solidarity and reciprocity, forgets to give enough weight to the alternative analysis that arises from the local reality. In order to correct this inadequacy, which is ultimately a problem of translation, I will later turn to a revealing essay by Sabine MacCormack on Inca history. MacCormack, also interested in giving meaning to the past, explains how difficult it is to translate into a Western language the conflictive pasts that lie buried in subaltern memory.

Contrary to Taussig's explanation, which reduces peasant and miner to a duality governed by irreconcilable modes of production that succeed one another with the passage of time, the peasants were never necessarily horrified by the commercialization of their economy. To the contrary, as Pascale Absi asserts (Absi 2005: 125), there was a voluntary dimension to their participation in the market. As it happened, *kajcheo* itself—a practice that allowed workers in colonial times to work abandoned mines illegally during weekends—was an indigenous market innovation that contributed to the reproduction of Andean communities. Indians were not, and are not, strangers to Western technology and Western exploits. We could speak of an "Andean modernity" within the framework of a rationality that is not precisely rationalist or empiricist, but that considers science (knowledge) to be the accumulated collective wisdom (*sophia*) that has been transmitted from one generation to another. In this sense, "knowledge" never was, and is not, the result of an intellectual effort; rather, it is the product of a broad life experience. Likewise, the appearance of money did not mean, as Olivia Harris reveals, the forced adoption of surplus value to the detriment of reciprocity and use value. We should also bear in mind that the formation of a mining worker class such as the one Taussig describes (wage-earning, proletarianized, and so on) was subsequent to the entrance of the market in peasant communities, refuting the argument that the indigenous workers discovered capitalism for the first time in the mines.

Aside from the critiques mentioned here, I would like to emphasize that the simultaneous existence of the modern and the nonmodern calls into question the historicism on which Taussig's analysis is based. Indeed, the continuity, the linear process of the semantic universe of the Tío—a figure that had abandoned the peasant cosmology based on belief in the Pachamama, the Mother Earth—is untenable.[13] To support his thesis, Taussig argues that the transition from the Pachamama to the cult of the Tío occurred only because of the peasants' transformation into new proletarians. This is thus a secular explanation that, by framing itself in the linear process of history, fails to convince. Indeed, rather than anything specific to neophyte proletarians, the dangerous nature of the Tío and his man-eating abilities, which Taussig interprets as the expression of the evils of the capitalist mode of production, in reality results from his identity as a *saqra*, that is, from his being one of the wild, undomesticated creatures of the world (Absi 2005: 125).

The secular history of the diabolical world in the Andes, as carried out by Taussig, has a very hard time understanding that labor not only produces metal and miners, but also influences the socialization of the supernatural forces of the universe. Dwellers in the subterranean spaces of the mine galleries, the Tío and the Pachamama are deities torn from the violent, evil world of the saqras and incorporated into the reproductive circuits of human society. This contradicts the idea that the Pachamama, as an Andean deity, has given up her place to the Tío, symbolic representation of evil capitalist witchcraft. Taussig forgets that both are complementary deities that directly influence the relationship between the wild and the domesticated. Living forces of the universe, the two deities fulfill a complementary role, passed over by secular history, which has neglected to incorporate the interaction between man and the underworld into its analysis. And this interaction can be viewed in terms of a relation of production that cannot be explained by the secular transformation of precapitalist culture into the evil of capitalist commodity fetishism. Such a rationalistic explanation is nullified, bypassed, by the ritual that calls forth the genetic powers of the Tío and the Pachamama, together with the protection of other Andean deities that dwell in the mountains, where they scheme to alter the lives of human beings. At the same time, each miner's own ritual and the relationship it creates with the deity confirm its location in the social organization of production.

As present-day forms derived from subaltern pasts, the Pachamama and the Tío, as Absi explains (2005: 81), are not transcendent deities but rather dynamic principles that acquire social meaning when they relate to the workers: the fertility of the ore, on the one hand, and the order that governs the interaction between the miner and the living powers of the mine, on the other. So a close relationship exists between the Pachamama and the Tío: she is identified with the mountain in whose womb the ore is found; he, appearing in devil form, is the chthonic lord of the mine and its veins, whose exploitation he organizes. They have a close reciprocal relationship with the mine workers, who receive protection and safety from the deities and in turn must feed them through sacrifices and satisfy them with veneration. To break this reciprocity would lead to punishments that might include illness, fatal accidents, and the disappearance of the veins of ore.

As Tristan Platt (1983) and Carmen Salazar-Soler (1990) have explained, then, there is continuity between the miners' cosmology and the beliefs surrounding agriculture among Andean peasants. Both associate the underground with the violent and wild powers of the world, with wealth, and with danger. And this symbolic unity, which favors the integration of peasants in the mine and has grown through constant exchanges between the mines and the countryside, breaks with the linearity of historical time and parts from the rational explanations of secular things that reduce that union to a dubious syncretism between the prehispanic religious world and the religious beliefs of the Spanish colonizers.

As archetype of the mine worker, the Tío embodies the dialectic of the rupture and continuity between mine and countryside. His figure, sketched out like that of the Pachamama by the rural representatives of the underworld, reflects the miners' agrarian legacy, for in this sense they have not entirely ceased to be peasants. But at the same time, his professional specialization, his mastery over money, and his eternal intimacy with the underground world are clear signs of the rupture between the mine and the peasant world. Rural heirs of the Tío, whom they hold to be a living, virulent power, the miners are much closer to the world of agriculture than to that of the city. However, as Absi (2005: 313) has noted, unlike the Pachamama and other mountain deities, the Tío is linked not to any lineage or region, but to an occupation. His foundation is built not on kinship or ethnicity but on a profession and a corporate group, and based on a sexual division of labor—women cannot enter the mines without arousing the wrath of the Tío—unknown to the rural world. Exclusively associated with mining tunnels, the Tío cannot leave the underground world except on special occasions, such as Carnival week; he may not trespass on the countryside, where his presence, feared by peasants, wreaks havoc. Peasants and miners also agree that fields sown by a miner possessed by the Tío are barren. In this respect, Taussig is right in saying that the intimacy that leads a miner to fuse with the Tío is the sociocultural rupture that marks his passage from the category of peasant working temporarily in the mine to the category of miner. By becoming the Tío, the miner ceases being a peasant, but that does not mean he takes on the spirit of a bourgeois or that he becomes a city-dweller like any other. Hence the miner's ambiguous nature: he is an ex-peasant, a "refined Indian," which confirms his marginal character.

In addition to the limitations indicated here of the "disenchanted" explanation of the mining world, there are other aspects that contradict the secular view that Taussig applies to subaltern pasts: there is, of course, the complementarity between the genetic powers of the mountain and the Tío's orienting role (Absi 2005: 99); there is also the distinction that the miners draw, which Taussig does not take into account in his analysis, between their "collective pacts" with the Tío, which the miners accept as normal, and "private pacts," which they perceive as amoral and negative. There is a certain similarity here between the rejection of the greed of those capitalist partners who, in the miners' mentality, assured themselves of access to exceptional veins of ore through equally exceptional offerings to the Tío, and the need to repress the selfish impulses that Peirce, cultivator of ex-centric thinking, questioner of capitalist modernity, invoked in his essay on "evolutionary love," demanding the sacrifice of self-interest in favor of the collectivity, the community. Only through the breaking of the world of greed can Peirce's "agapism" come about, a type of human solidarity that also makes room for the mediation of the supernatural as a counterforce to Social Darwinism. Likewise, the miners' solidarity is the power that permits them, thanks to the organizing abilities of the Tío, who distributes the daily labor tasks, to face up to their harsh and dangerous struggle with the mountain. "Individual pacts" throw this order, supernaturally imposed by the community, off balance. Finally, there is the topic of the circulation of money, another aspect that contradicts the disenchanted explanation that, in attempting to translate the supernatural, robs the miners of their ability to relate monetary matters with the patron deities. All of these imbricated aspects increase the difficulty that Taussig's analysis faces for translating into a strictly rational logic the subaltern themes that concern us here.

I have elaborated on the fact that the Tío, the most diabolical and sociable of the saqras, demonstrates, with the close connection he draws between the genetic powers of the mountain and his ability to order the miners' daily lives, the aspects that most clearly refute the linearity of historical time: the complementarity and dependence between the secular and supernatural worlds in the relations of production. Thanks to Absi's detailed research, I have also been able to establish the attributes that the Pachamama and the Tío have in common. Moreover, the pioneering works of June Nash (1979) and Olivia Harris and Thérèse Bouysse-Cassagne (1987) help Absi to enumerate the points that the Tío and the Pachamama have in common. These overlapping points between the miners' devil and the spirit of the mountains are due to the unifying role of the mountains, which have articulated the set of saqra forces in the world. But human labor socializes the supernatural by means of mining activity. Absi (2005: 277) relates that a few decades ago, when mining activity at the Cerro Rico de Potosí was less intense, miners who were off their shifts would rest in specific places, rest areas called *samanas*, that constituted domestic enclaves within the violent, barbarous environment of the mountain. In these places, miners got their breath back out of reach of the saqras, deities whose violence was placated through offerings of the men who chewed coca leaves and offered libations. Thus, the miners' journey inside the mines was an unending pilgrimage, which domesticated through human activity the existence of the Tío and the Pachamama as socialized deities from the saqra world. The complementarity of the supernatural and the secular was clear. However, as soon as a miner left his work, or if his relationship with the Tío were interrupted, the Tío would return to his violent, savage saqra state, undoing his insertion into the social network of transactions that domesticate the deities and give civilizing power to human labor.

Given that labor humanizes the deities, there is also a complementarity between money and the gods, who receive the miners' tribute. In clear contrast to capitalism and its ethics of labor, the dominion of the Tío and the Pachamama over metal extends to money. This translates into the idea that the profits of the mine belong to the devil and are doomed, like all buried treasure, to being extravagantly squandered. Indifferent to saving or investment, the miners enter a system of reciprocity that attempts to appease the Tío's unchecked desires, which call for alcohol and women. The money of those who make collective pacts with the Tío is frittered away in the cantinas and brothels of the city, while the miners are conscious of the fact that the veins of ore in the mines are doomed to disappear.

The miners' wives seem to have a very different relationship with money. Indeed, Absi has recently shown (2009) that while the miner sells his labor to make money—to "manufacture money," which he then squanders—his wife, dedicated to retail trade, generates income that "appears not to be a reproduction of money but rather the reproduction of capital" (2009: 120). Thus the role of money in the feminization of commerce also ties the secular and supernatural ritual together. In fact, according to Absi, the semantic field of the reproduction of capital in both Spanish and in the Quechua of the women traders is constructed through loan words from the vocabulary of raising livestock. Capital is called "the mother of money" (*maman*), and when it reproduces, the results are called "the offspring" (*uñan*).

In short, contact with the underground world transmits to the miner the saqra power that allows him to perform his job. The transference of the Tío's force to the workers gives rise to a reciprocal relationship in which the miners, imbued with this force, radiate a vital and sexual energy that reveals the genetic powers of mine, which allow the devil to be the master of labor there. So the function of their labor is not exclusively material, because the immediate economic aspect also implies human participation in the reproduction of the world. In other words, the Tío depends on the workers, and they depend on him.

Given that the Tío organizes the miners' activity, he is not a straightforward evil deity but an ambiguous one, sometime even contradictory. Owner of the veins of ore and of the miners' labor, the Tío allows men to discover the mineral beds in exchange for their offerings. Day after day, he distributes metal to those who deserve his favors, moving the veins from one place to another in the galleries, sometimes bringing ore from other mountains, on vicuña back, tied down with snakes, and so fertilizing the Pachamama. A tireless laborer, he is the workmate of the miners, in solidarity with them.

Related to the supernatural nature that the Tío so lavishly bestows on the miners, the theme of solidarity is another aspect that can be seen as a beneficial force, as a form of energy that moves the community. Taussig's analysis cannot see that, in contrast to the mere mechanical individualism of the capitalist mode of production, the Tío's supernatural solidarity balances out the excessive greed of the "individual pacts" created by capitalist owners. This supernatural solidarity, as much sexual as it is, in a sense, religious, is an argument of some weight in favor of the agapastic theory developed, among others, by Peirce and by Charles Taylor, whom I will discuss below. It is a check on utilitarianism, the theoretical sidekick of the individualism that modernism puts forward. The solidarity that the Tío offers is a propulsive force, an example of Peirce's "energetic projaculation," which, as an animating force, transmits to the miner the energy (*callpa* in Quechua: force, bravery, spirit) they need to take up their struggle with the mountain. As a consequence, the energy and courage that the miners display are qualities that cannot be separated from their relationship of solidarity with the Tío.

The bestowal of energy, which is the foundation of Peirce's agapism, is connected here to the cohesive force that transmits the supernatural. As

Carmen Bernard (1986: 185–186) observes, this energy should be understood as the intrinsic quality of the wild world. It is the power of the non-"civilized" places and entities of the world, of the force that harmonizes life and communicates with living beings, including the animals and plants. So the force that the Tío transmits is a form of energy that brings the mythical ancestors into the present, the animating powers of the *otorongo*, a sixteenth-century feline that the miners had asked for strength; powers that had been transmitted to the Tío.

When they invoked this energy, the miners analyzed by Taussig no doubt insisted on the Tío's humanity, on his status as a miner and as their workmate. The most human manifestation of the saqra universe, the Tío is, according to Absi's observations (2005: 276–277), an intermediary between the wild world and work. With his heterogeneous and contradictory attributes, he personifies the uncomfortable ambivalence that the miners recognize in their own religious practice, which has been unable to overcome the contradictions between their adherence to Christianity and their continued involvement in older forms of worship, now Satanized. It would be wrong, however, to apply the traditional concept of syncretism to the Tío—that is, to explain his existence as a fusion of elements from diverse historical traditions. And even though his figure juxtaposes elements with diverse origins without mixing them together, drawing a distinction between the "precapitalist indigenous deity" and the "proletarian deity" would not explain his reversible structure: a kind of dynamic continuity that allows the Tío's vital energy to circulate among the miners, sometimes emphasizing his saqra qualities, at other times stressing his domestic, social, human nature, thus conforming to the logic of supernatural transfiguration. Let us take a closer look at this reversibility.

Viewed from the capitalist mode of production, as Taussig argues, the Tío can pass for a figure of alienation, of separation, of disjunction, but the Tío is more than that: he is a reversible structure that seeks, by fluctuating between the capitalist mode of production and peasant precapitalism, to harmonize the miner's everyday life and to show solidarity with him. This means that their differences can be correlated and broad enough points in common can be found to overcome their asymmetries and the alienating differentiation that has characterized the division of labor and commodity fetishism up to the present day, attempting instead to turn that alienation upside down. In this way, between the precapitalist peasant world and the capitalist world, the Tío is a model that works as disjunction and as conjunction. He is like the lip of a glass, which, in separating the inside from the outside, also unites them and bestows them with meaning. He is the other, which, like a mediating *différance*, divides and unites.

A totalizing social factor, in the sense that he condenses various dimensions and meanings, as the symbol and "illumination" that he is, the Tío, reversible and ambivalent, is part of the system of precapitalist reciprocity marked by exchanges—gifts and countergifts—that bypass the abstract mediation of exchange value. And in this system, which insists on the obligatory nature of giving and receiving, the Tío goes beyond any linear explanation of history, for he symbolizes a spontaneous, impulsive form of action, a vital energy that, coming from the saqra world, admits of no rational control. The system of reciprocity places value on the division of labor based on a preexisting sacred symmetry under which accepting a gift without presenting a countergift unbalances the just measure of things. Nevertheless, precapitalist reciprocity is forced to coexist with the social asymmetries that capitalist power and domination generate. Thus, reciprocity must confront the equally continual splintering force of the division of labor introduced by capitalist domination. Opposing forces both resist comparison and create a way of acting much like what Elias Canetti—an ex-centric Sephardic writer who, like other writers and thinkers of Eastern Europe, translated his ideas into German, that is, into an adoptive language—described in his study of the exercise of social power.

In *Crowds and Power*, Canetti ties power to the "command," which "consists of *momentum* and *sting*" (1978 [1962]: 305). "Momentum" is what motivates a person to act; it is the domination that one exercises over another, creating an asymmetrical and unbalanced world. "Sting," on the other hand, is the often supernatural and invisible recourse that the dominated turns to in order to balance in the imaginary what the market economy has destabilized. Well concealed, the sting waits patiently, perhaps hibernating in the memory of the dominated, for a chance to seek revenge and overturn the original command. Consequently, it is a way of expressing the idea of the return of otherness as an a priori structure of social organization.

Like Canetti's "sting," the Tío is a way of contrasting capitalist alienation to the labor of imaginary reconstruction and ideological restructuring that endeavors to maintain the social whole undivided. It is worth noting, however, that this action takes place not in the immediate, tangible real world, but in a supernatural and metalogical state of suspension. It is not too much to propose that, as a model for structuring human society, the Tío, the master who regulates the development of the miner's everyday life underground, could be useful to the elaboration of a new way of focusing the public sphere, understood as the structure of a public organization of experience in which the religious and the supernatural are also taken as potential historical agents.

6. THE PROBLEMS OF TRANSLATION

Modernity, of course, considered religion to be a "survival" from an already obsolete era that was out of touch with modern advances in knowledge.[14] But though it was relegated to the background, religion found ways to keep from disappearing from politics in the most advanced capitalist societies. Even important liberal theorists such as John Rawls have had to recognize the need to incorporate it into their reflections. Indeed, while Rawls initially excluded religion from politics, considering it a subject that should be aired in the private sphere, in his later work he recognized that religiously motivated arguments should be taken into account as publicly valid, so long as they could be translated into secular demands that required no religious interpretation. Going even further, the recent works of Jürgen Habermas have accepted religion as an important resource in the exercise of politics in democratic societies (Calhoun 2011).

But the fact that religion has been partially recognized in the public sphere, and that it is now said as a result that industrial society is entering a "postsecular" age in which we are no longer counseled that public reason should admit entry only to exclusively secular arguments, does not mean that the difficulties of translating religious ideas into secular language have disappeared. Habermas, for example, recognizes the enormous difficulties entailed in assuring that religious arguments are not "encumbered with an asymmetrical burden" in debates with secular arguments in the public sphere (Habermas 2006: 11). This forces us to question whether "translation" is, in and of itself, an adequate conceptualization for everything involved in making religious arguments, complex as they are, also accessible to other, secular participants in the public discourse. Without denying the importance of translation, Craig Calhoun (2011: 86) asserts that participants often undergo a "transformation": that is, that the people involved in the exchange become ready to change, to become different and better people, as a result of the process. That is the only way we might aspire to a "culture of integration" based on citizen solidarity, for which individualist utilitarianism is a poor recipe. In the case of Western societies, this would also involve abandoning the notion of a secular public sphere, within which religious arguments are illegitimate because they do not lead to reason-based communicative action.

Translation implies that the differences between languages can be overcome without interference from other more complex and problematic inequalities, such as, for example, cultural differences.[15] While translation from one system of knowledge to another entails the construction of a highly complex model, the situation becomes even more complicated when it is a matter of translating religious arguments into a language that will be accessible to secular citizens. But the situation becomes even more dramatic when the meaning of the arguments is embedded in much more vast and complex cultural situations, such as the supernatural practices arising from subaltern pasts like those I am analyzing in this chapter. You can see, then, how hard it is to translate enchanted situations such as those narrated by Taussig into the disenchanted prose of modernity, for which the historical process is explained in secular terms that must not take notice of the complexity of the multiple aspects that characterize the supernatural.

In an article on memories of the ancient past in early colonial Peru, MacCormack (1995) has precisely described the gaps left by translation, pointing out that the past that interested Western thought was very different from the past that occupied the memories of the subaltern past. By contrasting the historical past (the past of Spanish Peruvians) to the subaltern past (the "Andean knowledge of the past"), MacCormack revealed the huge disparity between the two modes of conceptualizing history. Spanish Peruvians, being Eurocentric in that they thought from Europe, could not help but orient the historical process linearly. Indeed, they "considered their own past and their own social order to be the necessary framework within which the social order and the Andean past could be understood and judged" (1995: 5). Therefore, they "saw the invasion of Peru by Francisco Pizarro and his followers as the culmination of a historical process that began in Spain and that considered the Inca Empire to be a side question, like a prelude" (1995: 5). As Andeans were much better informed about local affairs, "the Andean knowledge of the past . . . changed significantly in the process of translation into Spanish and in being recorded as writing by the foreigners" (1995: 5). Given that this knowledge had been kept on *khipus*, the knotted cord devices used to keep records in the Andes before the European invasion, their substitution by colonial documents written in Spanish produced the problems of translation that MacCormack analyzes. The ones who had this detailed knowledge of the past were the *khipukamayuq*, "astrologer-poets" who interpreted "the path of the sun, the moon, the eclipses, the stars, and the comets" (Guamán Poma 2006 [1615]: 278) and who kept the public records of the Incas. Under the rule of colonial officials, these khipukamayuq lost their traditional role, which consisted in keeping the information that was recorded on the khipus (numerical and narrative, historical and calendrical information, lists of deities, sacred places, settlements, and the labor prestations that the Incas demanded from their subjects) and in keeping accounts of the sacrifices to be offered to the *waqas* (prehispanic ancestors and divinities) and of those that had already taken place. The subaltern past, then, was contained on these khipus, and the information that they contained and that was preserved by the khipukamayuq differed from what the Europeans learned.

Unlike early modern European governments, the Incas did not impose tribute on their subjects. Instead, they required their subjects to devote a certain portion of their time to them in the form of labor, as a kind of reciprocity with their rulers. This productive capacity of the Andean people that was placed at the disposal of the state was recorded in khipus, which also kept accounts of the resources and populations of the different regions in the empire, in addition to delegating the organization of various tasks to less important administrators. As MacCormack relates, thirty years after the conquest, Spanish officials were still amazed by the efficiency of their system for recording information and for delegating and distributing the responsibility for carrying out various public obligations among high and low-ranking authorities. The khipus, however, were replaced by new documents that were recorded by colonial officials and so lost the khipukamayuqs' communicative ability to report the responsibilities that members of a community had to each other and to their wider surroundings. With the khipus replaced by new documents written in Spanish, the meaning of information itself changed: it no longer arose from within the society itself, for the simple reason that the questions asked by Spanish officials reflected the requirements of the colonial state and the administrative and fiscal worries of its representatives. As Spanish officials began to absorb the Andean knowledge of the past into their own past and their own social order, that knowledge changed markedly in the process of its translation into Spanish, the information being recorded in a foreign writing system that distorted it. It seems to me that the translation problems that MacCormack skillfully describes with regard to Spanish colonial officials also occur in the way Taussig "Westernizes" the subject of the Tío when he translates it into the historical process advanced by the capitalist mode of production.

Historical pasts and subaltern pasts arise from diametrically opposed economic systems. The Andean knowledge of the past corresponded to a labor system that benefited the Incas through the labor of their subjects. Their subjects, in turn, acquired the food, clothes, and other material goods they needed to survive. In this way, the subjects gave the state part of their time, but they kept their property intact. The Spanish Crown, on the other hand, demanded not only labor from the Indians, but also finished goods and a payment of tribute in cash (Spalding 1982: 321–342). As MacCormack notes, this new principle of wealth extraction profoundly changed the relation between the colonial state and its subjects, and therefore the very nature of the information recorded in public documents, which no longer had any place for the notion of reciprocity.

Then again, the labor that the Incas demanded from their subjects kept their communities functioning as parts of a coordinated whole, which ultimately meant a reaffirmation and validation of the individual's and the group's social identity. In *Religion in the Andes: Vision and Imagination in Early Colonial Peru* (1991), MacCormack observes that labor was evoked as a public celebration: people recalled going to work singing, then coming back home to celebrate the finished tasks with festivities. Naturally, this agapastic view of the world disappeared with the coming of the money economy: commercialization dealt a heavy blow to community solidarity.

The changes in economic organization from the prehispanic past also affected the religious practices that had celebrated labor on behalf of the Incas and the deities of the Inca state. Stripped of public validation by Spanish colonial officials, the meanings that were once socialized and shared by the collective community became private, even secret. It should come as no surprise that by the late sixteenth century the worship of the Andean deities had been made a crime against the colonial state. This move was of tremendous importance, because the religious discontinuity between the Christian present, tied to historical time, and the subaltern past, linked with the time of the gods that had been expelled from the public sphere, widened into a cultural and social discontinuity with enormous consequences. The earlier time of the gods came into conflict with history, a development registered in the way that the subaltern past was understood by the Incas and their subjects before the Conquest and was translated by crown officials afterward.

The indigenous community, the *ayllu*, was important not only because it constituted the basic unit of the prehispanic economy, but also because it formed a kinship group that created and maintained the memory of the past through the worship of its dead ancestor. The ayllu thus kept alive the memory of an important event that was retold from generation to generation in an oral tradition that was also recorded on khipus. In the case of royal ayllus, the mummies of the most ancient kings, which were kept in the empires central Temple of the Sun in Cusco, were displayed on great holidays and given offerings of food. Moreover, poetic recitals commemorated the achievements of the dead, who were not only remembered but were also present, as mummies, among the living. Like living kings, the mummies owned fields and flocks of llamas, the products of which financed the celebrations in their worship; their financial interests did not disappear, because they were represented by their ayllus. The important part of all this, the reason it is relevant for understanding the time of the now, is that by upholding the interests of a dead ancestor, the members of an ayllu were also representing their own interests. As MacCormack shows in another work (1990), for the subaltern mentality the past was a resource for the present; therefore, living in the present entailed a commitment to the past, to the time of the dead. It could thus be said, in line with Benjamin's reflections on the "time of the now," that the members of the ayllu not only remembered its past but also commemorated it in the present.

Once the conquest had occurred, the newly subjugated subjects demanded that their memory be respected. Spanish notaries began to record narratives of the conquests and victories of important figures that were undoubtedly historical recitals representing these events not merely with the aim of celebrating the memory of the dead, but with the intention of bringing them into the present (Rowe 1985). During the sixteenth century, after many similar requests had been processed in colonial Cusco, Spanish historians began to question these odd Andean pasts. The result was the elaboration of narratives that were strikingly different in kind, for they changed the basic outline of a declaration of ancestral merit, which contained the sequence of topics recorded on khipus. Historical narratives written in Spanish tended to transform this sequence, interpolating or omitting items from its ordered contents. With notable exceptions, such as the text by Juan de Betanzos (Salomon and Urioste 1991), Spanish historians tended to construct their narratives according to rhetorical principles that were quite different from those that governed Quechua narratives, losing the voice of the original storyteller. Clearly, in the process of translating the information, two irreconcilable views of history clashed: this became obvious in the questions asked by the Spaniards, which differed radically from those posed by the subjugated people. At bottom, the times in which they told their histories were different. MacCormack carried out a detailed accounting of the problems that beset the translation of ancestral memories into Spanish. I am referring only to the theme of chronology, which is the most fundamental one.

Accustomed to counting years from the incarnation of Christ or from the creation of the world, the European historian conceptualized chronology as the union of classical culture and the Judeo-Christian tradition. This system, which made possible the connection between the various civilizations of the Mediterranean and the national histories of Europe, could also be applied to any other reality. Thus the primacy of chronology, of the linearity of history, created this seeming continuity between mythical and historical events. This meant that the biblical myths could serve as a historical frame for telling the story of the discovery of America and the conquest of Peru.[16] And given that the Andes had no chronological system that might be correlated with the linear European system, there could be no satisfactory answers to the questions that Spanish historians asked. In this way, the historians took on the task of understanding the Andean past by placing the Inca Empire on the European historical coordinates. They integrated the histories preserved by the different royal Inca ayllus into a continuous narrative that started with the biblical Genesis and was arranged according to a chronological order that was foreign to it. Andean myths turned into indistinctly remembered versions of European history.

In the end, Spanish historians faced up to the challenge of incorporating the khipus and oral traditions of the various royal ayllus into the continuum of European history: they created a historical narrative that was valid in Spain but had never existed in the Andes. In other words, by incorporating the khipu recorded kept by the Inca royal ayllus into a single narrative, they translated Andean reality into a Spanish, European language. In this project, the problem was not just to distort Inca history. In addition, by applying foreign historiographies to the evidence they found, the historians ended up paying less attention to the supernatural, to what was unfamiliar to them, than to the typical topics of European historiography.

7. A "CULTURE OF INTEGRATION"

The cultural conflict created by translating the religious into the secular makes it necessary to reflect on the fact that modernity does not fully explain our passage through the world. The problematic decision to put everything into "the hands of history" is controversial today because the secular public sphere must give in to the evidence that the supernatural, the metalogical, also has arguments that participate in public life. This makes it necessary to rethink the principles that led us to draw a sharp distinction between public and private, religious and secular. It would not be too outlandish, then, to speak now of a need to construct a "culture of integration" that, thought about from the viewpoint of postsecular public reason, could get past the two factors that historicism seems to have forgotten: the complementarity of the secular and the religious, including the supernatural and the metalogical; and human solidarity, including effective and concrete respect for human rights and the responsibility that each of us has to procure the well-being of our fellows. It seems to me that this "culture of integration" calls for the Law of Love and that therefore Peirce's agapism isn't a superficial concept that deserves to be forgotten. Quite the contrary: today it is being rethought and brought up to date.

Even though I am aware how naive it might seem to contrast the "evolution of love" and the greed generated by the capitalist system, it seems to me that we shouldn't forget that philosophy and wisdom are, above all, loving experiences. If the ties that bind science and love are broken, science becomes an anemic, lifeless body. That is why, despite the seemingly mad nature of Peirce's proposal, as seen from the West it constitutes a basic religious principle, without which Christian doctrine itself would lose its reason for existence. On the other hand, and together with this principle, science itself is no longer synonymous with blind faith in a secular reason that invokes the constant perfecting of knowledge and projects that it will lead to a heightened understanding of the human totality. To continue this reflection on the basis of human solidarity in love, let me turn to Calhoun's observations on Charles Taylor, the Canadian multicultural theorist who has insisted on rethinking agape, the law of love, in his latest work, *A Secular Age* (2007).

One of the central arguments of Taylor's book, on which Calhoun (2011) places special emphasis, is that European secularism has grown used to thinking of the world as an immanent reality that it is almost impossible to transform. To this immanence Taylor contrasts transcendence, that is, the need to go beyond the present world, seeking to modify it spiritually and materially. By anchoring his thought in this world, in the spiritual transcendence of the material—the reader will recall that Mariátegui said something similar in his reflections on Andean religion—Taylor argues that the world today is suffering from serious limitations. The first of these limitations is the narrowness of the individual ego, which reduces everything to the need to satisfy one's own needs, forgetting about the common good. In his *Critique of Modernity*, Alain Touraine also reflects on the split that it has created between the spiritual and the temporal (1995: 104). The former is guided by the need to satisfy collective needs; the latter is circumscribed by individual profit. This conflict between collective needs and individual profit leads him to pose a question about the ego: how could we overcome the narrowness of the ego and disperse the illusion of a social order that ignores the need to construct ethical values that will defend life, sometimes against technology, and the continuity of collective interests as against the discontinuity of the individual? Taylor answers this question with the need to construct an earthly "other world" that is agapastic, loving, that transcends the limitations of the individual ego that keep us from bettering the human condition.

The second limitation is the loss of the notion of the common good, and with it, what Taylor conceives as the lack of a moral horizon that can compete with quantitatively measured material achievements. Transcending the human impulse of accumulating goods is a categorical imperative that insists that personal interest not be set in opposition to the human community. So the object of agapism, of living together in harmony, is that people, motivated by the primarily financial values of modernity, should transcend the passivity with which they accept the world and the limitations of observing it as it is. Hannah Arendt (1968) spoke of the duty we all have to "make the world," not merely observe it as if we were simply spectators. We transcend this limitation when we transform our very beings, when we struggle together in solidarity for a better world, and when we participate in the construction of human values that can better the lives of others. In carrying out this principle, the logos of exchange, of dialogue between cultures, would not be a given that precedes and directs the dialogue, but something to be constructed in the act (Estermann 2009).

What would the repercussions on societies undergoing decoloniality be of this transformation proposed by Taylor, to construct with great difficulty genuinely public spheres that aimed at producing the common good? Do we have any examples of how the common good might be built, balancing the secular present with subaltern pasts that relied on religion and the supernatural? Is it possible to overcome the limitations of translation as imposed by modernity?

In her book *Milenarismo y movimientos sociales en la amazonía boliviana* (1999), researcher Zulema Lehm draws interesting connections between the millenarian movement known as the Búsqueda de la Loma Santa (Search for the Holy Hill) among the Moxo or Mojeño people in the Amazonian lowlands of eastern Bolivia in the 1880s, and the Marcha por el Territorio y la Dignidad (March for Territory and Dignity) that took place in 1990. Both movements, particularly the Búsqueda de la Loma Santa, revived social scientists' interest in the study of messianism and millenarianism. As we shall see—and this is the main merit of Lehm's work—this connection allows the author to counter the evolutionist postures of historicism, which look at millenarian movements as anachronisms that should be replaced by modern political movements. Contrary to this dominant position, Lehm's book shows that the millenarian movement is a resource from the past that the present, the here and now of the March for Territory and Dignity, reclaims. Her book also demonstrates that the secular does not present the drastic ruptures that would supposedly separate it from the supernatural.

The millenarian Búsqueda de la Loma Santa movement reflected the libertarian desires of the Moxos, a people oppressed by a neocolonial society that was insensitive to the pain of others. Sacred but also profane, this movement, like all millenarian movements, was characterized by Lehm as this-worldly, collective, imminent, total, and miracle-working (Lehm 1999: 131). Thus, rather than being messianic in the sense of producing the social redemption that Benjamin wrote of in his "Theses on the Philosophy of History," the Búsqueda de la Loma Santa movement was millenarian, centered on the discovery of a "land without evil" that did not need to await the coming of the Messiah—a communal place in the Amazonian rainforest southwest of Bolivia's Beni department, where a utopia with a better future for the Moxos would be located. After overcoming the domination of whites and mestizos, the source of the evil that would supposedly disappear with a cataclysm like the one that the sixteenth-century Taqui Oncoy millenarian movement in Peru awaited, the Moxos would find their paradise in this "Holy Hill" and would enter into a period of abundance, peace, and freedom there. This millenarian movement displayed a communal anticolonial content aimed at reversing the domination of the whites and mestizos who invaded Moxo territory and wrested from the indigenous people their ability to administer it autonomously. But as Lehm observes, this movement also had the peculiar characteristic of restoring the balance within the indigenous communities themselves, overcoming their internal conflicts through the permanent revitalization of Moxo culture.

By joining Christian doctrine to prehispanic Guaraní and Moxo beliefs, the Búsqueda de la Loma Santa ideology spoke to the wide sector of indigenous society who worked as rubber collectors, thus serving as a catalyst for indigenous consciousness, and also as a major tool for transforming the millenarian movement into a social movement based in the socioeconomic exploitation of the Moxo people. This connection between the two movements, millennial and social, removes them from linear historical processes through a recurrent interaction between the secular and the supernatural.

The March for Territory and Dignity of August 15, 1990, was the product of a number of regional meetings and *cabildos* among the indigenous peoples of the department of Beni. The aim of the march was to bring the protests of the Moxos, with their demands for recovering their territory and the right to self-determination, to La Paz, the capital of Bolivia.

Though the millenarian and social movements were mutually related and committed to the march, they were different in nature. The objective of the Loma Santa movement was to move into the rainforest, beyond any contact with national society; the new social movement, on the other hand, sought recognition from the state, and to that end it made use of wide coverage by social media. In other words, the March for Territory and Dignity sought its own peaceful integration into the public sphere.

Authorized by the Bolivian state itself, the March for Territory and Dignity called forth a solidarity such as had rarely been seen in the country's history. It was supported by workers' unions through the Central Obrera Boliviana; by the nongovernmental organizations belonging to the Coordinadora de Solidaridad con los Pueblos Indígenas; and by Andean settlers in the country's tropical zones. At the climactic moment of the march, the marchers were met by representatives of the Andean peoples (Aymara, Quechua, Uru, and Chipaya) who had set off from different starting places to join this communal "intercultural encounter," which can be considered a local example of a "culture of integration." In La Cumbre, an important point in the western range of the Bolivian Andes (almost five thousand meters high) and the gateway to La Paz, they carried out the Andean ritual of *wilanch'a*, the ritual sacrifice of a llama as a propitiatory offering to Pachamama. This act created a prophetic atmosphere and a sense of general awe, which was perceived not only by the Moxos, steeped in the millenarian ideology of the Búsqueda de la Loma Santa, but also by the Andeans. As Lehm explains, it could also be said that the summit in La Cumbre signified the meeting of two millenarian traditions, the Andean and the Amazonian, mediated by a new, collective spirit of participation.

The secular character of the March for Territory and Dignity, dedicated to achieving the integration of the Moxos into the public sphere and to fighting for their rights as citizens, contrasted with the supernatural nature of the Búsqueda de la Loma Santa, yet the latter nevertheless exerted an important political power. In this way, the Búsqueda de la Loma Santa, which promoted the recovery of indigenous territory, coincided with the secular aim of the march. A process was thus created in which the translation of the supernatural fed the secular demands of the social movement. Likewise, indigenous leaders interpreted the supernatural aspirations of the searchers for the Loma Santa, whose demands they translated and made intelligible to the state and civil society. As can be appreciated, we have here an interesting interaction between the supernatural and the secular public sphere. Indeed, the process of translating millenarianism into secularized codes also implied the reverse: the secular participated in the millenarian quest as well, in the search for the supernatural.

In conclusion, it could be said that the translation problems that MacCormack studies in her analysis of the Inca past were "solved" by the millenarian movement studied by Lehm. Indeed, both the Búsqueda de la Loma Santa and the March for Territory and Dignity carried out an interchange between the secular and the supernatural based on the same millenarian cultural starting point and created an interesting example of the way in which the religious created an ideology that allowed the indigenous leadership to demand the citizenship that had been denied the Moxo people for centuries under colonial domination. Thus, while the leaders of the new movement called for their secular demands to be heard, the seekers for the Loma Santa constructed the ideology that made it possible for this secular mission to be affirmed by the supernatural. In this task, both forces, the secular and the supernatural, had a place in the here and now, which, on the part of the indigenous leaders meant translating secular demands into a millenarian code. This code, aimed at the "inner world," legitimated the leadership of the latter and made possible the reproduction of the new social movement.

8. BY WAY OF CONCLUSION

Lehm's analysis shows that complying with modernity is not an indispensable condition for oppressed social groups to enter the public sphere where the meaning of the nation is organized. In a similar way, we should be very careful when we assert that all historical movements must be constructed by stages that come linearly, one after the other. The subaltern history recounted by Lehm also radically questions the belief that moving beyond the nonmodern, the supernatural, should still be the sine qua non that allows access to citizenship. Likewise, denying the supernatural means remaining under the dominion of a history and a political system that tend to be ignorant of the historiographical project of subalternity. It therefore seems to me that various cases presented in this chapter, those from MacCormack and Lehm, look critically at modernity and refute the linear path implicit in historicism. These are also cases of other possible social happenings in which the supernatural resists disappearing. Thus, influenced in part by insurgencies such as that of the Aymara, there are countless cases that fuse the return of ancestral beliefs and myths to the actions of current forces that deal hard blows to traditional historiography. As a result, situating ancestral practices as hoary recollections of an earlier mode of production that ought to be left in the past would return us to an evolutionary concept of history and to a historicist framework that does not do a good job of explaining reality. Indeed, such a modernizing framework keeps us from responding creatively to the challenges arising in political thought and philosophy due to the recent participation of novel indigenous movements.

Nourished by ancestral logics, the mode of action of the peasant masses obliges us to question the premise that capitalist modernity, inaugurated by nationalist movements, necessarily constructs bourgeois relations of power that may be considered hegemonic. If Andean modernity juxtaposes the bourgeois to the prebourgeois, if the secular lives alongside the supernatural, and if both are located in the sphere of the political, this does not happen because capitalism and political modernity have remained "incomplete." According to the judgment of Ranajit Guha, this is instead a matter of a state capitalism that was unable to construct hegemonic bourgeois relations of domination; to the contrary, we are living inside a "dominance without hegemony" (Guha 1997) of the modernizing elites who could not get the larger sectors of the nation to believe in and feel the interests of the elites as if they were their own. And, as Chakrabarty has also observed, it is believed incorrectly, under the influence of modernity, that humanity is a totality guided by a secular, homogeneous historical time. To this Western conception, which simplifies things to the point of erasing them, contrast the fact that thinking political modernity in and from the viewpoint of decoloniality necessarily implies admitting the opposite: historical time is not comprehensive, nor does it even concord with itself. Thus, the linear and celebratory discourse of modernity, of the forward progress of the human race, propelled by technology to new and magnificent historical destinies, is seriously called into question. This is why we say that European thinking is necessary but insufficient; that there is a need to renew it "from" the peripheries, both European and postcolonial.

In the spirit of Peirce and Taylor's studies on the evolution of love, I wonder whether it would be possible now to reincorporate human values into the way the economy functions. To cover this theme, we must go beyond the Western theory of "social capital," which follows the monotheistic view of the economy, and accept the alterity and polarity of indigenous economies that create social ties that put into circulation gifts, words, feelings, and rituals, all of these foreign to the logocentric reasoning of the West.[17]

Aware of colonial reality, of what Edgardo Lander (2000) has termed the "coloniality of knowledge," which forces us to see the world from the epistemic Western point of view, we must begin to think from the "colonial differentiation" that is concealed behind modernity, organizing and giving form to an alternative world of understanding things. We would thus have to think about "colonial differentiation" (indigenous communities and their ethical and economic modes of reproduction) from a critical borderland liminality that relates modern economic rationality to values and knowledges that were suppressed and made subaltern for whole centuries of colonial domination. These are nonepistemic knowledges, according to the canon of modernity, such as religious beliefs, gifts, rituals—in general, all nonacademic knowledges.

It seems to me that a reading of reciprocity should be situated in place of knowledge that approaches that of Peirce or Taylor. Peirce demonstrated very clearly, as Cochran notes, that the contemporary historical problem derives from the split that divides the notion of agency and historical comprehension (Cochran 2001). Even though the idea of agency is most often discussed as an attribute of subjectivity, it is actually tied to the ongoing discussion of this disappearance of universals in modernity. In the critical era through which we are living, which corresponds precisely to the profound instability of these universals, we now see an effort to make up for the inability of history to help us understand its own movements. Aware of this seeking in times of crisis, decoloniality questions all the discourses of cultural identity that take progress, the implacable historical continuity between past, present, and future, as a proven fact. If, as Peirce argues, love explains historical evolution in the opposite way from one ruled by self-interest regulated by economic exchange, then historical agency should also take place more because of harmony than because of conflict. In this way, human values would be born from reciprocity with each other and with nature, rather than exclusively from economic exchange based on greed. So, parting ways with Western critical reasoning, we must relativize secularism, empiricism, and individualism, the dominant values of modernity. Given that these values give us the theoretical tools to rationalize production, work, and consumption, we must hold them up against the principle of the complementarity of opposites, which softens and balances the weight of economic exchange and reciprocity.

Naturally, there are differences between the way Peirce perceived modernity from late nineteenth-century Western society and the way it looks today from poor, peripheral, and still colonized societies. And because we belong to different times, we also experience different traditions in the philosophy and epistemology of modernity. Today, when I am writing these words, I am aware that we must not ignore the historical and epistemological subalternization of decolonial intellectuals, thus we cannot take Peirce and Taylor as interpretive "models" of our reality, either. By doing so, we would continue covering up colonial differentiation by promoting intellectuals, who undoubtedly contributed decisively to the critique of modernity, but among whom colonial differentiation cannot have as much violent and oppressive force as it has for those who suffer subalternization. Theorizing via Peirce and Benjamin means doing it in parallel, always mindful of the critique that each of these intellectuals made of modernity and its economic model, inspired by the context of a Christian civilization whose temporal vision of history began with Saint Augustine's thinking.

To my mind, the originality of Peirce's works resides in the fact that this North American analytical philosopher was opposed to the idea of translating all forms of knowledge into modernity's language of economic rationality at the expense of other, equally valid forms of knowledge. Indeed, the secular code of historical time in the humanities, divorced from gods and spirits, ends up being, in the rationalist mentality, an inescapable universal in which "differentiations" are not recognized by the code and the historical agency of the dominated is denied.

Aren't the *apus*, the patron deities of the snowy Andean mountain peaks, integral to practices that are as real as the belief in the ideologies that govern modern life? However, they are invoked in community rituals that do not belong to the world of rational beliefs. The *ch'alla* ritual that "sanctifies" taxis and minibuses, though every bit as real as obtaining a vehicle insurance certificate, is very difficult to translate into the language of modern commercial transactions. Indeed, translating it would merely demonstrate the poverty of a functionalist approach, which, pushed forward by the "explanations" of secular narrative, would blur its sense entirely. Given the conflict between the cultures, it is hard to translate these particular worlds into universal economic and sociological categories. It is also hard to believe in histories that speak of mythical pasts that skip over the linear continuity of history.

Institutional history, with its linear time, and subaltern history, with its time of the now, do not follow parallel tracks; instead, being in conflict, they are interwoven with each other. This interweaving is not a clash but a "process of social mobilization from the bottom up and of political transformation from the top down" (Gilly 2003: 30). And it is in this interweaving, this peculiar combination of having recourse to modernity, of its laws and its institutions, with the timeless character of the ties of experience and customs, that we find the authentically original character of political autonomy for the indigenous peoples in the face of the state and its authorities.

This constant interaction of the politics and economy of the dominant classes with the habits and customs of indigenous communities transforms subaltern political activity and lends it a "remarkable capacity for combining legalism and violence, horizontal organization and mediation with the sphere of domination, autonomous social mobilization and negotiation" (Gilly 2003: 37). An extraordinary activity thus arises, which, like the Angel of History, becomes visible when you least expect it, and reappears, like a shooting star, in each new and unpredictable present.

It is to be expected that this interaction should also affect the scope of modernity, that its attachment to Newton's formulas should invoke the sense of "gravitation" more than that of "gravity" (González 2004). With love and reciprocity, gravitation brings us closer together, whereas gravity kills us with the physical (mechanical) sentence of falling bodies. As Peirce saw over a century ago, and as Touraine has recently reminded us (1995), the main thing is not to fall headlong into a pattern of fattening our egos, but rather to get our lives to gravitate into the "orbit of dignity," steering clear of the biased and discriminatory exercise of subordination.

Chapter Four

THE DIMENSIONS OF THE NATION AND
THE DISPLACEMENTS OF SOCIAL METAPHOR IN BOLIVIA

In his essay "Humanism in a Global World," the Indian historian Dipesh Chakrabarty introduces his vision of contemporary humanism with a phrase that helps explain the recent transformation in the social imaginary that was forged over the past century: "As we leave the shores of the 20th century to move into the uncharted waters of the twenty-first, we look behind to take our bearings for the future" (2009: 23). This observation weaves a suggestive spatial/temporal image, a provocative construction of fluvial metaphors that could be applied to the reality of Bolivia, one of the most interesting contemporary Latin American societies due to the political significance of its present-day ethnic movements. Indeed, by leaving behind the twentieth century, and by moving into the "uncharted waters of the twenty-first," we are capable of distinguishing the metaphorical construction for the two explanatory processes of the course of the Bolivian social imaginary: first, the developmentalist and pedagogical dimension of the nation-state; second, a more fluid conversation about whether, and how, cultural diversity might be recognized not by attributing it solely to the politics of the state. Let's call this the "dimension of deterritorialization." By "deterritorialization," I mean a cultural flow that contemplates the metaphorical displacement of the nation-state. This imaginary event does not only express the shifting of terrestrial spaces, but the "whole landscape of persons who constitute the shifting world in which we live" (Appadurai 1966: 33). I am talking here of "a society in movement" (Zibechi 2006), of an "ethnoscape" (Appadurai 33) that is changing the politics of the Bolivian nation to a hither unprecedented degree. While a lot could be said about the cultural politics of deterritorialized nations and the large question of displacement that it expresses, it is appropriate to reinforce here the idea that the term is not a reflection on migratory forces, on the shifting of spaces, but a question of the temporal asynchronies that affect the relationship between indigenous and mestizo identities. As we will see later on, this relationship in Bolivia is an embattled one. It is possible to say that in this country the nation and the state have become one another's projects. They are at each other's throat and the hyphen that links them implies a disjunction rather than a conjunction. This disjunctive relationship may be detected through the battle of the imagination, beyond the nation-state and its pedagogical dimension. Fluvial metaphors, I believe, are at the core of this debate.

1. THE NATION'S DEVELOPMENTALIST AND PEDAGOGICAL DIMENSION

The developmentalist and pedagogical dimension of the nation-state was dominant for most of the twentieth century. The developmentalist concept was imbricated in the construction of the "imagined community," the prime organizing principle of the nation since the early nineteenth century (see chapter 2). This order of events remains controversial to this day. It is no coincidence that a relatively unpublicized study by Bolivia's Constituent Assembly Coordinating Unit (UCAC) recently traced the source of the country's current political conflict to "differing concepts of the nation, among which there are two prevailing definitions that influence contemporary public discourse: the civic nation and the ethnic nation" (Mayorga and Molina Barrios 2005: 31).

Since these definitions derive from different traditions—the civic nation corresponds to the French model of voluntarism, while the ethnic nation arises from the German organicist model—political scientists themselves are unable to agree on which of the two types of nation should take precedence in their analyses. The civic nation highlights the construction of the imagined community, the changes introduced by mass media, and the geospatial shifts that are experienced over time that give rise to historicism, that is, to developmentalist thought. Without necessarily opposing the social imaginary of modernity, the ethnic nation explores the traditions (sometimes calling them "preexisting situations") that make it necessary to think the nation from an "organicist ethnic-genealogical spirit hailing back to the ancestral community, respectful of blood and language" (Mayorga and Molina Barrios 2005: 32).

It is thus problematic, though not impossible, to think that the two concepts—the traditional and the modern—can be complementary; that they can come together peacefully in the building of the nation-state; that both the organization of the modern community of citizens, founded on binding rules, and that of the cultural community, based on ancestral rituals and languages, can join forces to seek the common good. Reality, however, always resisted taking the two as equivalent. The confrontation between tradition and modernity gave rise to the temporal conflict that has been a recurrent theme in this book and will once more take center stage in this chapter.

Obviously, any view of the world must take place in both space and time; no space exists outside time, nor time outside space. In this chapter, however, I argue that the "spatialization of time," that is, prioritizing the analysis of "space" over the concept of "time," which is now being questioned by anthropologists and ethnologists, privileges the "territoriality" of civic institutions over the analysis of ethnic traditions that are localized in different senses of conflict-ridden times. Following Harootunian and Bloch, I call them noncontemporary temporal registers.[1] Later in this chapter, I will pay special attention to the growing effort to make identities "flow" like calm, orderly rivers, without letting this effort at postmodern explanation of identity observe with equal care that the new constructions of identity flow in tumultuous, disorderly streams, like those "currents" and "corners" of time that Ernst Bloch (1991: 106) and Reinhart Koselleck (2004) theorized about under the rubric of "the contemporaneity of the noncontemporaneous."

I agree with studies that analyze movement between "porous" spatial boundaries, because they show how rural life has been turning into urban life; at the same time, however, it worries me that the subject of temporality might be set aside, for its relative abandonment and subordination to reflections on space continues to affect social and historical analyses. The spatial turn seen in some recent research on the "refounding" of the Bolivian nation is related to the importance taken on by migratory movements. This social event leads me to think that the "spatialization of time," regulated by modernization and development, conceals the temporal asynchronies, the conflict-ridden times, which are so forcefully suggested by the social migrations taking place right now in the world.

As the relationship between space and time should be of key importance to those who wish to impart a balanced meaning to reality (Harootunian 2005), it seems to me that an analysis of reality can bear fruit only if it pays attention to what Bloch has described in these terms: "The *objectively* non-contemporaneous element is that which is distant from and alien to the present; it thus embraced *declining remnants* and above all an *unrefurbished past* which is not yet 'resolved' in capitalist terms" (1991: 108, emphasis in original). I think it is also important to bear in mind Bloch's assertion about history: "History is no entity advancing along a single line, in which capitalism for instance, as the final stage, has resolved all the previous ones; but is a polyrhythmic and multi-spatial entity, with enough unmastered and as yet by no means revealed and resolved corners" (1991: 62).

Since many historians and social scientists refuse to reflect on the nation from the repressed past, their analyses have solely to do with the construction of the civic nation. This willful renunciation of the conflict between the civic and the ethnic leads me to take a more detailed look at the struggle between these two concepts.

2. THE NATION'S TWO FACES

Following Eric Hobsbawm, the Mexican historian Tomás Pérez Vejo asserts that the history of the past two centuries is unintelligible without the term "nation" (2003: 276). Indeed, the nation has become the hegemonic form of collective identity for modernity, as well as the most important source of legitimacy for political power. An unavoidable reality since the eighteenth century, the nation, a concept that regulates the greater part of the aspects of collective life, became, together with progress, the new religion of the West. Even more than the other myths of modernity, including reason and progress itself, the nation is the only social construction that has remained untouched by the historical convulsions of the past century, so that, as Pérez Vejo says, "the goodness of the nation as a natural and desirable form of social organization continues to enjoy a wide consensus for most people around the world" (2003: 277).

But the nation is neither a "natural" nor a universal fact. It hasn't always existed, and it could cease to exist someday. Created by the development of modernity, the nation is merely a concrete historical response to the problems of identity and the legitimization of power. For that reason, and unlike other collective identities such as religions, classes, and family groups, the nation has a precise political nature that leads it to be confused with the state, so that Pérez Vejo considers the term "nation-state" a "semantic pleonasm" (2003: 280). Pleonastic to the extent that every state requires a nation and all nations aspire to be states, the nation-state correlates with the modernity of the nation, but not with the "existence of human communities that have been identified throughout the course of history as nations" (2003: 281). Thus, the term "nation" existed before European modernity, "but with a very different significance from what it began to have toward the end of the eighteenth century, in terms of both its meaning and, especially, its political use" (2003: 281).

If nations, as social constructions, are not objective realities but collective inventions—as we will see, the "modernist" theories of Hobsbawm (1990), Anderson (1983), and Gellner (1997) differ sharply from "primordialist" theories, particularly as elaborated by Anthony Smith (1986)—then they are not the product of a long historical evolution but the result of a relatively short "voluntarist" invention (the civic nation), as opposed to an "organicist" origin (the ethnic nation). Indeed, as the UCAC study observed in relation to Bolivia's reality, the civic nation and the ethnic nation are entities that, while contradicting one another, were substantially influential in the development of nationalism. Anthony Smith (1981, 1986) and Anderson (1983) agree that the two types of nation do not follow the same path. As a "primordialist," Smith hews much more closely to the past, to the fact that ethnic traditions continue to be active in the present, while Anderson, with his modern conception of the nation and following the logic of his imagined community, ignores traditions from the past that have nothing to do with the function of the mass media and the modernizing role of the state (Calhoun 2007: 28).

The civic nation is based on the loyalty that individuals, transformed into citizens, feel for the nation-state. In the civic realm, the nation-state is wholly political. Liberal in its inclination, civic life considers nationalism as anything but "rooted in a rhetoric of pre-existing ethnicity" (Calhoun 2007: 53). Invented by the French Revolution, the civic nation is thus founded on the notion of citizenship and the ideology that all men are equal, proclaiming the people's sovereignty throughout the country's territory as the only form of legitimization of power. In this way, the nation becomes a voluntarist concept, a "civic and territorial elective contract that leads to the nation-state and that presupposes a civil society, a people of citizens, liberty, and individualism" (Mayorga and Molina Barrios 2005: 31–32).

Recall that Walter Benjamin described the temporal nature of the civic nation as the "homogeneous empty time" of modernity (Benjamin 1968 [1940]: 262). German historian Reinhart Koselleck also describes it as historical time, that is, as a "horizon of expectation" that assimilates and subordinates the past and the present to the utopian future that never arrives because it is always under construction, so that "temporality robs the present of the possibility of being experienced as the present" (1985: 22), turning it into a "rational prognosis" of slowly forming "finite possibilities" (1985: 18).

The philosophy of progress guides the civic nation's temporality, turning it into a rational prediction that eliminates any past associated with ancestral traditions that lie beyond the reach of historical consciousness. While prognosis, as conceived by Koselleck, ties the past and the present to the future, this also means that the present can be understood only through the mental effort of constructing a philosophy of history (1985: 21–24). In this homogeneous time, events become a chronologically measurable and irreversible sequence, guided by the "before" and "after," the "pre-" and "post-" that order all historical events and distinguish them from mere circumstantial accidents. Such accidents presumably consist of phenomena that cannot be measured by history because they are fragments of the past, impossible to catalogue rationally. When the temporal sequence of events is organized, the chronological is subordinated to the historical, not the reverse.

The opening up of this "horizon of expectation" is thus the most important spatial-temporal characteristic of the civic nation. This is completely the opposite of the fragmented nature of the ethnic nation, whose essence lies beyond the reach of the notion of progress. Born from German Romanticism, the ethnic nation is an organicist concept (I will later relate it to the iconic metaphor of mestizaje) that emphasizes culture—language, blood, and land—as the foundation of nationhood.

Ever since Hans Kohn (1944) drew a sharp contrast between the ethnic nation and the civic nation, most specialists on the subject have considered the concept of ethnic nationality to be the opposite of enlightened liberalism.[2] More specifically, this concept was considered an attack on the possibility of constructing a unified humanity. Craig Calhoun notes that such unification would mean that nationalism should not be taken to be "the enemy of cosmopolitanism but a crucial if temporary mediator between individuals and global citizenship" (2007: 124). Civic life thus becomes a manner of expressing the emancipation of the individual, her liberation from old archaic bonds, and her potential for building a community bound together by intellectual interests rather than tribal ties. In the same way, civic nationalism differs from ethnic nationalism in that it is not the natural extension of nationality but rather its transformation by means of the notions of sovereignty and popular participation.

Going back to the case of Bolivia, the key fact is that both the civic nation and the ethnic nation were elitist concepts that resulted in the cultural form that I call "pedagogical," in which the most important essayists of the twentieth century engaged.

3. METAPHORS ABOUT "NATIONAL PEDAGOGY"

Hernán Vidal is one of the Latin American intellectuals who has worked the most diligently on the ways that narratives of identity are used to construct "national cultures." As in many of his other works,[3] in his essay "An Aesthetic Approach to Issues of Human Rights" Vidal defines the field of "the Humanities . . . as the study of the ways in which human beings create analogical, symbolic systems to give meaning to their environment, relationships, and purposeful actions therein" (2009: 14). For Vidal, human beings experience their aesthetic acts "as coherent fields of intellectual-emotional-bodily responses" to the problems they encounter in society (Vidal 2009: 14). For Vidal, whose concept of "narratives of identity" I draw upon, essays are clearly part of the narratives that found the nation.

Spread through literary texts—the *crónicas*, essays, and novels that represented through the imaginary the contemporary situation of the country's culture—the historical process of nation building had a long and important trajectory, which in the case of Latin America was related to widely read essays that guided the formation of the various "national cultures."

Linked to the print capitalism studied by Benedict Anderson,[4] the "foundational" essays that I will cover briefly in this section were written during the first half of the twentieth century.[5] These essays were constructions of social imaginaries, that is, sui generis historical interpretations that articulated metaphorical-symbolic fields capable of giving an orientation to the established social order. Heavily involved in building the nation, the letrados were able to represent public reality without actually being true historians, sociologists, or social scientists. They were, instead, "men of letters" who were "in symbolic relationship with their time," as Edward Said so aptly described writers of this type (1994: 43).

I must particularly emphasize the fact that we often forget the "representational" nature of these foundational essays; that is, we forget that they were not sociological investigations or historical documents aimed at directly explaining reality, but representations of reality that drew on social imaginaries. Between realism and representation, what mattered more than the facts themselves was the way they were organized, always bearing in mind that nations were not objective realities but individual and collective "inventions." Mediated by symbols and metaphors, the foundational essays of the Bolivian nation were the imaginary representation of the way in which certain groups and social classes reproduced their existence, following or breaking with patterns established by the hegemonic political power.

One of these essays, considered controversial by the intellectual elite of the time, was the first to develop the "cult of anti-mestizaje."[6] This was the book-length essay *Pueblo enfermo* (1937 [1909]) by the polemical essayist Alcides Arguedas from La Paz. Published in Barcelona, Arguedas's essay assumed a mechanical relationship between man and his environment and postulated a predominantly fatalist view of Bolivia's reality, full of racial prejudices. For Arguedas, the Indian was exclusively determined by the mechanical, unmodifiable action that the geography of the highland plateaus exerted on him. "The pampa and the Indian are but a single identity," Arguedas wrote, going on to assert that "the physical aspect of the high plains . . . has molded the spirit of the Indian in an odd way. Observe the hardness of character in the man of the altiplano, his aridness of sentiments, his absolute lack of aesthetic affections" (1937 [1909]: 180). And this deterministic relationship between human and environment, which would be extended to explaining the entire country's backwardness as a result of its convoluted geography, ignored other historical, economic, and social ingredients that had as much importance or more than the geographic, spatial factors Arguedas specified. According to his view of reality, under the degrading influence of mestizaje, any human being, whether Indian or white, would have grown sick and lost his ability to transform nature, transform reality. This loss, which made it impossible to organize a genuine project of "national culture," was linked to the profound state of degradation that Arguedas discovered in the nation's people. He therefore concluded that Bolivia did not possess the stability and harmoniousness necessary for progress to bloom or for the longed-for historical time of modernity to start ticking there. If Europe was a vast, uniform plain, Bolivia was an uncouth, chaotic space in which geography determined both the possibility and the impossibility of setting development in motion.

Unable to mold the "unique historical we" that is the nerve center of the modern nation-state (Vidal 2009: 32), Arguedas centered his observation of Bolivian reality on the metaphor of illness. Thus, "illness as metaphor," as Susan Sontag (1978) expressed it in the title of one of her books, became the iconic model[7] through which Arguedas represented the psychobiological degeneration of Bolivian society, a reality that he observed forthrightly.

Throughout Arguedas's essay, the incurable illness carried by the mestizo race explained the dysfunction of the social whole. Indeed, mestizaje as barometer of human degeneration was itself the disease that attacked the social body, that invaded all groups and all social sectors, including whites and the "indios acholados" (urbanized Indians, or Indians passing as non-Indians) who attempted to scale the social ladder. This "cult of anti-mestizaje," which revived the works of Gustave Le Bon (1995 [1895]) and his disciple Octavio Bunge in Bolivia, affirmed, in the words of Brooke Larson, that Arguedas "believed that hybrid races were characterized by psychological imbalances and moral deficiencies, and that contemporary Bolivia was suffering the consequences of a mixed race" (1998: 35), a fact that could be widened to include the hybridism of the Spanish-Arab conquistador.

But this concept of a "cult of anti-mestizaje" was not equally apt for explaining the thought of Franz Tamayo, the other great letrado of that moment and Arguedas's intellectual adversary.[8] Tamayo departed imaginatively from the anti-mestizaje that had been accepted by the positivism of that time, proposing to apply an "organicist" German approach toward taking a closer look at local culture, thus distancing himself from the Social Darwinism that dominated the social sciences in the early twentieth century. "Civilization" was the stage that was to be arrived at through instruction, through the development of the intellect, but at that historical moment—the first decades of the twentieth century—it was more important for the Bolivian nation to subordinate instruction to the exercise of the will. Education, the basis for "national pedagogy," was not the baggage of known facts that we keep stored in our heads, but what we forge with our own wills. More than ideas and facts acquired by the mind, what interested Tamayo was the learning accomplished by one's own will, by the local culture. Tamayo thus proposed, in his *Creación de la pedagogía nacional* (1975

[1910]), that education should be elevated above instruction. Instruction was objective, rational, but secondary, because it did not allow for the discovery of the nation's essence; education was subjective, transcendent, because it reached the depths of the soul and the character, reached the true power of the nation's life.

Since Arguedas had not accomplished the task of healing the nation, Tamayo proposed a regenerative response via a change in metaphor that recentered the social and enlarged local culture. This became the ethnic response, countering the social impasse created by the civic view of the nation. Through it, Tamayo could observe the vital power of nationhood. His *Creación de la pedagogía nacional* proposed a renovating iconic metaphor: the slender body of the Indian, governed by the mind of the mestizo. As can be appreciated, this metaphor exalted the Indian as "the storehouse of the nation's energy," though it also gave the mestizo's mind its place. This new metaphor reconciled the "internal" factors of the culture to the "external" factors of Western progress that indigenous vitality either did not take into account or openly disdained. As hardened as the environment in which he lived, the Indian resisted the attacks of Western civilization with peculiar tenacity. This resistance to change and to passive acceptance of the exogenous elements of civilization was a virtue, and also a defect, in the character of his race. The new metaphor therefore visualized, better than the racial illness expressed in Arguedas's essay, the Indian as a body and a will that would endure. His soul, withdrawn into itself, explained the Aymara's psychology. Devoid of intelligence, the Indian was pure will and character, a stranger to aesthetic imagination and metaphysical thought. It was pointless, then, to search the Aymara race for hints of a higher intelligence. That was one of the mestizos' qualities, with their facility for understanding, intellectual vivacity, and skill at picking up aesthetic forms. Mestizos, however, did not have the Europeans' will. Skilled at copying, but without sufficient will to create anything that was truly their own, mestizos were unable to put the stamp of their will on things.

In his construction of the ethnic nation, it was possible that the clear differences Tamayo found between the Indian and the mestizo could be overcome by applying different pedagogical roles to each race: the Indian's education called for a pedagogy of love and patience; the mestizo's instruction called for a disciplinary pedagogy that would develop the intellect. The two pedagogies clearly had different objectives, but they nevertheless complemented each other in an interesting way: the Indian's worked through his will and the superb physique of his body; the mestizo's worked through her head, her intelligence. This program conjured an ideal image, an image of "ideal mestizaje," which tied the Indian to the creolized mestizo, the Westernized mestizo, but which, keeping watchful control over the social imaginary, at all costs prevented the Indian from becoming a cholo and rising to political or social power.[9] This is the metaphoric displacement that I will develop below as part of "the nation's deterritorializing dimension." For the moment, let's just say that the "ideal mestizo" was not the cholo, a social type that Tamayo erased from the social imaginary. Indeed, it was not until the 1930s and 1940s that the lettered elite dropped the mystical aura in which they had wrapped this "ideal mestizaje" and created a new ideological project in its place, a broader and democratizing project that could tie ("suture") the civic to the ethnic. That was when important new letrados emerged, such as Augusto Céspedes and Carlos Montenegro, the intellectuals of an emerging middle class and important dissidents, who would forge the "nationalist revolutionary" trend.

Montenegro's tempering mestizo discourse overcame odious distinctions and racial controls, especially the separation between mestizos and cholos. His discourse thus became part of the lettered project of nation building, though with objectives distinct from those held by the people who promoted a "culture of mestizaje" and who promoted disciplining the subaltern Indian sector of society. The reformist and demythifying tone of Montenegro's *Nacionalismo y coloniaje* (1994 [1943]) attempted to establish a new interrelation—he called it a "social suture," because he argues for healing the wound that had been opened up by colonial-era racial domination—with the agrarian cholo and Indian sectors, which he no longer perceived as a threat to reformist elites, seeing them instead as transformed into a political force that could now be approached and addressed ideologically.

Nacionalismo y coloniaje marked the appearance of the collective "historical we" that Vidal demands for his "narratives of identity." Montenegro's work was fundamental for constructing the "foundational" novels that appeared during that decade. As Vidal observes, the "'unique historical we' is supposed to be the mythical core of the modern nation-State" (2009: 32)—"mythical" in the sense that the staging of its politics can be evaluated and deemed legitimate or illegitimate according to the principle of equality before the law. Following the lead of Guillermo O'Donnell, Vidal states,

> Two other myths emerge from this foundation—the notions of *citizenship* and *"the popular" (lo popular)*. Citizenship implies that members of a "unique historical we" have free access to all the rights, privileges, protections, and must carry all the obligations prescribed by the law. "The popular" implies that all defenseless, dispossessed, and aggrieved members of the "unique historical we," whatever their racial, ethnic origin or social status, have a right to full solidarity. (2009: 32)

Nacionalismo y coloniaje was a radical attempt to change the "cult of mestizaje" as it had been constructed by the relatively compact group of lettered oligarchic liberals. Armed with a new ideological project—the metaphor of "nation versus antination"—the group of dissident intellectuals was now called to replace the cultural sphere of liberalism. This new project, which was still a lettered project imposed by a revolutionary intelligentsia that thought through the viewpoint of the dissident sectors in the middle class, must have been much more accessible to the popular masses and able to connect with what Montenegro called the "'vital nerves' of our nationhood" (1994 [1943]: 51).

Throughout his book, Montenegro's nationalism is a relatively vague concept, but one that lends *Nacionalismo y coloniaje* a particular ideological orientation: the "nation" should win over against the dark forces of the past and serve as a bastion against the imperialist rapacity that had been allowed and consecrated by the traditional system, the "antination." Suggestively, though this fact has gone unobserved by exclusively political and sociological studies of this essay, he did not altogether get rid of the metaphor of "ideal mestizaje." The function of that bodily metaphor, once corrected and demythified, is tied to the political struggles of the early 1940s. Montenegro, who believed in the power of literature, interpreted this cultural metaphor through an extensive literary analogy, naming each chapter of his book after a different literary genre. Dressed up first as epic, then as drama, then comedy, mestizaje retained its place in the vision of nationalism that Montenegro left us. Finally, Montenegro applied his argument about the nation—that the content of the nation was degraded by the oligarchic and liberal "antination"—to the novel, seeing in it the possibility of creating a new form that, with the guidance of the masses, of the "true nation," might overcome the alienating past.

The metaphors that constituted the civic nation and the ethnic nations thus gave meaning to the "territorial boundaries" that, like so many walls or dams, impeded the free flow of identities and closely controlled the elitist construction of the social. Indeed, both concepts of the nation gave rise to "hard boundaries," as the Indian historian Prasenjit Duara called them in his study of modern China (1996). These hard boundaries were assumed by elites who could not construct genuinely hegemonic projects of "national culture." In its place, the "culture of antimestizaje," as well as that of "ideal mestizaje," founded on the metaphors of mestizo illness and Indian bodily regeneration, built the nation-state, subject to discourses of domination that "excluded the cultural values of indigenous peoples and most of the population with regard to the rights of citizens" (Mayorga and Molina Barrios 2005: 32). The civic nation may have been a project limited to the bureaucratic expansion of criollo identity, without any corresponding expansion in the rights of citizenship, but the ethnic nation was also elitist in that it sought to incorporate Indians under an abstract idealism that would consign them to concreteness. The ethnic nation claimed to be modeled after the project of a mestizo nation that was promoted by "civilizing" pedagogical ideas.

The tensions between the civic and the ethnic nation that dominated the first half of the twentieth century relaxed somewhat, but did not disappear, with the "revolutionary nationalism" that arose in the 1940s as the ideological framework for the bourgeois democratic revolution that would come about in 1952. This "revolutionary nationalism" was the boundary of the imaginary that came closest to building a "national culture" and incorporating the people into the political sphere. Nonetheless, this attempt to overcome the spatial-temporal differences between the civic and the ethnic was not really successful, as the study conducted by the Unidad de Coordinación de la Asamblea Constituyente has pointed out, and ethnic diversity did not succeed in manifesting itself in the homogenizing discourse of mestizaje (Mayorga and Molina Barrios 2005). Indeed, it could be said that the major problem with Montenegro's essay was that it reduced "colonialism" to a vision of some "feudal" (that is, precapitalist) stage that could only be overcome through a bourgeois democratic revolution that would eliminate the oligarchic "antination," the ally of imperialism.[10]

For the homogenizing practice of the official discourse of mestizaje, which reduced and simplified the complex reality of actual mestizajes, the civic nation, subjected to the pressures of state corporatism, was never consolidated. The ethnic issue was postponed, its place taken by an iron, authoritarian state culture, the best example of which was found in the essays of Fernando Diez de Medina (1969). To conclude this section on the developmentalist pedagogy of "revolutionary nationalism," I will turn my attention to Diez de Medina, whom I believe to be the clearest Bolivian example of the way an affirmation of the values of a "national culture" can turn into a dangerous authoritarian discourse that sets progress on a pedestal.

Inspired in equal measures by nationalist essays and by the modernist poetry of Franz Tamayo, Diez de Medina felt that the Andean lands held the spiritual power to combine the aesthetic, the ethical, and the religious. This spiritualization of the Bolivian landscape, with traces of German pantheism, was a mystical attitude very characteristic of Diez de Medina's intellectual project of making the territory his own, as he used his imaginary to turn the land into an aesthetic realm of truth. For this Bolivian letrado, it was in the highest mountain peaks that the foundations of human behavior were to be sought.

In 1953, when Diez de Medina was serving as the minister of education in the country's first National Revolutionary Movement administration (1952–56), he took on the "problem of our national culture" and set in motion the tempering process that equated mestizaje with the nation's spiritual growth. Literature once more played a fundamental role in this cultural construction. For Diez de Medina, Bolivian literature began in the mountains, in the great, solid, geographic myth of its nationhood. That was the "cradle of the nation's soul." Diez de Medina then said, in the same prophetic tones that liberals had used in prior decades, that "we can only speak of a genuine national literature when, instead of merely contemplating, we become the molders of the cosmos that surrounds us" (1953: 142). In this anthropocentric view of culture—I will see it again at the end of this chapter, when I look at the dangerous turn that the current plurinational Bolivian state seems to have taken—which Diez de Medina set forth in works such as *Nayjama* (1950) and *Mateo Montemayor* (1969), he called on themes and symbols that can be classified as constructed in the orbit of authoritarianism.

Moralistic and didactic—especially *Mateo Montemayor*, Diez de Medina's last novelized essay—this letrado's writings developed hierarchical and conservative cosmic and political systems. Static, solid symbols such as the mountain made the higher condition of the soul visible, according to Diez de Medina. Thus Illimani, the mountain that stands guard over the city of La Paz, turns into "a petrified hurricane of matter," a "final oracle on which are inscribed the destiny of the marvelous city and the fates of each of its children" (1969: 251). I should note that, in this vertical, authoritarian aesthetic, the Indian becomes "the good savage," regimented and educated by power.

The allegorical project of this "spiritual monumentalism" also refers to the "youth of America" by means of sociological laws of very dubious value, because they arbitrarily set up the interpretive "ups" and "downs" of reality. Diez de Medina's essays contain many theatrical soliloquies founded on spatial scenography whose monumentalized execution turns the solid mountain into the fetish of national sovereignty. Its spiritualized up, a zone of dazzling light that unites races and cultures in a "mestizo national type," is none other than the narcissistic, authoritarian aesthetic exercise that sidesteps the ethical topic of mending the public. Instead we get these ideal republics produced by great creative geniuses, that is, spiritualized ideological productions that seek to redeem a social reality that has been tattered and torn asunder by the years of authoritarian domination that include the "national revolution." In Diez de Medina's discourse we also find a clear equivalence between the content of the soliloquy, the monumentalized representation of reality, and the corporal posture of the mestizo protagonists. Virile, decisive attitudes and energetic, precise bodily movements form part of the kinesis that accompanies the mestizo's allegorical-symbolic search for national unity. I particularly note, however, that this discourse ignores any downs, any need to mend and give outlet to civil society. Instead, the solid, fixed nature of the nation-state and its mestizo ideal, consubstantialized as the mountain, are mere stereotypes that have little to do with society.

Today, however, there is a felt need to go further, to overcome the hard, fixed, homogeneous nature of this nation-state. Thus new arguments arise; many new ideological and discursive positions (postmodern, postcolonial, and so on) question the rigidity of the boundaries constructed by nationalism, the modern narrative regulating history. While contrasting this fixedness with the much more fluid and changing nature of the multiple identities that live within the nation—today in Bolivia we use the terms "plural nation" and "plurinationality"—the task of extracting the nation-state from the "hard boundaries" of modernity is a possibility that, while necessary, remains problematic. In any case, new demands for recognizing citizenship, arising from the internal migrations of recent decades, have caused cracks in these "hard boundaries," this mestizo condition, making the metaphor much more fluid, much more sensitive to the ethnic demands of new social movements. This is how "otherness" is built, a fact that reveals the limits of the nation conceived as a homogeneous community. I now turn to a new stage, a new interpretive dimension of the national.

4. DETERRITORIALIZATION AND METAPHORS OF FLOWING

It is time to leave the territorial boundaries of modernity behind and return to Chakrabarty's assertion that we have now sailed "into the uncharted waters of the twenty-first" century. Questions remain about the telos of modernity and preoccupations with development and with the old pedagogical policies that, in the case of Bolivia, derive from both the oligarchic-liberal state and the reformist nationalism of the second half of the twentieth century. Indeed, the "uncharted waters" themselves have headed off in a different direction in present-day Bolivia. They have moved beyond the sensory and territorialized dimension of mestizaje associated with the 1952 revolution, which introduced the social suture between the civic and the ethnic. How can this change be explained? What is this new kind of flow that modifies representation?

After three decades of predominance in the Bolivian social imaginary, in the mid-1980s "revolutionary nationalism" and its homogenizing version of mestizaje fell into a deep political and moral decadence. As social scientist and journalist Pablo Stefanoni recently wrote: "It was, paradoxically, the Movimiento Nacionalista Revolucionario (MNR) itself that proposed, in the midst of the economic collapse brought on by hyperinflation and the rise of neoliberalism in Latin America and around the world, abandoning state capitalism" (2010: 117). Indeed, this exchange of state capitalism for economic liberalism, which in Stefanoni's words had already been "perfected" by the skills of mining entrepreneur Gonzalo Sánchez de Lozada, dominated the neoliberal political agenda.[11]

Combining the recipes of the Washington Consensus with a heavy dose of multiculturalism, triumphant neoliberalism allowed for a series of initiatives to incorporate the "multiethnic, plurilingual, and multicultural" character of the Bolivian nation. These were the Law of Popular Participation, which gave rise to autonomous municipal governments and indigenous municipal districts; the education reform of 1995; and the introduction of single-member districts elected by plurality vote (*diputa-*

ciones uninominales). Stefanoni describes this process as an "attempted 'passive revolution' in the face of growing ethnic demands, within the framework of a process of technocratic democratization" (2010: 118). These neoliberal reforms were expressed above all in popular participation, which "transferred great sums of money to the rural municipalities and opened up new political opportunities for rural workers' unions to jump into institutional politics" (Stefanoni 2010: 118).

The field of education was not ignored. To the contrary, it once more became an important space for the national imagination. Indeed, the new Education Reform Act proposed "to reinforce the national identity by exalting the historical and cultural values of the Bolivian nation in all its multicultural and multiregional richness" (Stefanoni 2010: 119). In order to achieve this multiculturalism, the reform needed "to overcome distances and isolation and build the nation based on an intercultural vision of reality" (Stefanoni 2010: 119). Before neoliberalism appeared on the scene, the dominant pedagogy was that of the territorial nation-state, which put development before diversity; in its neoliberal version, diversity balanced cultural matters against economic development. Thus, the displacement of pedagogical policies since the 1980s have been the new ways of navigating waters that, as we will see, have been filled with conflict since the beginning of the twenty-first century. In the Bolivian case, I think that displacement was linked to the new trajectory taken by the iconic model of mestizaje, separated now from its modernity-based developmentalist discourse. I turn now to this displacement, which I will link to major migratory forces not considered heretofore; then I will connect it with one of the most interesting "deterritorialized" readings of the present, which was set forth by the economist Carlos Toranzo Roca, a sharp-eyed researcher of the pluricultural and multilingual face of Bolivia today.

The pluricultural and multilingual facet that was promoted during the neoliberal phase of the 1990s gave rise to a singular experience related to ethnicity that changed the course of Bolivian society. This sudden turn in favor of "pluri-multi" diversity was very handy for neoliberalism, because it helped weaken the nationalist state that had preceded it. Its "participative" face, which promoted popular culture, made the new system much easier to digest and allowed progressive sectors to swell the ranks of neoliberalism. By offering a more equitable division of wealth among the various ethnic groups, the neoliberal reforms also helped the indigenous communities and peasant unions to make use of and subsume "into their corporative and communal logics the Popular Participation Act, which was set up to expand liberal democratic institutionality into the rural area" (Stefanoni 2010: 120).

During these years of neoliberalism's triumph it became very clear that there was a newly constituted cholo-mestizo elite, composed of people who owed their rise in society to their successful entrance into the market.[12] In this way, the "discovery of the cholo" was closely related to the growing power acquired by a sui generis bourgeoisie, that is, by an ascendant social sector that had resulted from one of the great paradoxes produced by the 1952 revolution: the growth of state capitalism, which did not manage to create a solid industrial bourgeois but instead brought about, beginning in the 1970s, an urban sector formed of migrants from the countryside who worked in smuggling and informal commerce. The strongest portion of this booming sector was organized into a "cholo bourgeoisie," which, significantly, did not abandon its indigenous cultural roots.

The suggestive intellectual work of Carlos Toranzo Roca, in my opinion the most important promoter of "pluri-multi" discourse, covers the deterritorializing viewpoint of this neoliberal moment that has made the cholo so particularly visible. Toranzo states about one of his own books:

> *Lo pluri-multi o el reino de la diversidad* (1993) is not a sociological, political, culturalist, or ethnological analysis; it contains not a drop of academic research or conceptual debate. It was, above all, a descriptive essay that showed how Bolivian society, including its elites and its peasants (in 1993 it wasn't time yet to insist on their being indigenous or first peoples), was the product of a historical process of five centuries of mestizoization, of building many mestizajes, dozens of them. (2009: 51–52)

The books that Toranzo wrote in past decades were essays describing reality and targeted at local elites in the hopes that they, who loved to define themselves as "criollos," might understand that they were actually the products of the long process of mestizaje brought about by Bolivian history. Moreover, *Lo pluri-multi o el reino de la diversidad* was

> an indictment of homogeneities. Though it described the process of mestizoization, it did not speak of a single type of mestizo; that is, it departed from the homogenizing culturalist model of the 1952 Revolution, which understood that revolutionary history was going to construct only one model, a single, monocultural model of mes-

tizaje. Just as it differed from the revolutionary MNR [Movimiento Nacional Revolucionario, the leading political party after 1952], it also stood apart from the Soviet revolutionaries who intended to construct a different sort of homogeneity, the proletariat, while killing or obscuring every shade of diversity, or covering up the heterogeneities that were being cultivated every day and that continue to do so everywhere in the world. (2009: 52)

It is suggestive that, a century after the publication of Tamayo's essay, Bolivian reality still makes it necessary to keep "thinking" mestizaje. Note, however, that doing so now calls for a very different viewpoint. Indeed, Toranzo reinforced his conclusions from *Lo pluri-multi o el reino de la diversidad* in his article "Repensando el mestizaje en Bolivia" (2009: 45–61), one of the most interesting essays in *¿Nación o naciones en Bolivia?*, an anthology commemorating the twenty-fifth anniversary of the Graduate Program in Development Sciences (CIDES) at the Universidad Mayor de San Andrés and edited by the social scientist Gonzalo Rojas Ortuste.

"Rethinking" mestizaje means bearing in mind that racial differences, which were supposedly superseded by modernization and the rationalization of the state, are not a bygone matter but, to the contrary, continue to hold the interest of intellectuals today. At bottom, we can say that the homogenizing view of reality that seemingly cured Bolivia of the racial "illness" that had ailed it has now reappeared with unexpected force under the name of "the mestizo nation." The need to rethink mestizaje shows that the mestizo nation, just as it had been thought by last century's pedagogical policies, had to be reinterpreted by various sorts of new demands related to ethnicity, gender, the generations, regions, labor sectors, and so on. Therefore, at the end of the last century there were calls for studying the formation of "multiple mestizajes" (Toranzo 2009: 45). Indeed, Toranzo argued, by the 1990s "closing your eyes to the hundreds of mestizajes in this country simply means closing your eyes to the majority of Bolivians" (2009: 45).

But studying these "multiple mestizajes" or describing their long process in Bolivia, as Toranzo does in his recent essay, means being very aware that historical construction "is not linear but iterative, sometimes with moments full of violence" (2009: 46) that fill the process with "tonalities" that cannot be taken as homogeneous regularities, but as heterogeneities that require periodic reinterpretation. The reader should note, however, that reinterpreting does not mean starting over altogether. As

Toranzo says, "The idea of starting from scratch is fallacious, just as it is wrong to think that political phenomena begin from zero, as if they had never had any historical antecedents" (2009: 46). At bottom, Toranzo is suggesting the ordered flow in which mestizajes displace and mimic each other, as identities that "are constructed from the amalgam of past, present, and dreams of the future" (2009: 46). Therefore, this flow of identities contains the traces, good or bad, of the history that marks such processes. To deny them—as Toranzo says occurs in the cultural politics of today's Plurinational State, which promotes an indianismo that neglects and subalternizes the existing mestizajes—only makes it more difficult to see reality clearly. Given that "the" Bolivian identity cannot exist as a singular fact, Toranzo insists on mestizo *identities*, plural, to reestablish the need to construct a "common we" that can change the direction of the Republic of Bolivia, wrongly described by the current government as a "Plurinational State."

Now, the displacement of these mestizajes, their flowing in time, removes them from the terrain of pedagogy, from the "hard boundary" delineated by Tamayo and later imposed by the "revolutionary nationalism" of the early 1950s. For Toranzo, this nationalist model has not lost its relevance, but it has changed in the flow of time. He concludes that we Bolivians, whether rural or urban, are "facts of community and a presence of diversities" (2009: 49). We Bolivians, however, have changed iconic models (the phenomenon of identities being, basically, movement). I would like to emphasize this idea in particular, because it constitutes one of the most important observations in this last chapter, one that would surely have been ignored by a different reading, purely sociological in bent, that paid no attention to representation. I will concentrate, then, on this change, this "metaphor of flowing," which now represents identities from a very different viewpoint.

Reading a book by the Argentine historian Ignacio Lewkowicz, who has dedicated himself to the study of contemporary subjectivity (2004), I am reminded of the fact that we often talk about the "stream of consciousness," but we don't realize that we are using a metaphor that displaces itself in a very peculiar way: flowing like a stream, like a river that changes and is never the same. Thought of from its banks, Lewkowicz tells us, "the river is the image of fluidity conceived as 'change' into which we cannot 'step twice'" (2004: 235). But if everything in the river changes, the transformation follows an ordered, permanent meaning: a source, a course, and an outlet. Thus, "the river is the meaning of the water between its source and its outlet" (2004: 235).

This image of the river's ordered fluidity gives us a way to "rethink" mestizaje, because Toranzo uses this very image to explain, as I have noted, how "everything flows in time" because "no one is identical to what he was in the past" (2009: 50). Toranzo uses this Heraclitan metaphor to express the opening of the mestizo nation to historical processes that are much more complex, that leave no one unscathed, petrified in her original state: "No, there are no exactly identical copies in history; this is valid for all of society, even its elites, who have also changed over time" (2009: 58). The result of all historical processes is that no one is identical to what he was in the past. There cannot be, then, "an" unchanging mestizo nation; rather, there is a historical process, a flowing of races in permanent change. Note, however, that this flow of mestizajes has an end, an exact outlet: the nation and the republic.

The interesting but problematic aspect of this fluid multicultural construction of identities is precisely the postulation of the possible "common we" that can mediate our acts. This mediation can make it possible to administer real conflicts in such a way as to remove and resolve (miraculously, it must be said) the difficulty of constructing the human community. These same conflicts only deepen when they are determined and preceded by many demands of an ethnic nature.

At this point in the analysis, I should note that the ordered flow of identities is quite separate from the fact that the contemporary condition is configured, as Lewkowicz puts it, "between two different sorts of movements: on one hand, the collapse of the state; on the other, the construction of a subjectivity that inhabits that collapse" (2004: 220). And these distinct forms of subjectivity that grow up in the collapse of the state become a very different "we" than the one Toranzo assumes as a synthesis of the trajectory followed by identity construction. Lewkowicz describes it as a "contingent we" (2004: 277). The contingent we is "the pronoun of quick joy, the proper name of the unruly fiesta and of the state on the verge of dissolution" (2004: 231).

Where did this imprecise, strange, and precarious "we" originate? Given the "collapse" of the institutionality of the state, it seems to have come about quite unexpectedly, forming on street corners and in plazas, in assemblies that apparently left people with a new way of thinking. This "we" is the result of a different way of conceptualizing fluidity, because, given the collapse of the state, it corresponds to the dispersion of the contents for lack of a container. It is the water that flows like an uncontrollable, "uncharted" torrent, with no outlet and no dam that could contain it. I speak of troubled waters that can change, can transform, the ordered course of identities, such as Toranzo has thought them. Indeed, the "metaphor of the river," affirmed as it is in the flow of the historical process, ignores those "corners" that come from the past to create turbulence in the tranquil waters of mestizajes. It seems to me that this metaphor does not represent the avalanches of water and earth that come smashing down the current when rivers rise and flood. In other words, the "metaphor of the river" ignores the "ruins," the "whirlpools of the past" that disturb our present because they correspond to a beyond and a before that is suddenly rediscovered, a past that cannot be rationalized and that is useless for predicting the future. This "beyond" and this "before" that the "metaphor of the river" conceals is the "here" that, when it is present, feeds on our sleepless but fragmented memory. It is the "now" that runs just as it burrows vertically into a dense time that accumulates without synthesizing the experiences that I call "the embers of the past," product of a circular, mythical time that had been left behind but continues to disturb the present with anger and violence. I speak, then, of postponed longings, sunk in memory, which, as they bob to the surface, take on new and sudden social and political importance, giving rise to a "contingent consciousness" that, unlike proletarian consciousness, is the point of departure for the historical earthquake we are now experiencing. Avalanches, earthquakes, turbulence: all are incorporations of the remote past that the "metaphor of the river," in its ordered and tranquil flow, manages not to notice. Through these incorporations appear the social movements that today play a specific role in the dynamics of the social whole. The avalanche and turbulence express the return of the multitude, of the plebeians.

In this connection it seems useful to follow the path left by the "multitude form of the politics of vital necessities," the topic and title of an essay by Raquel Gutiérrez, Álvaro García Linera, and Luis Tapia, who describe in detail the "wave of humanity" (2000: 162) that the multitude generates. "Forma multitud de la política de las necesidades vitales" is the last essay in a book on the "return of the plebeian" that these three authors wrote. It amply reveals the changes that took place in Bolivia at the end of the twentieth century and the opening of the twenty-first. Actually, the events of April 2000 marked the beginning of the "collapse" of the nation-state, the crisis of the neoliberal system, and the emergence of the "contingent we" described by Lewkowicz.

The first months of 2000 saw the city of Cochabamba, located in the Bolivian hinterlands, become the epicenter of one of the most important social rebellions in Latin America in our time, the Water War. Between January and April of that year, the Coordinadora del Agua y de la Vida (Water and Life Coalition), a new organization without institutional precedents, was formed and successfully opposed the privatization of the city's water system under a neoliberal law passed in late 1999, which would have transformed water from a public good into a commodity.

This coalition brought together the associations of irrigation farmers of the high Andean valleys, the Federation of Cochabamba Manufacturers, the middle-class professional schools, the coca unions, and the members of the highland ayllus (indigenous communities), forming, according to the authors of this essay, "an organizational structure with new voices" who expressed the discontent of a "plebeian multitude" who represented themselves in a vast and spontaneous street assembly (Gutiérrez, García Linera, and Tapia 2000: 150). It was their "plebeian density" (154) that "swirled through the streets, plazas, and avenues" like a "human torrent" (163), giving rise to an unprecedented "deliberative council" (154). This multitude, which "overflowed the streets until it reached the city center" (157) was not a traditional union structure but a multitude composed for the most part of "agrarian blockaders, humble men and women from the outskirts of the city" (139). The multitude that gathered in Cochabamba in April 2000, rising up to demand respect for their "customs and traditions" (136), was a "centripetal pressure" (143) spontaneously invented by the mechanism—strange and precarious for any traditional political organization—of an assembly gathered on the streets and plazas of the city. As Lewkowicz put it with reference to the "contingent we," "The assembly first needed to gather on street corners or in plazas to think in this fashion. And even if it were later dissolved or weakened as an effective assembly, this modality of thinking remained. The assembly is the effective mechanism for the *we*" (2004: 221).

This renovated modality of thinking also called for a new metaphor that could express it more appropriately. I refer to the "avalanche," the "eddies" and "corners," that is, to the flowing metaphor of the uncharted here and now that is the present. The "avalanche" is the violent accumulation of asynchronicities, of conflicting, noncontemporaneous times that break from the ordered vision of history. Distanced from the beaches, the safe coastlines of modernity, and from the river that represents and contains them, thought from a different point of enunciation in conflict with the nation, the "metaphor of the avalanche," of turbulence, overflows, as did the Water Warriors in the social confrontations of the year 2000. The essay we have been citing about the "multitude form" goes on to reconstruct the days that followed the event that kicked off Bolivia's contemporary era: the Water War.

For these essayists, the Water Warriors who "descended on the city under the leadership of their indigenous authorities" did not temporize, but instead "swept away the mestizo elite in power" (Gutiérrez, García Linera, and Tapia 2000: 168). A "human wave that overwhelmed the state" (162), made up of cholos and campesinos like the revolutionary wave of 1952 that René Zavaleta Mercado described so vividly in *Bolivia: El desarrollo de la conciencia nacional* (1990 [1967]), the Water Warriors constituted "the intense aroma of the crowd who transformed the use of urban space in response to their sense of collective force and pride in movement" (Gutiérrez, García Linera, and Tapia 2000: 154). Thus, the dense avalanche of the insurgent plebeians of Cochabamba was the "multitude form" that, "spreading like water" (155), flooded everything, even the terrains that neoliberalism had depoliticized.

It is very suggestive that the authors of the essay on "the multitude form" concluded their piece on present-day Bolivia, on plebeian Bolivia, by referring to it as the "high tide mark of the politics of vital necessities" (Gutiérrez, García Linera, and Tapia 2000: 177), a metaphor that alters the ordered flow of the river waters and reveals their torrential and disorderly outlet into the sea. If the river is the endless flow, the endless becoming of mestizo identities, the "high tide mark" seems to be the contingent beginning of new social actors who no longer flow in an ordered way but quite the contrary, becoming the wave, the avalanche, the torrential current, the high tide and the line of driftwood it leaves behind, the everlasting beginning-over, the collapse of the sense of the stream and of the democratic institutions it represents.

A significant fact about this "human wave" at the dawn of the twenty-first century, which the essayists celebrate for its multitudinarious force, was its discovery of the weakness of the neoliberal mestizo state, particularly its discovery of the progressive loss of its "symbolic" capacity, its unifying function. To keep itself in power, the state had to resort to armed violence. The actions of the neoliberal state began to lose legitimacy in the eyes of people on the inside and the outside, but especially for those who were called upon to carry out the arbitrary commands of power. In this way, the "human wave that overwhelmed the institutions of the state" (Gutiérrez, García Linera, and Tapia 2000: 162) began the new, uncertain, "uncharted" cycle of "plebeian democracy," whose "high tide" would inundate the spaces formerly depoliticized by the ruling system and would once more open up the old nationalist schemes that seemed to have vanished with the neoliberal wave.

Having reached this point, I do not want to end this section without mentioning that the essay on the "multitude form"[13] concludes with a reminder that if one function of the "return of the plebeian" was the "rehabilitation of the customs and traditions of the oppressed" (Gutiérrez, García Linera, and Tapia 2000: 177), another function was to bring into the present day Marx's old dream that "the archaic" would return to modernity under superior conditions, giving renovated use to communal agrarian structures. Thus the essay reminds us that "two far-reaching social projects remain standing: political and economic self-rule, and the widened community or *ayllu*" (177). These are "the two discursive axes of the multitude in action" (177).

We are now well aware that the reign of capital was not overthrown in Bolivia—we have returned instead to state capitalism—and that the production of a new horizon of communal self-rule is further off each day. The current limitations on the "multitude form," which no longer seems to correspond to the flowing metaphor of high tide but rather to the line of flotsam that marks how high it reached, shows the uncertain direction of indigenous campesino nationalities that call upon their customs and traditions to defend themselves from the very same Plurinational State that, as it grows more invasive and authoritarian, contravenes the norms set by its own Constitution and by international treaties to which Bolivia is a signatory.

In conclusion, the "deterritorializing dimension" that supposedly explains our expansive and complex present has serious disadvantages for charting the future. This dimension sends us back to the doubts that Chakrabarty set out at the beginning of his essay on humanism. Without a genuine commitment to difference, there can be no dialogue, nor can a "culture of integration" (which I asserted as a social imperative in the previous chapter) be established. But the new dialogue will never become reality if we remain unable to integrate the baggage of our indigenous experience. This dialogue will have to be carried out in open communication with an ancestral home that, far from remaining static and petrified in its past, must also experience the modernizing changes of the present.

5. THE METAPHOR OF THE AMPHIBIAN

I think the deterritorializing dimension cannot remain stuck in the "uncharted waters" of Chakrabarty's image in his essay on humanism. The undertow of the "multitude form" obliges me to return to dry land in order to recover the theme of cultural integration with which I concluded the previous chapter. I refer to the need to recover the fruitful dialogue between "contemporaneously noncontemporaneous" spaces and times, such as that promoted by the first peoples of the lowlands in their March for Territory and for Dignity and Quest for La Loma Santa. Both of those mobilizations (discussed in chapter 3) led to powerful symbol-building, which, as the author of a recent book on the subject notes (Canedo 2011), created a new utopia, a "resignifying of territory," which argues for the establishment of a new social and economic order. The utopia created by these first peoples did not reject modernization; rather, it balanced modernization with ancestral symbols of identity that helped the inhabitants of the lowlands, of Amazonia, to resignify their territory. This return to the ancestors, to the mythical, religious past, promoted greater tolerance and understanding of the complex interaction between human beings and nature. In the same way, it generated new associations that crossed—defiantly yet peacefully—the territorial and pedagogical borders drawn by the state, including the limits on its current understanding of what "plurinationality" means.

The tenacity with which the indigenous people protected their land and their territory in that movement in 1990 led to a new modern way of thinking that does not simply give in to the plans already laid out by modernity; a way of thinking that scrupulously respects human rights but at the same time recovers Enlightenment humanism and turns it into a legacy for the dispossessed, for the rest of humanity. Since that time, the lowland movements have not sought to return to nationalism; instead, they have opted for something unprecedented, for something that searches, lovingly and with utter generosity, for the whole self that modernity denied when it opted for mere individualism. I think that this territorial resignification is sui generis, for it does not claim to encompass Europe, nor to apply the programs of progress and development unreflectively. The new program returns to nature with the hope that nature might shelter humanity without being attacked and devastated by the blows of modernity and its globalized capitalism. As Arif Dirlik has recently expressed it:

> The new times call for a new politics. The spaces for this new politics are to be found not outside of but in the contradictions of a globalized capitalism. The challenge presently is not to overthrow a globalized capitalism, or to replace the capitalist state with a socialist one, neither of which appears as an imminent possibility. The challenge rather is to build up a more just and sustainable society from the bottom up, to socialize the spaces offered by these contradictions. (Dirlik 2011: 54)

We noted earlier that, although the "pedagogical dimension" built the nation-state, its deterritorialization produced, as a countereffect, the flow of identities that ended in its dismantling. Beyond these two dimensions, here I postulate the concept of "integrating (re)territorialization," that is, the capability held by today's indigenous movements of building a dialogue, a cross-fertilization between modernity and their ancestral culture. It seems to me that the amphibian is the metaphor that best expresses this new displacement. This is the metaphor that Orlando Fals Borda used in his analysis of the riverine world of Colombia (1979). Today it is called for in analyzing countries and regions where cultural diversity is the source of renewed interpretive potential. The metaphor is useful because it "takes knowledge from one context and transfers it to another, reworking it in consequence of the new context" (Mockus 1994: 37). Let us take a closer look at this metaphor.

In a broad sense, the term "amphibious," meaning "adapted to both lives or both ways of life," applies to every community that "develops reliably in more than one cultural tradition and that facilitates communication between them" (Mockus 1994: 37). As a metaphor of communication between cultures, the image of the amphibian helps overcome the differences that crop up in contemporary societies with high levels of cultural diversity and social segmentation. On one hand, the metaphor brings the law closer to morality and culture, which is where discrepancies between different cultures traditionally lie. On the other, the amphibian can glimpse the possibility of overcoming the violence to which power resorts when it resolves conflicts. The metaphor of the amphibian illustrates the possibility of elaborating norms that are compatible with difference; it also shows that it is possible to build a dialogue between cultures.

Drawn from research by Basil Bernstein (1990) on education as a social process of the circulation of knowledge, the metaphor of the amphibian represents the capacity of cultural difference to "obey partially divergent systems of rules without a loss of intellectual and moral integrity" (Mockus 1994: 39). It is precisely this integrity that allows the amphibian "to select and rank bits of knowledge and morality in a given context in order to translate it and make it possible to appropriate it in another" (Mockus 1994: 39). This applies to the dialogue between the ancestral and the modern; the March for Territory and Dignity of the lowland first peoples is a revealing example of the "culture of integration" represented by the amphibian.

The March for Territory and Dignity put forward a social demand that completely changed the way in which land grants were made and the way in which land was occupied—two processes that had figured as exclusively material phenomena in Latin American agrarian history. In the Amazonian peoples' march, they were demanding that the state recognize not only their right to land, but an imbricated set of material and symbolic values. Territory was therefore transformed into a symbol for the claims to autonomy that the first peoples demanded from the state and from the power groups that had subordinated them. As Álvaro Bello puts it in his prologue to the recent book by Gabriela Canedo (2011), regarding the resignification of territory:

> In the face of the legalism of the state and of those who seek to appropriate indigenous land, territory is demonstrable, measurable physical evidence of their original "genuine rights," because it is an irrefutable "proof" of their belonging and of the "place" of their identity.
>
> This is the case for the Mojeños, who, as Gabriela Canedo shows, seek to represent through territory the central role of place for their existence and material reproduction, the role of the place where they hunt, fish, gather, and cultivate the food they live on. But it is also, she argues, the place where the symbols of their ethnic identity reside. Loma Santa, their symbolic territory, is a mobilizing utopia that propels them to establish a new social and economic order. And that is why the defense of Loma Santa motivates the Mojeños' collective action, for through this struggle they were able to position themselves as a political actor. (Canedo 2011: 12)

By living in modern life as much as in their ancestral life, the Mojeños were expressing the capacity that cultural difference has for crossing cultural codes, for demanding that legislation must not consign custom to oblivion but, to the contrary, must recognize and value it. Legalism as imposed from power was not enough, because the Mojeño—the lowland inhabitant, the interpreter and translator of cultures—insisted also that the written rule should not pretend ignorance of cultural customs. The marches in 1990 therefore demanded the cross-fertilization of law with morals and customs. And this fertilization also helped spread democracy, because it allowed what was legal to communicate with what was morally valid and culturally relevant, even if positive law did not specifically recognize them. In this way, the rise of new "soft boundaries," amphibian borders that can connect the modern with the ancestral, allowed for the "(re)territorialization" of concepts that interwove to provide novel, creative answers to the predatory forward march of developmentalism. Dirlik explains a view of amphibian borders that parallels my own:

> Place as metaphor suggests groundedness from below, and a flexible and porous boundary around it, without closing out the extra-local, all the way to the global. What is important about the metaphor is that it calls for a definition of what is to be included in the place from within the place—some control over the conduct and organization of everyday life, in other words—rather than from above, from those placeless abstractions such as capital, the nation-state, and their discursive expressions in the realm of theory. (2011: 57)

In the face of the subjugation of communal land, in the face of the colonization of rural spaces, the March for Territory and Dignity and the Search for the Loma Santa created the possibility that arguments from the distant past might "shortcut" the distance between customs and the law. Indeed, the power of culture sought to reduce the separation between ancestral customs and the specific procedures that were foreign to sacred interpretations and the ethical motivations that were beyond the grasp of positive law. The systemic functionality of law, its instrumental rationality, also subject to goals, exempted the law from having to attend to religious and cultural arguments, and it emphatically distinguished between legal arguments and arguments by those human groups that found the values that broadened their freedoms in their ancestral morality and customs.

Using cultural and religious arguments belonging to the time of the gods (see chapter 3) to influence the communicative acts that develop in the public sphere is tremendously difficult. Such arguments exceed the limits of the instrumental reasoning of power and of the positive law that legitimates it. But the amphibious peoples who cross and interrelate cultures seem to understand the urgency of making these systems compatible and of adapting them to the needs of the present. Hence the cross-fertilization of law with morals and culture is surprising current today, for it has confirmed that the struggle for land and territory is not just about protecting the human rights of indigenous Amazonian peoples, but about extending its protection to nature, making its recognition the "main political and epistemological problem of the twenty-first century" (Komadina 2011). Indeed, this "epistemological problem" appears with remarkable clarity in the recent march of lowland indigenous peoples in defense of TIPNIS (Territorios Indígenas del Parque Nacional Isiboro Sécure, or Indigenous Territories of Isiboro Sécure National Park), which I will explain below. By demanding in that march that the state recognize the legitimate rights of indigenous peoples, they were insisting on respect for the laws that guarantee them not only their human rights but also the rights that tie nature to the defense of territory. The observation of these rights also implies the need to investigate more deeply the very rationale of plurinationalism. Indeed, the rationale of the current Plurinational State of Bolivia is complicated when that state harms the very rights that it helped place in the Bolivian Constitution that went into effect in January 2009.

6. PLURINATIONAL STATE OR INTRACTABLE STATE?

In order to identify itself with the principles that flow from the civic nation and to guarantee the rights of its ethnic nationalities, the present Bolivian state—defined in Article 1 of its 2009 Constitution as a "Unitary Social State of Plurinational, Community-Based Law"—took an unprecedented step in Latin America, because by explicitly accepting the multivocality of the nation, it called into question the logocentric reductionism that had hitherto made the mestizo and criollo perspective the key to observing Bolivian nationality. The state defines itself as "unitary" because it safeguards the integrity of the nation's territory and guarantees unity among Bolivians, and as "plurinational" because it recognizes political, economic, and institutional pluralism. The current state thus links liberal democracy to communal democracy and respects the prior existence of the indigenous peasant nations and first peoples. Its plurinational nature also accommodates diverse forms of economic organization: communalist, state, private, and cooperative social organization. The new version of the state thus recognizes complex economic, social, political, and territorial structures that are embodied in different forms of institutional organization, at departmental, municipal, provincial, and community levels.

The Constitution defines the state as "plurinational" and "community-based" (*plurinacional, comunitario*) because it takes into account the diverse forms of community life at the economic, political, and cultural levels. The Constitution also institutionalizes the ancestral Andean principles of solidarity, reciprocity, economic complementarity, and equitable distribution of wealth. By recognizing the existence of nations and indigenous peoples predating the colonial period, it expressly affirms their ancestral dominion over their territories and guarantees their freedom of self-determination. The Constitution expressly recognizes indigenous peoples' right to self-government and allows for their consolidation as autonomous territorial bodies.

The recognition of regional and indigenous autonomy is linked to the right of first nations to be consulted before any action is carried out that might affect their territory. The Bolivian state has raised this right of consultation to a constitutional level by signing relevant treaties on human rights, particularly Convention No. 169 of the International Labour Organization (ILO), which guarantees the rights of indigenous and tribal peoples regarding their peaceful possession of their territories.[14] Similarly, the 2009 Constitution establishes that first peoples have the right to

> be consulted through the appropriate procedures, and in particular through their institutions, whenever legislative or administrative measures are adopted that might affect them. Within this framework, the right to obligatory, systematic prior consultation, realized by the State in good faith, shall be respected with regard to the exploitation of nonrenewable natural resources in the territory that they inhabit. (Article 30, section II, paragraph 15)

The Constitution recognizes a right to "free, prior, and informed" consultation with the people who would be affected by natural resource exploitation in their territory and to respect for "their norms and local procedures" (Article 352). In other words, consultation with indigenous peoples is to be "binding and obligatory," because it derives from an explicit mandate in the Constitution (Article 203). This mandate obliges the state to solicit the informed opinion of indigenous peoples. It also obliges the state to wait until the first peoples make a determination about proposals that might alter or modify their rights to their territory.

Despite the tremendous step forward that the Constitution represents in the recognition of the rights of first peoples, the logocentric model that limits "the national" to a homogenized perception of reality persists in the Plurinational State. This perception, which is now spreading to the recognition of plurinationality, falls short of fully becoming "an 'other' national agenda, thought from subjects historically excluded in the unitary vision of state, nation, and society" (Walsh 2008: 142). In other words, the fact that the Plurinational State is constitutionally obliged to recognize these rights is not enough, it seems, to guarantee that it will respect them.

Catherine Walsh notes that although "the project of the Plurinational State has been a central component in the decolonizing struggles and strategies of indigenous movements" (2008: 142), this refounding of the nation, conceived "from down below," is manifested in norms that still establish an epistemic comparison between "items of universal knowledge and the collective wisdom of the indigenous peasant nations and peoples, thus giving the impression that the former is scientifically superior to the latter" (146). In other words, Walsh broadens her view of the problem to include the Constitution itself, because it affirms that the anthropocentric vision is incapable of conceiving nature as a living thing with rights of its own. As Walsh notes, in the Constitution, humankind "continues to be the guardian of nature" (147). As a consequence, for both the Constitution and the social power that guarantees compliance with its provisions, ancestral logic and the time of the gods are still inconceivable and form "a threat to the rationalist optic, to economic stability, and to social control" (147). The Constitution, which continues to stand by the "coloniality of nature" (138) and of life itself, is based "on the binary nature/society divide, discarding everything that is magical-spiritual-social, the age-old relationship between biophysical, human, and spiritual worlds, including the world of the ancestors, which sustains the holistic systems of life and of humanity itself" (138).

The struggle between these opposing views of reality is not mere ingenuous speculation, for it is embedded in the core of the social upheavals now taking place in Bolivia's Amazonian lowlands. Indeed, I see the recent march in defense of TIPNIS—the Indigenous Territories of Isiboro Sécure National Park—as confirmation not only of the surprisingly current nature of the first peoples' struggle to defend land and territory, but also, and more importantly, of the renewed presence of paradigms of knowledge that are in conflict today. This clash can be observed in the two key metaphors. One is the primacy of the "highway," a metaphor of power, which, setting aside the roads that may lead to the liberation of the peoples who have been subjugated since colonial days, sums up the developmentalist project of the current state, obdurate in its industrialization process even if that means social imbalance and trampling on the rights of others. The other is the metaphor of the amphibian, which, as expressed by an inhabitant of Sécure Alto who said that "my highway is the Sécure river, I don't need any other" (Quispe 2011: 1), suggests a river flow very different from the sort of flowing we have observed, affirming the need that indigenous peoples have to commercialize their products. In this new flow of the river's waters, the amphibian rejects the "civilizing" process that remains embedded in the spheres of power, and instead demands that its legally agreed-upon rights should include the rights of nature—that is, that the reach of constitutionally guaranteed rights should also, as I have indicated above, make moral and cultural change possible. The amphibian metaphor is opposed to the social and economic "superhighway" metaphor envisioned by the state: opposed, because it trades it for a just and balanced social life that will be possible only if culture and morality can continue to play the regulating roles that are not sufficiently guaranteed by law.

Let's look at how the amphibian represents the situation of Bolivia's Amazonian lowlands. Covering nearly eleven thousand square kilometers (more than forty-two hundred square miles) between the savannah of Beni department and the Andean foothills of Cochabamba, TIPNIS is an indigenous territory and, at the same time, a national park that has enjoyed the protection of the Bolivian state since the 1990s. This territory nevertheless was under pressure from various socioeconomic demands that have impacted its ecosystems over the past twenty years. The south of TIPNIS, around the sources of the Isiboro, Moleto, and Ichoa Rivers, has been affected by the incursion of coca farmers and a road that Shell built for oil exploration in the 1970s. The forested mountains here thus underwent drastic transformations that have lowered the ability of its aquifers to replenish themselves and of its wildlife to reproduce. Central TIPNIS is in a better state of conservation; this is an immense region of rivers and tributaries that guarantees a good living for the indigenous peoples who hunt and fish there. The wetland forest in this central region teems with snakes, lizards, turtles, and a huge diversity of fish and birds. A third region, characterized by important riparian forests adjacent to the Isiboro and Sécure Rivers, makes it possible for a great diversity of wild grasses and fish to reproduce; this region is settled by peasant communities devoted to livestock raising. Finally, a fourth region lies in the upper Sécure River valley, an Andean piedmont zone settled by indigenous communities that are also devoted to hunting and fishing.

The state resolved to build a highway whose second phase would cross this protected area, from the Cochabamba foothills to the Amazonian flatlands of Beni. Financed by a loan from Brazil and built by a Brazilian corporation, the highway threw a spotlight on the importance of TIPNIS and the propositions and principles of the new Constitution of the Plurinational State. As I have explained above, the state had pledged to comply with the principle of "prior consultation" with the peoples who inhabit these territories and was legally unable to set aside or alter their rights unilaterally. In reality, the highway planned by the state would not have much of an effect on the southern region of TIPNIS, where the environment has already been heavily impacted by coca farming. However, by cutting through TIPNIS, it would have a very significant impact on the other regions. Not only would it alter the fragile ecosystem that makes human and animal life possible throughout the area; it would also split the central zone, carving in two the best-conserved rainforest anywhere in South America. Even if the highway were to skirt the piedmont region, it would disrupt the biological cycles that link the piedmont, the wetland forests, and the savannas. As social anthropologist Sarela Paz notes:

> If the path of the highway crosses the piedmont or follows the piedmont line inside TIPNIS, its economic, social, and cultural impact on the central region and the region where the Isiboro joins the Sécure will have several faces. Its first impact will become apparent in the medium term, directly affecting the system of cultural adaptation that the indigenous communities have achieved, which reproduces the basic pillars of the ethnic group's economy—that is, agriculture, hunting, fishing, gathering. (Paz 2011: 4–5)

Adding to her reflection on the amphibian character of human life in this territory, Paz points out that

> the indigenous communities that live in both regions have initiated a cycle of combined economy that integrates their ethnic economy with certain forms of commercial activity, such as cacao cultivation, the sale of snake skins, and livestock raising. We might think that, for activities such as these, the highway is an opportunity for commercial ties that would make it easier to transport their prod-

ucts. However, if the highway goes through or around the piedmont in TIPNIS, communities in both regions would see no benefit from the highway because it would be too far from their settlements. Neither their cacao agroforestry, nor their exploitation of reptiles, nor their livestock raising could possibly be moved closer to the highway. (Paz 2011: 5)

It should be added that the highway would also impact the indigenous political structure, which maintains the family and clan exchanges that reproduce the logic of the first peoples of the forest region, as well as the religious expressions that remain just as important as when the Mojeños undertook their Search for the Loma Santa. All this shows that the highway would have a very significant human and environmental impact if it were to enter this protected zone.

It was in defense of this territory that one of the most important fights to conserve the environment and to safeguard human rights and the rights of nature has been carried out since June 2011. This is the March for the Defense of TIPNIS, which, though violently suppressed by the state, has still not ended, despite the passage of a law by the Plurinational Legislative Assembly in October 2011 that prohibits the construction of the highway through the territory and declares the park an "untouchable" zone.

The march for TIPNIS is a second edition of the March for Territory and Dignity that was held in 1990. Indeed, the march is about the constitutional right of indigenous peoples to govern their own territory. Also, not only does it touch on deciding between a civil engineering project—the highway—and a national protected area; it also shows, as clear as day, the clash between two worldviews: the first is anthropocentric, devoted to the pronunciations of humankind as the lord and ruler of nature; the other is polycentric, because it conceives of nature as a legal subject with the "power to give speech to all those who gather there to argue over it. In any case, as shown by the conflict over TIPNIS, nature speaks a language that is incomprehensible to political power" (Komadina 2011: 1).

The anthropocentric view is the one the state takes on when it looks at the conflict. It is disquieting to see how the state unilaterally assumes the ability to define social dilemmas, twisting them and subjecting them to laws of refraction that distort them. I wonder, then, whether the Plurinational State isn't trying to reintroduce the "national culture" project that nationalist elites set in motion in the mid-twentieth century. Its developmentalist logic, which renews the old quest for national integration, seems to confirm the suspicion that, if it persists, it runs the risk of ending up as a form of authoritarianism just as irksome as what we have had in past decades.

Newly regulated by the teleological historicism flowing from the pedagogical and prospective dimension of nationhood, the highway has the same physical and symbolic importance as the old territorializing desires of the 1952 National Revolution. This developmentalism grew from the conviction that nature must be tamed, just as the Indian must be assimilated into the nation-state. And just as the development discourse of 1952 was an erasure of difference, those responsible for such erasure today are not just faraway development bureaucrats, but the very advocates of the Plurinational State, native leaders who have internalized the culture of developmentalism. This problem illustrates the complicity of all modernizing states in the erasing of differences. As Dirlik puts it:

> Indeed, it is difficult to say in historical hindsight which, a voracious capitalism ever invading places or a nation-state inventing homogeneities, has been the bigger problem in the creation of such generic categories. The question may ultimately be moot because the complicity of state and capital (or in the case of existing socialisms, of state and managerial bureaucrats) extends over the history of modernity. . . . It inevitably raises questions about the universality of categories of social analysis, which are all products of the same modernity that produced developmentalism, and are implicated in it one way or another. (2011: 58–59)

According to Carlos Romero Bonifaz, then minister of the presidency and official spokesperson for the Plurinational State, the highway across TIPNIS "will give cohesion and historical sense." This statement—a modernized version of the old paradigm of a struggle between "civilization" and "barbarism"—seeks to turn the supposed territorial "chaos" of the first peoples into a new nationalist strategy, constructed by a way of seeing that newly refracts, distorts, and breaks reality because it touches on objective truth—it is obvious that development is necessary—in certain selected points, in the same way that any highway project is concerned only with the path that the highway will take, discarding all other roads proposed by the indigenous people of this large territory as less spectacular. And this logic is well aware that reality can become a frail enemy when the state has armed itself with good rhetoric. Thus, the Bolivian reality that the minister sees is like a measuring rod placed in the water along the banks of a river: it first bends, then breaks. Refraction is the phenomenon I am describing here. Developmentalist thinking is refractory because it participated distortedly in reality, causing serious violations of human rights and nature. The minister's way of seeing is refractory, because his anthropocentrism understands human action as an interference in nature with the purpose of orienting it exclusively toward material productivity.

If the highway "gives cohesion and historical sense," that imposition emanating from power sets apart and relegates anyone who thinks differently, calling them "barbarians," enemies of progress. As an important member of the new team of epic builders, the minister counters ethnic pluralism and substitutes for it the coveted cultural homogeneity, which can be more easily administered, and whose manifest destiny is none other than to bear witness to the supreme victory of humans over the forces of nature. For that is what the highway will be, if it cuts across TIPNIS: a battlefield in which nature, the ancient enemy of progress, will at last sign its unconditional surrender. As Chakrabarty observes, the discourse of power is completely uncritical of modernization, making "the figure of the engineer"—or the highway builder—"one of the most eroticized figures of the postcolonial developmentalist imagination" (2010: 53). It is precisely this emphasis on development that marks the split between those who hold power and the subaltern sectors living in the farthest reaches of the territory. Behind this new pedagogical politics crouch the officials of the emerging Plurinational State, making excuses for their developmentalism at the expense of diversity.

The polycentric view, contrary to the anthropocentric, observes nature's ability to articulate a multiplicity of voices (Komadina 2011: 1). When it communicates the outcry of the first peoples, nature becomes polyphonic, for it harmonizes their demands not only with those of environmentalists and members of the scientific community who support the indigenous protest, but with the sentiments of the general citizenry. Nature communicates "the surprising capacity of Bolivian society to mobilize in rejecting state violence" (Wanderley 2011: 1). The protest slogan, "TIPNIS is all of us—another kind of development is possible," translates the feelings of a citizenry who "demand that the promises of a 'process of change' be carried out: deepening democracy, social and political inclusion for historically excluded groups, environmental sustainability within the framework of a new model of development" (Wanderley 2011: 1).

Beyond the old developmentalism, a genuinely post-neoliberal and postcapitalist state now faces the challenge of setting public policy on a path "towards a new, post-extractivist pattern of wealth generation and distribution" (Wanderley 2011: 1). This effort will call for new institutional mechanisms capable of connecting civil society with the state, above and beyond the corporate interests that ultimately represent the people who have power. In this new quest, the presence of cultural amphibians can no longer be left behind, forgotten; their arguments—not only economic ones, but moral and religious as well—must be recovered and explicitly taken into account. Consequently, these new mechanisms will inevitably call into question our ways of knowing and will demand a knowledge that serves the purposes not of capital or the state, plurinational or not, but of human survival and justice. Since knowing and living are intricately interrelated in the "culture of integration," there is no distinction in these convictions between knowledge and ethics.

Since a human being cannot be the lord and master of nature, the statement "My highway is the river, I don't need any other" conflicts with the anthropocentric view of reality. The metaphor of the cultural amphibian is displaced between cultures and follows the route of the river to examine roads and paths that situate human action as one part, one fragment of reality, one more inscription in the constellation of signs.

If nature "speaks and feels" through natural disasters and through the countless voices that represent it, its demands are not contrary to the "other" modernity, which respects ancestral traditions and customs. But its spatial-temporal view is different, because it requires the past to rejoin the present. Indeed, while Mojeños speak in the language of the past, the language is informed more by vision than by empirical evidence that the vision had been realized anytime in the past. Mojeños, in other words, have a strong utopian religious present.

Fundamental to any claim to Mojeño identity is an assertion of an inalienable connection between community and land, and, by extension, between society and nature. As one of the directors of TIPNIS has stated, "There's a need for a view of development in which people are linked via rivers and roads without killing them off; in which merchandise can be transported without destroying territories, and which generates development without leading to the disappearance of the fauna" (Bustillos Zamorano 2011: 2). For cultural amphibians, affirming what is indigenous does not imply denying modernity but rather balancing it, through respect for customs and traditions, which, like embers of the past, return in the present.

Today we are witnessing a fight between two paradigms, which, as they face off against one another, clearly express the disagreements between the notions of "progress" and "decolonization." For the logic of progress, "knowledge and the acts of knowing and learning" do not go "beyond individual, instrumental means-ends rationality," whereas for the logic of decoloniality, "ancestral wisdom has the status of 'knowledge.' Its relevance and importance are not for indigenous peoples alone, but for everyone; it is part of a new constitution articulating a plural form of knowledge, giving concreteness and meaning to being plurinational" (Walsh 2008: 145).

A basic aspect of decolonial logic is that knowing is interwoven with living. Decoloniality

> opens up and challenges modern epistemology of the sort that makes us think that "you get at the world through knowing about it," instead cherishing a different epistemological logic, the one that prevails and makes sense for the majority. This logic is: "you get at knowledge through the world," and it points to what I have mentioned elsewhere as "a decolonial epistemology and pedagogy," ... a principle that is not only social and economic (as is usually the case with the idea of "living well" in Bolivia's Constitution), but that is also epistemic. (Walsh 2008: 146)

As noted above, the current Constitution, aiming at the development of society as a whole, establishes a distinction between universal knowledge (*conocimientos universales*) and collective wisdom (*saberes colectivos*); it also specifies that the former are scientifically superior to the latter. Indeed, nature is considered in the Constitution not as a subject of rights, but rather as a collection of natural and environmental resources that must be protected by the state. At base, the Constitution continues to assert the superiority of the rationality for which thinking through ancestral forms of logic is not only inconceivable but an actual threat to economic stability and social order. As Walsh puts it:

> The "good life" is not simply the "living well" considered in the Constitution, but the possibility of conceptualizing and having agency in an "other" way, a different way, conceptualized from one's ancestral difference and its principles, but thought through for society as a whole. This poses the possibility of a social contract rooted in the ethical relationship and coexistence between humans

and their environs, with the desire to challenge fragmentation and promote interculturality. (Walsh 2008: 148)

Violently suppressed by the state, the March in Defense of TIPNIS is a clear example showing that the paradigm of "the good life" is not tolerated by the state. The same thing happened decades ago to "revolutionary nationalism," whose pedagogic dimension and plans for colonizing the Amazonian lowlands was impervious to indigenous demands and whose reformism called for a homogenizing mestizaje—which, as I noted in the case of Diez de Medina, in the end stood by authoritarianism.

If colonizing territories was always the way to justify the destruction and nonobservance of the rights of nature, developmentalist discourses that hide such destruction serve to remind us that human thought has never constructed absolute truths. Today the risk is that political power, that Gorgon turning anyone who looks it in the eyes into stone, will just take out its refracting wand and make reality fit its interests. The discourse of power is often inexact and immoral—inexact because it has lost the Aristotelian ethical precept that it is necessary to adjust means according to what the occasion demands, as we see in the art of medicine and in navigation; immoral, because the essence of morality includes compassion and a commitment to keeping your neighbor from suffering. The inconsistencies of power reveal, in the two cases examined in this chapter, that of Diez de Medina and that of the current Plurinational State, that developmentalist gospels are characterized by refraction. The Plurinational State will deserve no credit from future generations unless it adjusts its viewpoint and pays attention to the demands of those who question it with well-founded right. Not to do so implies a presbyopia or myopia, which in the recent TIPNIS case would call into question the very construction of plurinationality. I will say it quickly, without anesthetics: we have changed the country's name and its Constitution, but the doubt remains whether we have done this in order to integrate the voices of the voiceless. Let us hope we have not acted like a snake shedding its skin, only to plunge headfirst once more into the depths of authoritarianism.

Notes

INTRODUCTION

1. The colonial matrix of power should be understood as an enterprise that works on all five levels of human experience: (1) the economic, particularly the expropriation of land, the exploitation of work, and the control of finances; (2) the political, primarily the control of authority; (3) the civic, especially the control of gender and sexuality; (4) the epistemic, that is, the origins and subsequent control of knowledge; and (5) the subjective/personal, that is, the control of subjectivity.

This colonial matrix most often works invisibly, so that it is imperceptible to the distracted gaze. As it happened, a combination of an expansionist ideology (Western Christianity) and the transformation of mercantile trade into an enterprise of land ownership and massive labor exploitation aimed at producing goods for the globalized market engendered this colonial matrix of power. For a more complete analysis of this subject, see Quijano 2001.

2. An interesting decentering of the "universals" created by modernity can be found in José Rabasa's latest book, *Without History: Subaltern Studies, the Zapatista Insurgency, and the Specter of History* (2010). For Rabasa, abstract universals are being questioned today by "the voices, the daily practices, the forms of memory, and the strategies of mobilization that subalterns have devised" (p. 3). Up against the *telos* created by Western modernity, we have, according to Rabasa, an expanding present that allows indigenous populations to recover their unfulfilled pasts. The "now" of these increasingly strong subjectivities resists being transferred to or delegating power to "important" institutions, the supposed bearers of the "universals" created by the European Enlightenment.

3. According to Mignolo (2003: 27–28; my translation), "'border thinking' is precisely what is found in the grumbling of those who have been dispossessed by modernity; those for whom their experiences and their memories correspond to the other half of modernity, that is, to coloniality. It would not be right, indeed it would be dangerous to generalize border thinking and remove it from

the historicity from which it has arisen," from the logic of thought historicized in and by "the coloniality of modernity." Thus, "border thinking" arises from the dispossessed, from their pain and their rage at the shattering of their histories, their memories, their subjectivities, their biographies, as clearly seen in, for example, Waman Puma de Ayala or in the Frantz Fanon of *Black Skin, White Masks*.

4. It is interesting that this hybridism began by regulating the principles articulated in Bolivia's new Constitution, which was approved by national referendum on 25 January 2009 and passed into law on 7 February 2009. As Jorge Komadina Rimassa has observed (2009: 103–104), the institutions and republican principles spelled out in this Constitution, which are liberal in origin, articulate individual rights and liberties through a body of collective and communitarian rights that can be applied to indigenous-peasant nations and peoples.

5. Maurice Merleau-Ponty used Edmund Husserl's term *Lebenswelt* (lifeworld), a useful neologism that the German phenomenologist coined to designate the worlds—that is, the living contexts, the spaces and times—in which human beings interact and create their intersubjectivity. In his essays, Merleau-Ponty asserts that "I discover myself in the other, just as I discover consciousness of life in consciousness of death" (1964b: 68). Merleau-Ponty is less concerned with the future than with the living present (*lebendige Gegenwart*), that is, the "hardened" present that includes the past as well as the future (1964a: 90).

6. Mariátegui cannot be understood without taking into account the "double consciousness" that characterizes his border thinking: his consciousness of belonging to an Indo-mestizo culture branded by a deep "colonial wound," but also, as I argue in chapter 2, his clear-eyed declaration that he couldn't have thought Peru if he had not had the necessary "European apprenticeship." Only after making this declaration did Mariátegui feel secure enough to be able to assert that he couldn't be thought of as an exclusively Western thinker.

I do not believe Mariátegui can be classified as an "orthodox Marxist," as Mario Vargas Llosa called him in *La utopía arcaica* (1996). Mariátegui's thought was heterodox, mediated not only by Marx, with whose work he was superficially familiar, but also by the no-holds-barred fight between indigenous mysticism and the radical Christianity of Georges Sorel. This made Mariátegui's view of things much more complex. His shunning of any kind of orthodoxy, and his ability to assimilate European ideas "from" Peru, helped Mariátegui forge in his essays the decolonizing abilities that distinguish him deeply and genuinely from other well-known Latin American essayists.

7. Mignolo (2003: 27) refers to this *paradigma otro* ("a paradigm other") as "thinking based on and from colonial difference. Not transforming colonial difference into an 'object of study,' to be studied from the epistemological perspective of modernity, but thinking from the pain of colonial difference; from the

cries of the subject." Regarding the "cries of the subject," see also Hans Hinkelammert (1998).

8. In his suggestive essay "Porcelain and Volcano" (1989 [1969]), Gilles Deleuze makes some observations about time that are very much to the point of this strange "hardening" of the present that I am explaining. For Deleuze, "the alcoholic does not live at all in the imperfect or in the future, the alcoholic has only a past perfect. In drunkenness, the alcoholic puts together an imaginary past, as if the softness of the past participle came to be combined with the hardness of the present auxiliary: I have-loved, I have-done, I have-seen.... Here the past perfect does not at all express a distance or a completion" (1989: 180). Much like Deleuze's explanation of verbal tenses as used by the alcoholic, Andean subjectivity also seems to cling to the use of this hardened past perfect, which, faded and powerless, leaves the future hanging, replacing it with the hardness of this present that is related to the "effect of flight of the past" (1989: 181). Thus, "everything culminates in a 'has been,'" lacking any precise object; in an alcohol effect that can also be produced by other events: a loss of money, a loss of social prestige, a loss of one's community of origin. This connection between alcohol and the loss of one's community of origin is a salient aspect of Bolivian filmmaker Jorge Sanjinés's *La nación clandestina (Secret Nation)* (1989). Like other Third World Latin American intellectuals, Sanjinés focuses not on how the grammatical and linguistic aspects of alcoholism affect Andean subjectivity, but on how alcohol is related to colonization and the dismantling of the local Aymara culture. We could speak of the alcohol effect of the broken individual due to the colonial wound.

9. I am aware of the subversive capacity of other literary genres, especially poetry. José Rabasa has written of the "rage without ends" that Arthur Rimbaud showed in his poetry (2010: 263). Devoted to the repopulation that came about with the Paris Commune, whose struggle to achieve autonomy went well beyond the limits imposed by the state, Rimbaud exemplifies the "poetics of resistance" to the multiple singularities that tried to dismantle it (see Rabasa 2010: 138–147).

CHAPTER 1. THE CHANGING FACES OF HISTORICAL TIME

1. It seems to me that Cornejo Polar's observations associate mestizaje with an elaboration of iconic "root metaphors," that is, with the construction of a model of representation that does not merely describe but also explains reality as a homogenous whole. An in-depth study of this kind of metaphor can be found in Richard Harvey Brown (1989).

2. This chiliasm, this absolute "here and now," had, as Mannheim notes, "its period of existence in the world of the decaying Middle Ages, a period of tre-

mendous disintegration. Everything was in conflict with everything else. It was the world of nobles, patricians, townsmen, journeymen, vagabonds, and mercenaries, all warring against each other. It was a world in upheaval and unrest, in which the deepest impulses of the human spirit sought external expression" (1997 [1936]: 204). One of the main figures in this world in conflict was Thomas Müntzer (1490–1525), a radical preacher during the Protestant Reformation, a defender of Anabaptism (a doctrine that rejected the baptism of infants and children; baptism was to be a conscious act of those who had first made a confession of faith), founder of the League of the Elect, and a revolutionary leader of peasant movements. In 1524, Müntzer delivered his famous "Sermon to the Princes," in which he asserted that laymen and poor peasants could see things more clearly than their disoriented and corrupt rulers. Particularly striking was his revolutionary interpretation of Romans 13:1–7, from which he drew the conclusion that if the authorities do not carry out their role properly, "the sword will be taken from them." Müntzer joined forces with the peasants and in 1525, at the Battle of Frankenhausen, in which more than six thousand peasants lost their lives, was captured, whipped, tortured, and beheaded. A novelized version of these events, *Q*, has been written by four young Italian activists under the pseudonym Luther Blisset (2003).

3. The *Oxford English Dictionary* online version (December 2012) defines "catachresis" as "improper use of words; application of a term to a thing which it does not properly denote; abuse or perversion of a trope or metaphor." The Spanish definition (here, from the 1972 *Pequeño Larousse ilustrado*) gets to the *purpose* of catachresis, which is what I wish to focus on: "primitive rhetorical figure that entails using words in a meaning distinct from their own, because of the lack of a term that can express an idea literally."

4. *Ya es otro tiempo el presente* ("Times are different now," or, more literally, "The present is another time now") was the slogan of the Jesús de Machaca rebellion in 1795, when the memory of the great Tupac Katari insurrection was still fresh in the region around La Paz. The slogan reappeared in 1899, when the *comunarios* of the four ayllus of Mohoza rose up against a military squadron that had committed abuses against the population. It reemerged a few months later in the Paria region, during an uprising against the authorities named by the central government. The motto also serves as the title of a collection of essays on four moments of indigenous insurgency, by Forrest Hylton, Félix Patzi, Sergio Serulnikov, and Sinclair Thomson (2003). Their book illuminates the experience and consciousness of the indigenous forces at historical moments of insurgency, from the precursor movements that led up to the great insurgency of Tomás Katari and Tupac Katari in 1780–1781, to the indigenous, peasant, mining, and urban insurgencies of the early twenty-first century.

5. On this point, there is a certain similarity between conservative thinking and the apocalyptic thinking of chiliasm spread by social movements. However,

the salvational future of conservative tradition, with its Christian roots, is not of this world. Social movements, on the other hand, aspire to establish the salvation of the elect here and now.

6. Étienne Klein has presented the consequences of thinking of history as the "arrow of time." From such a perspective, all we can do is observe irreversible, temporally oriented phenomena. Klein states that "if we film any scene from everyday life and then project the scene backward, we can tell from the very first images that the film has been reversed." He then adds, "This comes from the fact that at the macroscopic scale, in general, we cannot redo what has been undone, nor undo what has been done" (2005: 89–90).

7. On mimicry, see Homi Bhabha's essay "Of Mimicry and Man: The Ambivalence of Colonial Discourse" (2002).

8. The colonization of the concepts of time and space has a long history. Indeed, the concept of modernity is the final stage of a progressive transition that resorted to the colonization of both concepts to create the dominant narratives mentioned here. Thus, the imperial languages were based on the Christian religion and on the Greco-Latin world in order to colonize time. As Johannes Fabian shows in *Time and the Other* (1983), temporal difference appeared in the late eighteenth century in the idea that "primitive" peoples (which replaced the previous belief in "barbarous peoples") should be denied what Fabian calls "coevalness." But as Walter Mignolo explains (2007), this "denial of coevalness" was actually preceded by the Renaissance colonization of space and construction of the "colonial difference of space." If temporal difference is expressed through the notion of "the primitive," spatial difference came about with "the barbarous," an idea taken from the historical experience of the Greeks and modified in the sixteenth century to be applied to peoples located in spaces that were taken to be inferior. Reconceptualized, the idea of the barbarous appeared as Western Christianity employed Latin and the vernacular Western languages to construct the narratives of its own identity. In contrast to it, situated in inferior spaces, in colonized spaces, there appeared the peoples "without history."

The concept of "the primitive" was introduced in the eighteenth century, incorporating the temporal dimension into the earlier spatial difference. Thus, modernity not only stood in opposition to the Middle Ages and the barbarous territories; it was also intended to overcome the idea of "tradition." By the late eighteenth century, when modernity was entering the stage of the Enlightenment, in the lineal history of Christian Europe, the exploitation of the New World (mines, plantations) was complete and had been tied to the slave trade from Africa. Holland and England began to expand their influence throughout South Asia. In America and Asia, the great human settlements allowed ascendant Europe to adopt a temporal consciousness that conceptualized those societies as "backward," classifying them as "primitive." "Barbarous people" were connected with space, while "the primitives" were stuck in time. So the "primitive" peoples were perceived as foreign "objects" from outside Europe, impervious to the changes of modernity. As is known, the geopolitical invention of the outsiderness of the other was constructed to secure the inland identity of the European subject and to safeguard the primacy of the place of enunciation, that is, the primacy of European knowledge.

When the outsiderness of the other was established and the other was left behind in history (time) and marginalized in production (space), her situation grew even worse in the early nineteenth century with the idea that time, measured in terms of progress and the forward march of Western civilization, was being transformed. It was Hegel who redefined the classificatory system so that History, with a capital *H*, turned into the development of the Spirit through time, just as Nature became the development of the Idea in space. Through this reordering of time and space, through Hegel's efforts to situate Germany (space) as the world's first nation (time), the "heart" of Europe (including France and England) was being constituted. To its south, the Mediterranean countries occupied the margins of Empire. The states to its northeast—Poland, Russia, the Slavic nations—showed up "late" to this carving up of History, forming and perpetuating their connection to Asia and thus constituting the imperial difference. As Mignolo asserts, the Hegelian heart of Europe (Germany, France, and England) became the object of desire: to belong to modern, imperial Europe.

CHAPTER 2. IS THE NATION AN IMAGINED COMMUNITY?

1. I will discuss this topic in greater detail in chapter 4.

2. This diagnosis, the product of observation and a detailed description of nature and the human types who inhabit it, is in this sense comparable to *Os sertões* by the Brazilian writer Euclides da Cunha (English translation: *Rebellion in the Backlands*). But, as I observe in this chapter, the similarities should not make us lose sight of the sharp differences in the models of observation used in each of these works. *Facundo* never expresses doubt about future progress; *Os sertões*, with its tragic view of reality, does question progress. Within Brazil itself, da Cunha's tragic vision can be distinguished from the model of constructing a national identity proposed by Gilberto Freyre (Rodríguez Larreta and Giucci 2007).

Both Sarmiento and da Cunha give unquestioned pride of place to politics, above any literary considerations. This also reveals the precarious nature of Latin American intellectual institutions. What Antônio Cândido wrote about Brazil is also true of Spanish America: writers gained social prestige from the recognition of their "patriotic and sentimental" contributions to political and social causes (Cândido 1973: 81). This is why literary activity was merely a hobby for most intellectuals. Even José Hernández thought of his masterpiece, *Martín Fierro* (1872), as a distraction from his more important work as an Argentine senator.

3. There is no doubt that "lettered cities" were counterposed to rural "orgies," cut off from "civilization" and therefore lacking all rationality. Thus, the "lettered city"—which, in Latin America, was not an organic social fact like the "public spheres" of eighteenth-century Europe but rather a top-down fabrication—arose to counteract and cancel out the chaotic reality of rural life. To this end, lettered culture inscribed a "regime of visibility," which, by fusing the material (the city center) with the metaphoric / symbolic (the institutions of power), created the analogy between the city and state hierarchy; this analogy made the city a "readily legible text" of social control (Dabove 2007: 221).

4. I am referring to the crisis of all logocentric models for observing reality.

5. The quarrel between liberals and conservatives gave rise to alternative projects within the dominant discourse of modernity. These projects never challenged the dominant position of the oligarchy or the coloniality of power.

6. In his reading of *Os sertões*, Juan Pablo Dabove (2007) retains Anderson's theoretical framework of the nation as an imagined community. Later in this chapter I will explore the differences that Dabove's smart reading presents regarding the critical perspective on the imagined community that guides my view of da Cunha's book.

7. My observations about Mariátegui agree with Antonio Cornejo Polar's analysis in "Mariátegui y su propuesta de una modernidad de raíz andina" (1993: 58–63). In this essay, Cornejo Polar notes that Mariátegui argued for a modernity different from the kind that the societies of Western Europe had attained, as well as from the modernity of the socialist states that were then coming into being. Instead, Peru's modernity should develop in its own way, based on the country's own particular social, historical, and cultural circumstances: a modernity with Andean roots and an Andean spirit.

8. According to Peruvian critic José Antonio Mazzotti, Sorel argued that members of the working class relied on myth as a central part of their identity and their program of action. It was as a function of the revolutionary myth that the masses acted in an organized and decisive way as subjects to destroy the bourgeois state. Sorel, however, did not bother to explain what constituted that myth, beyond the political exigencies of the moment. Thus, Mazzotti explains, the importance of myth in Sorel's work "is basically instrumental, for it allows him to avoid the determinism of an evolutionist view of bourgeois society as a function of technological advancements" (Mazzotti 2009: 140). Mazzotti goes on to point out that Sorel criticizes Marx himself for "presenting a determinist, teleological, and linear picture of human history, ending with the final instatement of socialism as the stage that dialectically overcomes all the contradictions in the capitalist mode of production" (2009: 140–141).

9. Placing himself outside modernity, José Rabasa carries out one of the most

radical readings of the "multitude." Noting that the concept of "the people" simply carries out a "domesticating function," he argues that it cannot be harmonized with the "subaltern rage" contained in the category "multitude." Rabasa opts for the latter as making possible the "people *without* History" that calls all institutionalized spaces into question. See Rabasa 2010, especially chapter 8, "On the History of the History of Peoples *without* History" (138–147).

CHAPTER 3. "NOW TIME"

1. Chilean authoritarianism is well documented by Alfredo Jocelyn-Holt Letelier in his book *El peso de la noche* (1997).

2. I am referring here to "group psychology," which gave a racist aspect to the theories of Gustave Le Bon (1995 [1895]) and Hippolyte Taine (1920). The same group psychology was called upon by many of the Spanish American letrados who were devoted to explaining their nations' backwardness. If they found useful Le Bon's studies on the dividing line between the normal and the pathological, they justified the backwardness of our countries by using Taine's depiction of French society as a social organism threatened by the eruption of the popular masses. The important point was that these group forces, which they linked to Indian culture or mestizo "degeneration," lacked any internal consistency: they were merely the pernicious result of instinctive racial impulses that society found it difficult to control. On the topic of distortions of the mob, see Laclau 2005: 37–88.

3. Here I should emphasize the fact that Western culture is not homogeneous. When the geopolitics of knowledge speak of the West as a dominant culture, they are referring to the logocentric knowledge that has ruled since rationalism organized its worldview, its universal *Weltanschauung*. But as Milan Kundera correctly points out (2007), Europe is also a set of small nations, each with its own destiny. The "great Europe" of logocentric modernity, the Europe created by History, may be the one we know best, but there are still small European nations that remained in the "waiting room of history" (Chakrabarty 2000: 8), giving rise to the insuperable inequality between these Europes. And it is precisely in opposition to History that nations such as Poland, Czechoslovakia, and Romania assert their identity.

Unlike France, where the notion of the state cannot be distinguished from the construction of the state, the small nations are a mosaic of heterogeneous identities unable to organize the nation-state and therefore obliged to resort to building mediating contexts that serve to give them an identity. Thus, Central Europe is an identity concept similar to Latin America, another geographic zone where homogeneous and fully modern nation-states have not managed to be built.

In short, the "Great Europe" imagined by universal thinkers turns out to be "provincial," because it is incapable of seeing its own culture in the greater context that includes the small nations. For their part, those nations remain, as Benjamin perceived, the "other side" of modernity.

4. Later in this chapter I will introduce the distinction between messianic utopia and millenarian utopia.

5. It is interesting that the reasons I have for turning to Benjamin's "Theses" coincide with those of Fernando Coronil, who uses the theses to rethink the academic role that the Program in Anthropology and History should play at the University of Michigan. In the first of his own theses—he calls them "pieces of a puzzle to be assembled"—Coronil calls for "critical evaluations of the history, premises, and politics of Western knowledge—its teleological narratives, disciplinary classifications, and complicity with eurocentrism, racism, sexism, elitism, and other modalities of dominative knowledge" (2011a: 301). Leaning more toward "representations of the world as fragments of an unfolding totality" (number 5, p. 303), Coronil asks for life to be restored in the image of the "freed grandchildren" rather than in that of their "enslaved ancestors" (number 8, p. 304). The "silences of the past" that he recovers for the present (number 3, p. 302), as in Michel-Rolph Trouillot's reflections on this subject, seem very much like the function I assign to the here and now that aims at reclaiming the ruins of the past.

6. See Taussig 1980: 34–35. I will analyze this text later in this chapter.

7. Referring to Andean reality (*lo andino*) as a "non-rational rationality," Josef Estermann (2009: 112–114) argued that "the main method of 'approaching' the reality of human beings in the West is—to express it paradoxically—through 'gnoseological distancing,' the most typical expression of which is 'sight' (*theoria, visio*). Through sight, the human being is distanced from the visible as a transcendent object—in other words, is set apart, and at the same time is brought close through the incorporation of the object as 'image' in the subject." Estermann then adds: "Western philosophy and cultures are highly 'visual,' as reflected in the predominant value placed on visual means of communication and the 'mania for reproduction' (libraries, film archives, art galleries, newspaper libraries, even genomic libraries)." Given that sight served as a cognitive model for the history of philosophy, "reason (*ratio, nous, Verstand, Vernunf*) became the most proper way to 'see' reality, for in grasping it, it turned it into concept."

8. Pascale Absi (2005), who gives me the elements that allow me to take a critical look at Taussig's analysis of the devil in the mines, explains that the term *Tío* has more than one origin and many connotations. A heterogeneous semantic field—I will later argue that it can be conceived as a reversible structure of meaning—the Tío suggests, in the miner's mind, a series of linguistic and symbolic connotations, signifying both the possibility of finding the mineral in the mines (the devil here being a positive deity and supportive of the miner) and

trickery and temptation (related to production surplus and capitalist profits). In either connotation, the name Tío ("uncle" in Spanish) alludes to the family ties that bind miners to their underground master, and their tendency to conceptualize their relation with the deities in kinship terms. The term *lari*, for example, associated with the world of the saqras, the primitive, savage, diabolical deities who live inside the mountains, also once meant "maternal uncle" (Bouysse-Cassagne and Harris 1987: 258). It is striking that the figure that steals human fat from people—known in the Andes as Karisiri, Lik'i siri, or Pishtaku—is called Tío Mantequero (Uncle Fatman) in Andalucía (Molinié-Fioravanti 1986: 174).

The Tío also recalls the figure of the Spanish "familiar," which in the seventeenth century was a minor demon who performed small favors in the home. In the Andes, this term for minor demon was translated as *supay* (Estenssoro 1998: 83).

The Tío is also a common figure in the oral tradition of the Andean countries (Paredes Candia 1972). He appears in Quechua folktales as the figure of the fox, a predator linked to the saqra world of the mountains, one that embodies a seductive, crafty trickster character. Sometimes he is associated with the figure of the mestizo who deceives the indigenous people.

The appearance of the Tío, as built in statues that represent him in the mine galleries, is that of a diabolical figure, with horns, a long tail, and goat feet, drawn from stereotypes of the devil dating from the European Renaissance, according to Bouysse-Cassagne (1998).

In any case, the Tío is the chthonic master of mineral veins and the animating force of the mining world.

9. In the "deconstructive" sense of the term. Spivak's reflections on catachresis and "deconstruction" are discussed in chapter 2.

10. For a development of this theme and its connection with the concept of "reification," see Lukács 1960 [1923].

11. With another nod to the importance of Walter Benjamin's "Theses on the Philosophy of History" in Taussig's thought.

12. This is precisely the notion of "reification" that Lukács has developed.

13. Both the Pachamama and the Tío are closely associated with the Andean mountain deities. The identification of one particular mountain, Cerro Rico, with the Pachamama is specific to Potosí, however. Indeed, in Potosí, where Taussig carried out his fieldwork, the Pachamama is the wife of the Tío (Absi 2005: 87–88). The connection between the Pachamama and the Tío is related to the fact that she is an archetype that generates the ore that miners extract from underground. The image, then, is that of the mountain-Pachamama as a womb in which mineral ores grow and mature, representing an obstetric vision of mining activities (Absi 2005: 88–89).

14. "Reasonable pluralism" is the frame used now when religion is incorporated into an analysis of the public sphere; see Habermas 2006.

15. For a more detailed analysis of this problem, see Calhoun 1995.

16. See Allen 1949.

17. See Javier Medina's preface (2004) to *La reciprocidad y el nacimiento de los valores*, the first of three volumes titled *Teoría de la reciprocidad* by Dominique Temple (2004).

CHAPTER 4. THE DIMENSIONS OF THE NATION

1. The spatialization of time is one of the most important characteristics of modernity. It is a "ghostly and spectral" cultural form that conceals the past time built into its production. In tension with the synchronic production of space, time is asynchronous: it revives earlier images of the presence of the capitalist mode of production. These are "preexisting" images that create conflict because they contradict the spatial metaphor of expanding, developing society. When they are connected with space on a plane of equality, the condensation of time gives rise to the presence of the contemporaneity of the noncontemporaneous. To show that such noncontemporaneous concepts exist is to prove that the capitalist system desynchronizes things and produces inequalities. On this, see Harry Harootunian's essay "Some Thoughts on Comparability and the Space-Time Problem" (2005).

2. Hans Kohn was the most important source for the contrast between civic and ethnic nationalism, as well as that between the Western and Eastern versions of modernity. His *Idea of Nationalism* (1944) has been well explored by Craig Calhoun (2007).

3. Vidal's essays have been collected in *La literatura en la historia de las emancipaciones latinoamericanas* (Vidal 2004).

4. Anderson uses the term "print capitalism" to refer to three things. First, educated language (Latin and the languages derived from it) was of supreme importance in nation building. Nationalism privileged the use of vernacular languages over that of Latin. Thus the alignment of capitalism and print technology put language in close relation to nationalism. Second, certain languages—the ones that had acquired a fixed shape and stable grammar—had the ability to dominate the administrative mechanisms of the state. And third, print capitalism entailed the construction of a "high culture" that could dominate society and define it according to its own "totalizing" abilities (Anderson 1983).

5. See the more detailed analysis of the essays of Alcides Arguedas, Franz Tamayo, and Carlos Montenegro in my book *Mestizaje Upside-Down* (2004).

6. The historian Brooke Larson (1998) coined the term "cult of anti-mestizaje" to refer to the early twentieth-century liberal essayists who, in their zeal to build

the nation-state and strongly influenced by the Social Darwinism of the time, thought that "the mestizo race did not join or fuse Indians and whites, but rather embodied the worst of both races: the audacity, adventurism, and fanaticism of the Spanish and the passivity, primitiveness, and faintheartedness of the Indian." In other words, "mestizaje eliminated the redeemable qualities of these 'pure races,' while, by perpetuating the debased characteristics of conqueror and conquered, the hybrid race embodied a volatile mix of ungovernable people" (1998: 33).

7. For a detailed study of social metaphor, see Richard Harvey Brown, *A Poetic for Sociology* (1989: 77–171).

8. For a critical review of this "cult of anti-mestizaje" that coincides with my evaluation of the intellectual figure of Franz Tamayo, see the recent book by Ximena Soruco Sologuren, *La ciudad de los cholos: Mestizaje y colonialidad en Bolivia, siglos XIX y XX* (2011).

9. Recent studies show that the control exerted by the image of "ideal mestizaje" ran throughout the "narrative of identity" up to the nationalist project that was crystallized in the National Revolution of 1952. See Soruco Sologuren 2011.

10. In this sense, the thesis of *Nacionalismo y coloniaje* clashes with the theories about Latin America that André Gunder Frank and the dependency theorists would later develop. For dependency theorists, the bourgeois democratic revolutions and their populist programs did nothing but reproduce and intensify dependency. See Frank, "The Development of Underdevelopment" (1966).

11. Stefanoni's book is an interesting and agile reading, but its observations on Arguedas and representation are insufficient. At the outset of his critical study of "internal colonialism" and postcolonial reflection in Bolivia, Stefanoni asserts that "the topics regarding Indiannness in Bolivia have derived from two opposing images: the 'bronze race' and the 'sick pueblo.' . . . Various versions of indigenismo were based on this ambivalence, which recurs throughout the national ethnic imagination" (2010: 9). Unlike Stefanoni, I think that the "sick pueblo" (*pueblo enfermo*) image conflates the metaphor of illness with the social whole, not with the Indian alone. It does not represent the Indian, nor is it a metaphor that contradicts his basic condition. For Arguedas, this "bronze race" degenerates only when it comes into contact with mestizaje. In other words, the Indian loses his vitality and "falls sick" only when his condition changes, when he transforms into a cholo.

12. Soruco Sologuren's recent work (2011) shows the repercussions that the weakness of the elites in the nineteenth and twentieth centuries had on the mestizo sectors. The rise of that sector, which according to Soruco has not yet received the attention it deserves from official historians, reveals an intense process of accumulation. Indeed, the emergence of modernity, understood as a process of constituting criollo identity with its Darwinist discourse and purity cam-

paigns, made it impossible to see the rise of the cholos, with their aesthetic codes and cultural affiliations.

13. Its antecedent is an essay with a less celebratory tone, "Forma clase y forma multitud en el proletariado minero en Bolivia," which Zavaleta Mercado wrote in late 1970 (Zavaleta Mercado 1983 [1970]).

14. Anticolonial struggles after World War II, but especially from the 1960s, also empowered indigenous peoples and brought them together across national boundaries, a process that led in 1975 to the founding of the World Council of Indigenous Peoples. The United Nations and other international organizations, such as the ILO, provided a novel political space for indigenous self-assertion. These efforts culminated in 2007 in the UN Declaration on the Rights of Indigenous Peoples (see Dirlik 2011).

References

Aboul-Ela, Hosam M. 2007. *Other South: Faulkner, Coloniality, and the Mariátegui Tradition*. Pittsburgh: University of Pittsburgh Press.
Absi, Pascale. 2005. *Los ministros del Diablo: El trabajo y sus representaciones en las minas de Potosí*. La Paz: PIEB / IRD / IFEA / Embajada de Francia.
———. 2009. "Trabajo, género e ingresos entre los comerciantes minoristas de Potosí." *Tinkazos: Revista boliviana de ciencias sociales* 12, no. 26: 69–90.
Adorno, Theodor W. 1991. "Introduction to Benjamin's 'Schriften.'" In *On Walter Benjamin: Critical Essays and Recollections*, edited by Gary Smith, pp. 2–17. Cambridge, MA: MIT Press.
———. 2000 [1958]. "The Essay as Form." In *The Adorno Reader*, edited by Brian O'Connor, pp. 91–111. Oxford: Blackwell.
———. 2005 [1951]. *Minima Moralia: Reflections on a Damaged Life*. Translated by E. F. N. Jephcott. London: Verso.
Albó, Xavier. 2009. "Prólogo." In Javier Sanjinés C., *Rescoldos del pasado: Conflictos culturales en sociedades poscoloniales*, pp. xi–xxiii. La Paz: PIEB.
Allen, Don Cameron. 1949. *The Legend of Noah: Renaissance Rationalism in Art, Science and Letters*. Urbana: University of Illinois Press.
Anderson, Benedict. 1983. *Imagined Communities: Reflections on the Origin and Spread of Nationalism*. London: Verso.
Appadurai, Arjun. 1996. Modernity at Large. Cultural Dimensions of Globalization. Minneapolis: University of Minnesota Press.
Arendt, Hannah. 1968. *Between Past and Future*. New York: Viking.
Arguedas, Alcides. 1937 [1909]. *Pueblo enfermo*. 3rd ed. Santiago de Chile: Ediciones Ercilla.
Arguedas, José María. 1985 [1941]. *Yawar Fiesta*. Translation of *Yawar fiesta*, by Frances Barraclough. Austin: University of Texas Press.
———. 2000 [1973]. *The Fox from Up Above and the Fox from Down Below*. Translation of *El zorro de arriba y el zorro de abajo*, by Frances Barraclough. Pittsburgh: University of Pittsburgh Press.

Aricó, José, ed. 1980. *Mariátegui y los orígenes del marxismo latinoamericano*. México: Ediciones Pasado y Presente.

Barth, Fredrik, ed. 1969. *Ethnic Boundaries*. Oslo: Norwegian University Press.

Benjamin, Walter. 1968 [1940]. "Theses on the Philosophy of History." In *Illuminations*, translated by Harry Zohn, pp. 253–264. New York: Harcourt, Brace, and World.

Bernard, Carmen. 1986. *Enfermedad, daño e ideología: Antropología médica de los renacientes de Pindilig*. Quito: Abaya-Yala.

Bernstein, Basil. 1990. *The Structuring of Pedagogic Discourse*. London: Routledge.

Beverley, John. 1999. *Subalternity and Representation*. Durham, NC: Duke University Press.

Bhabha, Homi. 2002. "Of Mimicry and Man: The Ambivalence of Colonial Discourse." In *Race Critical Theories: Text and Context*, edited by Philomena Essed and David Theo Goldberg, pp. 113–122. Oxford: Blackwell.

Blissett, Luther (pseudonym of Roberto Bui, Giovanni Cattabriga, Federico Gugliemi, and Luca Di Meo). 2003. *Q*. Translated by Shaun Whiteside. London: Heinemann.

Bloch, Ernst. 1991 [1935]. *Heritage of Our Times*. Translated by Neville Plaice and Stephen Plaice. Berkeley: University of California Press.

Bouysse-Cassagne, Thérêse. 1998. "Attention! Un diable peut toujours en cacher un autre: A propos de l'introduction des images de l'enfer chez les Indiens de l'Altiplano bolivien." *Traces* 34. México: CEMCA.

Bouysse-Cassagne, Thérêse, and Olivia Harris. 1987. "Pacha: En torno al pensamiento Aymara." In *Tres reflexiones sobre el pensamiento andino*, pp. 11–60. La Paz: Hisbol.

Brown, Richard Harvey. 1989. *A Poetic for Sociology: Toward a Logic of Discovery for the Human Sciences*. Chicago: University of Chicago Press.

Buck-Morss, Susan. 1977. *The Origin of Negative Dialectics: Theodor W. Adorno, Walter Benjamin, and the Frankfurt Institute*. New York: Free Press.

Bustillos Zamorano, Iván. 2011. "En el TIPNIS o nace o aborta el nuevo Estado Plurinacional." *La Razón* (digital edition), 19 September. www.la-razon.com/version.php?ArticleId=2231&EditionId=2649&idp=42&ids=441.

Calhoun, Craig. 1995. *Critical Social Theory: Culture, History and the Challenge of Difference*. Cambridge, MA: Blackwell.

———. 2007. *Nations Matter: Culture, History, and the Cosmopolitan Dream*. London: Routledge.

———. 2011. "Secularism, Citizenship and the Public Sphere." In *Rethinking Secularism*, edited by Craig Calhoun, Mark Juergensmeyer, and Jonathan VanAntwerpen, pp. 75–91. New York: Oxford University Press.

Cândido, Antônio. 1973. *Literatura e sociedade: Estudos de teoria e história literária*. São Paulo: Editora Nacional.

Canedo Vásquez, Gabriela. 2011. *La Loma Santa: Una utopia cercada*. La Paz: Ibis / Plural.

Canetti, Elías. 1978 [1962]. *Crowds and Power*. Translated by Carol Stewart. New York: Seabury.

Chakrabarty, Dipesh. 2000. *Provincializing Europe: Postcolonial Thought and Historical Difference*. Princeton, NJ: Princeton University Press.

———. 2009. "Humanism in a Global World." In *Humanism in Intercultural Perspective: Experiences and Expectations*, edited by Jörn Rüsen and Henner Laass, pp. 23–36. New Brunswick, NJ: Transaction.

———. 2010. "The Legacies of Bandung: Decolonization and the Politics of Culture." In *Making a World after Empire: The Bandung Moment and Its Political Afterlives*, edited by Christopher Lee, pp. 45–68. Athens: Ohio University Press.

Cioran, E. M. 1970. "Encounter with the Void." Translated by Frederick Brown. *Hudson Review* 23, no. 1 (Spring 1970): pp. 37–48.

———. 1983. "After History." In *Drawn and Quartered*, translated by Richard Howard, pp. 33–45. New York: Seaver Books.

Cochran, Terry. 2001. *Twilight of the Literary: Figures of Thought in the Age of Print*. Cambridge, MA: Harvard University Press.

Cornejo Polar, Antonio. 1993. "Mariátegui y su propuesta de una modernidad de raíz andina." *Anuario mariateguiano*, vol. 5, pp. 58–63. Lima: Empresa Editora Amauta, Editorial Gráfica Labor S.A.

———. 1997. *Los universos narrativos de José María Arguedas*. 2nd ed. Lima: Editorial Horizonte.

Coronil, Fernando. 2011a. "Pieces for Anthrohistory: A Puzzle to Be Assembled Together." In *Anthrohistory: Unsettling Knowledge, Questioning Discipline*, edited by Edward Murphy, David William Cohen, Chandra Bhimull, Fernando Coronil, Monica Patterson, and Julie Skurski, pp. 301–316. Ann Arbor: University of Michigan Press.

———. 2011b. "The Future in Question: History and Utopia in Latin America (1989–2010)." In *Business as Usual: The Roots of the Global Financial Breakdown*, edited by Craig Calhoun and Georgi Derluguian, pp. 231–292. New York: New York University Press / SSRC.

Costa Lima, Luiz. 1992. *The Dark Side of Reason. Fictionality and Power*. Translated by Paulo Henriques Britto. Stanford, CA: Stanford University Press.

Courville, Mathieu E. 2010. *Edward Said's Rhetoric of the Secular*. London: Continuum.

Dabove, Juan Pablo. 2007. *Nightmares of the Lettered City: Banditry and Literature in Latin America, 1816–1929*. Pittsburgh: University of Pittsburgh Press.

Da Cunha, Euclides. 2010 [1902]. *Backlands: The Canudos Campaign*. Translation of *Os sertões: Campanha de Canudos*, by Elizabeth Lowe. New York: Penguin.

Deleuze, Gilles. 1989 [1969]. "Porcelain and Volcano." In *The Logic of Sense*, translated by Mark Lester with Charles Stivale, pp. 176–185. New York: Columbia University Press, 1989.

Diez de Medina, Fernando. 1950. *Nayjama*. La Paz: Gisbert.

———. 1953. "El problema de una literatura nacional." *Cuadernos Americanos* 68: 135–144.

———. 1969. *Mateo Montemayor: Un relato del hombre sudamericano para sus hermanos del mundo*. La Paz: Cooperativa de Artes Gráficas E. Burillo.

Dirlik, Arif. 2011. "Globalization, Indigenism, Social Movements and the Politics of Place." *Localities* (Korea) 1, no. 1 (November): 47–90.

Duara, Prasenjit. 1996. "Historicizing National Identity, or Who Imagines What and When." In *Becoming National: A Reader*, edited by Geoff Eley and Ronald Grigor Suny, pp. 151–177. Oxford: Oxford University Press.

Eller, Jack David. 1999. *From Culture to Ethnicity to Conflict: An Anthropological Perspective on International Ethnic Conflict*. Ann Arbor: University of Michigan Press.

Escobar, Arturo. 2009. "Una minga para el postdesarrollo." *América Latina en movimiento* 445: 26–30.

———. 2010. "Latin America at a Crossroads." *Cultural Studies* 24, no. 1: 1–65.

Estenssoro Fuchs, Juan Carlos. 1998. "Du paganisme a la sainteté: L'incorporation des Indiens du Pérou au Catholicisme (1532–1750)." Doctoral thesis, EHESS, París.

Estermann, Josef. 2009. *Filosofía andina: Sabiduría indígena para un mundo nuevo*. La Paz: ISEAT.

Fabian, Johannes. 1983. *Time and the Other: How Anthropology Makes Its Object*. New York: Columbia University Press.

Fals Borda, Orlando. 1979. "Investigating Reality in Order to Transform It: The Colombian Experience." *Dialectical Anthropology* 4: 33–55.

Fanon, Frantz. 1963 [1961]. *The Wretched of the Earth*. Translated by C. Farrington. New York: Grove.

Favre, Henri. 1998. *El indigenismo*. México: Fondo de Cultura Económica.

Flores Galindo, Alberto. 1989. *La agonía de Mariátegui*. Lima: Instituto de Apoyo Agrario.

Foucault, Michel. 2008 [1967]. "Of Other Spaces (1967)." Translated by Lieven De Cauter and Michiel Dehaene. In *Heterotopia and the City: Public Space in a Postcivil Society*, edited by Michiel Dehaene and Lieven De Cauter, pp. 13–28. New York: Routledge.

Francovich, Guillermo. 1956. *El pensamiento boliviano en el siglo XX*. México: Fondo de Cultura Económica.

Frank, Andre Gunder. 1966. "The Development of Underdevelopment." *Monthly Review* 18, no. 4: 17–31.

Frye, Northrop. 1957. *Anatomy of Criticism: Four Essays*. Princeton: Princeton University Press.

Gellner, Ernest. 1983. *Nations and Nationalism*. Oxford: Blackwell.

———. 1994. *Conditions of Liberty: Civil Society and Its Rivals*. New York: Penguin.

———. 1997. *Nationalism*. New York: New York University Press.

Giddens, Anthony. 1990. *The Consequences of Modernity*. Stanford, CA: Stanford University Press.

Gilly, Adolfo. 2003. "Historias desde adentro: La tenaz persistencia de los tiempos." In *Ya es otro tiempo el presente: Cuatro momentos de insurgencia indígena*, edited by Forrest Hylton, Félix Patzi, Sergio Serulnikov, and Sinclair Thomson, pp. 15–50. La Paz: Muela del Diablo Editores.

Godoy, Ricardo. 1984. "Small Scale Mining among the Jukumani Indians of Bolivia." PhD diss., Columbia University.

González, Nelson. 2004. "La caída de la inteligencia." *Juguete rabioso* (La Paz, Bolivia) 3, no. 97 (1 February): 3.

Gramsci, Antonio. 1992 [1930–1932]. *Prison notebooks*. 3 vols. Translated by Joseph A. Buttigieg. New York: Columbia University Press.

Guamán Poma de Ayala, Felipe. 2006 [1615]. *The First New Chronicle and Good Government*. Translated by David Frye. Indianapolis: Hackett.

Guha, Ranajit. 1983. *Elementary Aspects of Peasant Insurgency in Colonial India*. Delhi: Oxford University Press.

———. 1985. "Nationalism Reduced to 'Official Nationalism.'" *Asian Studies Association of Australia Review* 9, no. 1: 103–108.

———. 1997. *Dominance without Hegemony: History and Power in Colonial India*. Cambridge, MA: Harvard University Press.

Gustafson, Bret, and Nicole Fabricant. 2011. "Introduction. New Cartographies of Knowledge and Struggle." In *Remapping Bolivia: Resources, Territory, and Indigeneity in a Plurinational State*, edited by Bret Gustafson and Nicole Fabricant, pp. 1–25. Santa Fe, NM: School for Advanced Research Press.

Gutiérrez, Raquel, Álvaro García Linera, and Luis Tapia. 2000. "La forma multitud de la política de las necesidades vitales." In *El retorno de la Bolivia plebeya*, edited by Alvaro García Linera, Raquel Gutiérrez, Raul Prada, and Luis Tapia, pp. 135–184. La Paz: Muela del Diablo Editores.

Habermas, Jürgen. 2006. "Religion in the Public Sphere." *European Journal of Philosophy* 14: 1–25.

Hardt, Michael, and Antonio Negri. 2000. *Empire*. Cambridge, MA: Harvard University Press.

———. 2004. *Multitude: War and Democracy in the Age of Empire*. New York: Penguin.

Harootunian, Harry. 2005. "Some Thoughts on Comparability and the Space-Time Problem." *boundary 2* 32, no. 2: 23–52.

Harris, Olivia. 1978. "Phaxsima y qullqi: Los poderes y los significados del dinero en el Norte de Potosí." In *La participación indígena en los mercados surandinos*, edited by Harris, Brooke Larson, and Enrique Tandeter, pp. 235–280. La Paz: CERES.

Hinkelammert, Hans. 1998. *El grito del sujeto*. San José, Costa Rica: DEI.

Hobsbawm, Eric. 1990. *Nations and Nationalism since 1780: Programme, Myth, Reality*. Cambridge: Cambridge University Press.

Hylton, Forrest, Félix Patzi, Sergio Serulnikov, and Sinclair Thomson. 2003. *Ya es otro tiempo el presente: Cuatro momentos de insurgencia indígena*. La Paz: Muela del Diablo Editores.

Jakobson, Roman. 1976. "Metalanguage as a Linguistic Problem." In *Selected Writings*, vol. 7, pp. 113–121. Gravenhage: Mouton.

Jay, Martin. 1993. *Force Fields: Between Intellectual History and Cultural Critique*. New York: Routledge.

Jocelyn-Holt Letelier, Alfredo. 1997. *El peso de la noche: Nuestra frágil fortaleza histórica*. Buenos Aires: Ariel.

Johnson, M. C. Ariana. 2005. "Subalternizing Canudos." *MLN* 120, no. 2: 355–382.

Kedourie, Elie. 1993 [1960]. *Nationalism*. Oxford: Blackwell.

Klein, Étienne. 2005. *Chronos: How Time Shapes Our Universe*. Translated by Glenn Burney. New York: Thunder's Mouth.

Kohn, Hans. 1944. *The Idea of Nationalism: A Study in Its Origins and Background*. New York: Macmillan.

Komadina Rimassa, Jorge. 2009. "Identidad democrática y proceso de cambio." In *¿Nación o naciones boliviana(s)?*, edited by Gonzalo Rojas Ortuste, pp. 99–110. La Paz: CIDES-UMSA / Embajada de Francia en Bolivia / CAECID / Universidad Complutense de Madrid.

———. 2011. "Derechos del TIPNIS." *La Razón* (digital edition), 19 September. www.la-razon.com / version.php?ArticleId=137505&EditionId=2653.

Koselleck, Reinhart. 1985. *Futures Past: On the Semantics of Historical Time*. Translated by Keith Tribe. Cambridge, MA: MIT Press. Repr., New York: Columbia University Press, 2004.

———. 2002. *The Practice of Conceptual History: Timing History, Spacing Concepts*. Translated by Todd Samuel Presner et al. Stanford, CA: Stanford University Press.

Kundera, Milan. 2007. "Die Weltliteratur." *New Yorker*, 8 January, 28–35.

Laclau, Ernesto. 2005. *On Populist Reason*. New York: Verso.

Lander, Edgardo. 2000. "Ciencias sociales: saberes coloniales y eurocéntricos." In *La colonialidad del saber: Eurocentrismo y ciencias sociales*. Buenos Aires: CLACSO.

Larson, Brooke. 1998. "Indios redimidos, cholos barbarizados: Imaginando la modernidad neocolonial boliviana (1900–1910)." In *Visiones de fin de siglo: Bolivia y América en el siglo XX*, edited by Dora Cajías, Magdalena Cajías, Carmen Johnson, and Iris Villegas, pp. 27–48. La Paz: IFEA / Coordinadora de Historia / Embajada de España en Bolivia.

Le Bon, Gustave. 1995 [1895]. *The Crowd*. London: Transactions. (Originally titled *La Psychologie des foules*.)

Lefebvre, Henri. 1995. *The Production of Space*. Translated by Donald Nicholson-Smith. Oxford: Blackwell.

Lehm Ardaya, Zulema. 1999. *Milenarismo y movimientos sociales en la amazonía boliviana: La Búsqueda de la Loma Santa y la Marcha Indígena por el Territorio y la Dignidad*. Santa Cruz de la Sierra: APCOBCIDDEBENI–Oxfam America.

Lewkowicz, Ignacio. 2004. *Pensar sin estado: La subjetividad en la era de la fluidez*. Buenos Aires: Paidós.

Lomnitz, Claudio. 2001. "Nationalism as a Practical System: Benedict Anderson's Theory of Nationalism from the Vantage Point of Spanish America." In *The Other Mirror: Grand Theory through the Lens of Latin America*, edited by Miguel Ángel Centeno and Fernando López-Alves, pp. 329–359. Princeton, NJ: Princeton University Press.

Lukács, Georg. 1960 [1923]. *Histoire et conscience de classe: Essais de dialectique marxiste*. Translated by Kostas Axelos and Jacqueline Bois. Paris: Éditions de Minuit.

———. 1974 [1910]. *Soul and Form*. Translated by Anna Bostock. London: Merlin. Repr., New York: Columbia University Press, 2010.

MacCormack, Sabine. 1990. "Children of the Sun and Reason of State: Myths, Ceremonies and Conflicts in Inca Peru." *1992 Lecture Series, Working Papers 6*, Department of Spanish and Portuguese, University of Maryland—College Park. www.lasc.umd.edu / Publications / WorkingPapers / 1992LectureSeries / dta6.pdf.

———. 1991. *Religion in the Andes: Vision and Imagination in Early Colonial Peru*. Princeton, NJ: Princeton University Press.

———. 1995. "'En los tiempos muy antiguos . . .': Cómo se recordaba el pasado en el Perú de la Colonia temprana." *Procesos: Revista Ecuatoriana de Historia* 7: 3–33.

Mallon, Florencia. 1995. "Comas and the War of the Pacific." In *The Peru Reader. History, Culture, Politics*, edited by Orin Starn, Carlos Iván Degregori, and Robin Kirk, pp. 168–186. Durham, NC: Duke University Press.

Mannheim, Karl. 1997 [1936]. *Ideology and Utopia: An Introduction to the Sociology of Knowledge*. New York: Routledge.

Mariátegui, José Carlos. 1971 [1928]. *Seven Interpretive Essays on Peruvian Reality*. Translation of *Siete ensayos de interpretación de la realidad peruana*, by Marjory Urquidi. Austin: University of Texas Press.

———. 2011 [1925]. "Man and Myth." *José Carlos Mariategui: An Anthology*. Edited and translated by Harry E. Vanden and Marc Becker. New York: Monthly Review Press, pp. 383–389.

Marx, Karl. 1971. "Formas que preceden a la producción capitalista." In *Elementos fundamentales de la crítica de la economía política (Grundrisse)*, vol. 1. Buenos Aires: Siglo XXI.

Mayorga, Fernando, and Ramiro Molina Barrios. 2005. *La asamblea constituyente y las representaciones sociales de nación/naciones*. La Paz: UCAC (Unidad de Coordinación de la Asamblea Constituyente de Bolivia).

Mazzoti, José Antonio. 2009. "La fuerza del mito (andino): Apuntes sobre los '7 ensayos' y la deconstrucción de Sorel por Mariátegui." In *José Carlos Mariátegui y los estudios latinoamericanos*, edited by Mabel Moraña and Guido Podestá, pp. 139–150. Pittsburgh: IILI.

Medina, Javier. 2004. "Dominique Temple y la teoría de la reciprocidad." Preface to Dominique Temple, *Teoría de la reciprocidad*, vol. 1, *La reciprocidad y el nacimiento de los valores humanos*. La Paz: Plural Editores. Reprinted in *El juguete rabioso* (La Paz, Bolivia) 3, no. 97 (1 February): 6–7.

Merleau-Ponty, Maurice. 1964a. *The Primacy of Perception and Other Essays*. Translated by William Cobb. Evanston, IL: Northwestern University Press.

———. 1964b. *Sense and Non-sense*. Translated by Hubert Dreyfus and Patricia Allen Dreyfus. Evanston, IL: Northwestern University Press.

Mignolo, Walter. 2000. *Local Histories/Global Designs: Coloniality, Subaltern Knowledges, and Border Thinking*. Princeton, NJ: Princeton University Press.

———. 2003. "'Un paradigma otro': Colonialidad global, pensamiento fronterizo y cosmopolitismo crítico." Preface to the Spanish translation of *Historias locales/Diseños globales: Colonialidad, conocimientos subalternos y pensamiento fronterizo*, translated by Juan María Madariaga and Cristina Vega Solís, pp. 19–60. Madrid: Ediciones Akal.

———. 2005. *The Idea of Latin America*. Oxford: Blackwell.

———. 2007. "The Rhetoric of Modernity, the Logic of Coloniality and the Grammar of De-Coloniality." *Cultural Studies* 21, nos. 2–3: 449–514.

Mockus, Antanas. 1994. "Anfibios culturales y divorcio entre ley, moral y cultura." *Análisis Político* 21: 37–48.

Molinié-Fioravanti, Antoinette. 1986. "El regreso de Viracocha." *Bulletin de l'IFEA* 16 (3–4). Lima: IFEA.

Montenegro, Carlos. 1994 [1943]. *Nacionalismo y coloniaje*. La Paz: Editorial Juventud.

Mosès, Stéphane. 2009 [1992]. *The Angel of History: Rosenzweig, Benjamin, Scholem*. Translated by Barbara Harshav. Stanford, CA: Stanford University Press.

Nash, June. 1979. *We Eat the Mines and the Mines Eat Us*. New York: Columbia University Press.

Paredes Candia, Antonio. 1972. *Diccionario mitológico de Bolivia*. La Paz: Los Amigos del Libro.

Paris, Robert. 1980. "El marxismo de Mariátegui." In José Aricó, *Mariátegui y los* orígenes del marxismo Latinoamericano, pp. 119–144. México: Ediciones Pasado y Presente.

Parker, Patricia. 1990. "Metaphor and Catachresis." In *The Ends of Rhetoric: History, Theory, Practice*, edited by J. Bender and D. E. Wellbery, pp. 60–73. Stanford, CA: Stanford University Press.

Paz, Sarela. 2011. Unpublished working paper.

Peirce, Charles Sanders. 1935 [1893]. "Evolutionary Love." In *Scientific Metaphysics*, vol. 6 of *Collected Papers*, pp. 190–215. Cambridge, MA: Harvard University Press.

Pérez Vejo, Tomás. 2003. "La construcción de las naciones como problema historiográfico: El caso del mundo hispánico." *Historia Mexicana* 53: 275–311.

Platt, Tristan. 1983. "Religión andina y conciencia proletaria: Qhoya runa y ayllu en el Norte de Potosí." *Hisla* 2, Lima.

Pratt, Mary Louise. 1987. "Linguistic Utopias." In *The Linguistics of Writing: Arguments between Language and Literature*, edited by Nigel Fabb, Derek Attridge, Alan Durant, and Colin Maccabe, pp. 48–66. New York: Methuen.

Propp, Vladimir, 1968 [1927]. *Morphology of the Folktale*. Translated by Laurence Scott. Austin: University of Texas Press.

Quijano, Aníbal. 2000. "Colonialidad del poder y clasificación social." *Journal of World-Systems Research* 6, no. 2 (Summer / Fall): 342–386.

———. 2001. "Colonialidad del poder, cultura y conocimiento en América Latina." In *Capitalismo y geopolítica del conocimiento*, compiled by Walter Mignolo, pp. 117–131. Buenos Aires: Ediciones del Signo.

Quispe, Jorge. 2011. "Sin carretera aún, el bloque indígena TIPNIS se agrieta." *La Razón* (digital edition), 28 November. www.la-razon.com / suplementos / especiales / carretera-bloque-indigena-TIPNIS-agrieta_0_1514848618.html.

Rabasa, José. 2010. *Without History: Subaltern Studies, the Zapatista Insurgency, and the Specter of History*. Pittsburgh: University of Pittsburgh Press.

Rama, Ángel. 1996. *The Lettered City*. Translated by John Charles Chasteen. Durham, NC: Duke University Press.

Rawls, John. 1971. *A Theory of Justice*. Cambridge, MA: Harvard University Press.

———. 1987. *Time Wars: The Primary Conflict in Human History*. New York: Simon & Schuster.

———. 1999. *The Law of Peoples*. Cambridge, MA: Harvard University Press.

Rodríguez Larreta, Enrique, and Guillermo Giucci. 2007. *Gilberto Freyre, Una biografia cultural: A formação de un intelectual brasileiro: 1900–1936*. Rio de Janeiro: Editora Record.

Rowe, J. H. 1985. "Probanza de los Incas nietos de conquistadores." *Histórica* (Lima) 9, no. 2: 193–245.

Said, Edward. 1975. *Beginnings: Intention and Method*. New York: Basic Books.

———. 1994. *Representations of the Intellectual*. New York: Vintage.

———. 2002. *Reflections on Exile and Other Essays*. Cambridge, MA: Harvard University Press.

———. 2003. "The Other America." *Al-Ahram Weekly Online*, 20–26 March. http://weekly.ahram.org.eg/2003/630/focus.htm.

Salazar-Soler, Carmen. 1990. "Pratiques et croyances religieuses des mineurs de Julcani, Huancavelica, Pérou." Doctoral thesis, EHESS, Paris.

Salomon, F., and J. L. Urioste. 1991. *The Huarochiri Manuscript: A Testament of Ancient Andean and Colonial Religion*. Austin: University of Texas Press.

Sanjinés C., Javier. 2004. *Mestizaje Upside-Down: Aesthetic Politics in Modern Bolivia*. Pittsburgh: University of Pittsburgh Press.

———. 2009. *Rescoldos del pasado: Conflictos culturales en sociedades poscoloniales*. La Paz: PIEB.

Sarmiento, Domingo Faustino. 1977 [1845]. *Facundo. Civilización y barbarie*. México: Editorial Porrúa.

Scholem, Gershom. 1991. "Walter Benjamin and His Angel." In *On Walter Benjamin: Critical Essays and Recollections*, edited by Gary Smith, pp. 51–89. Cambridge, MA: MIT Press.

Siles Salinas, Jorge. 1969. *Ante la historia*. Madrid: Editora Nacional.

Smith, Anthony. 1981. *The Ethnic Revival in the Modern World*. Cambridge: Cambridge University Press.

———. 1986. *The Ethnic Origins of Nations*. Oxford: Blackwell.

Sontag, Susan. 1978. *Illness as Metaphor*. New York: Farrar, Strauss and Giroux.

Sorel, Georges. 1907. *La decomposition du marxisme*. Paris: Librairie des Sciences Politiques et Sociales.

Soruco Sologuren, Ximena. 2011. *La ciudad de los cholos: Mestizaje y colonialidad en Bolivia, siglos XIX y XX*. Lima: IFEA / PIEB.

Spalding, Karen. 1982. "Exploitation as an Economic System: The State and the Extraction of Surplus in Colonial Peru." In *The Inca and the Aztec States, 1400–1800: Anthropology and History*, edited by G. A. Collier, R. Rosaldo, and J. Wirth, pp. 321–342. New York: Academic.

Spivak, Gayatri. 1988. "Can the Subaltern Speak?." In *Marxism and the Interpretation of Culture*, edited by Cary Nelson and Lawrence Grossberg, pp. 271–313. Urbana: University of Illinois Press.

Starn, Orin, Carlos Iván Degregori, and Robin Kirk. 1995. *The Peru Reader. History, Culture, Politics*. Durham, NC: Duke University Press.

Stefanoni, Pablo. 2010. *Qué hacer con los indios . . . y otros traumas irresueltos de la colonialidad*. La Paz: Plural Editores.

Taine, Hippolyte. 1920. *Essais de critique et d'histoire*. Paris: Hachette.

Tamayo, Franz. 1975 [1910]. *Creación de la pedagogía nacional*. 3rd ed. La Paz: Biblioteca del Sesquicentenario de la República.

Taussig, Michael. 1980. *The Devil and Commodity Fetishism in South America*. Chapel Hill: University of North Carolina Press.

Taylor, Charles. 2007. *A Secular Age*. Cambridge, MA: Harvard University Press.
Toranzo Roca, Carlos. 1993. *Lo pluri-multi o el reino de la diversidad*. La Paz: ILDIS.
———. 2009. "Repensando el mestizaje en Bolivia." In *¿Nación o naciones boliviana(s)?*, edited by Gonzalo Rojas Ortuste, pp. 45–61. La Paz: CIDES-UMSA / Embajada de España en Bolivia / CAECID / Universidad Complutense de Madrid.
Touraine, Alain. 1995. *Critique of Modernity*. Oxford: Blackwell.
Valcárcel, Luis E. 1927. *Tempestad en los Andes*. Lima: Editorial Minerva.
Vargas Llosa, Mario. 1996. *La utopía arcaica: José María Arguedas y las ficciones del indigenismo*. Lima: Alfaguara.
Vidal, Hernán. 2004. *La literatura en la historia de las emancipaciones latinoamericanas*. Santiago de Chile: Mosquito Comunicaciones.
———. 2009. "An Aesthetic Approach to Issues of Human Rights." *Hispanic Issues On Line* 4: 14–43, hispanicissues.umn.edu / assets / pdf / VIDAL_HR.pdf.
Walsh, Catherine. 2008. "Interculturalidad, plurinacionalidad y decolonialidad: Las insurgencias político-epistémicas de refundar el Estado." *Tábula Rasa* (Bogotá) 9: 131–152.
Wanderley, Fernanda. 2011. "El TIPNIS somos todos: Otro desarrollo es posible." *La Razón* (digital edition), 14 October, www.la-razon.com / version.php?ArticleId=138520&EditionId=2671.
White, Hayden. 1978. *Tropics of Discourse: Essays in Cultural Criticism*. Baltimore: Johns Hopkins University Press.
Wieviorka, Michel. 2001. *La difference culturelle: Une reformulation des débats*. Colloque de Cerisy. Paris: Éditions Balland.
Williamson, Edwin. 1992. *The Penguin History of Latin America*. London: Penguin.
Zavaleta Mercado, René. 1983 [1970]. "Forma clase y forma multitud en el proletariado minero en Bolivia." In *Las masas en noviembre*. La Paz: Libreria Editorial Juventud.
———. 1990 [1967]. *Bolivia: El desarrollo de la conciencia nacional*. La Paz: Editorial Los Amigos del Libro.
Zibechi, R. 2006. *Dispersar el poder: Los movimientos como poderes anti-estatales*. Buenos Aires: Tinta Limón.

Index

Absi, Pascale, 119, 120–24, 191n8
Adorno, Theodor W., 107–8; essay and, 15–16, 18, 20; negative dialectics and, 19, 109
"Aesthetic Approach to Issues of Human Rights, An" (Vidal), 149
Albó, Xavier, 21
Amauta (journal), 79
amphibian, metaphor of, 169–72, 180; highway and, 174–76
Anatomy of Criticism (Frye), 87
Anderson, Benedict: essay and, 149; homogeneous, empty time and, 63, 65, 109; imagined communities and, 26, 58, 61–63, 72, 74, 95, 189n6; linear time and, 65; nation and, 26, 61–62, 74, 95, 147; print capitalism and, 149, 193n4; social heterogeneity and, 64
Ante la Historia (Siles Salinas), 36, 40
Appadurai, Arjun: deterritorialization and, 143
Arendt, Hannah, 134
Arguedas, Alcides, 17, 68, 193n5, 194n11; "cult of anti-mestizaje" and, 150–52
Arguedas, José María, 29–34, 47, 54; Mariátegui and, 50–51; Montenegro and, 50–51; mythic past and, 30–33; temporal categories and, 25; transculturation and, 15, 29
Ariel (Rodó), 70
Arielismo, 76, 80

"arrow of time," 42, 47, 49, 71, 187n6
Asto (fictional character), 29–32
avalanche, metaphor of, 32, 34, 164–66

Beginnings: Intention and Method (Said), 20
Bello, Álvaro, 170
Benjamin, Walter, 18, 102–3, 106, 114–15, 140, 191n5, 192n11; allegory and, 98, 115; Angel of History and, 101, 104, 108–9, 111, 141; "awakening of the dead" and, 108; categories of "rememorization" and "redemption" and, 104, 111; historical agency and, 109–10; historicism and, 104, 107–9; homogeneous, empty time and, 63, 109, 113, 147–48; "illuminations" and, 98, 108; image of the future and, 107–8; indexicality and, 108–9; messianism and, 101, 107, 111, 135; philosophy of history and, 13; presence of the now and, 107–8; rejection of progress and, 109–11; revolution and, 107, 111; speculation and, 104–5; "time of the now" and, 53, 108, 110–11, 131; utopianism and, 104
Bernard, Carmen, 125
Bernstein, Basil, 169
Betanzos, Juan de, 131
Beverley, John, 86, 89
Bhabha, Homi, 86, 187n7
Black Skin, White Masks (Fanon), 184n3
Bloch, Ernst: contemporaneity of the non-

Bloch, Ernst (*cont.*)
contemporaneous and, 4, 145–46; noncontemporary temporal registers and, 145; persistence of "then" within "now" and, 13, 58
Bolivia, 6, 23, 26; border thinking and, 7; civic and ethnic nation and, 144, 146, 149, 152, 153, 158, 172; communal politics and, 9–11; Constitution of 2009 and, 167, 172–74, 181–82, 184n4; "cult of antimestizaje" and, 150–51; decolonization and, 7–10; indigenous peoples and, 10–11, 27, 36, 135–38, 144, 150–51, 165–67, 172–77; leftward turn and, 6, 9; mestizaje and, 153, 159, 161–62; metaphors of flowing and, 143–44, 162; modernity and, 25; Montenegro and, 44–46, 49–50; multitude and, 164–67; national culture and, 150, 156, 177; national pedagogy and, 149, 151–52, 182; nation-state and, 27, 143–44, 157, 159, 177, 180; nature as legal subject and, 172, 174–82; neoliberalism and, 7–8, 158–60, 164, 166–67; pluri / multi diversity and, 159–60; plurinationality and, 157, 162, 167, 172–74, 177–78, 180–82; popular movements and, 9–10; revolution and, 36, 43–44, 46, 158, 160, 178, 194n9; revolutionary nationalism and, 158, 162, 182; social imaginary and, 143–44, 153, 158; societies on the move and, 10, 143; temporal categories and, 25, 27, 48–49; Water War and, 10, 165–66
Bolivia: El desarrollo de la conciencia nacional (Zavaleta Mercado), 166
border thinking, 7, 18, 183n3, 184n6. *See also* Mignolo, Walter
Bouysse-Cassagne, Thérèse, 122
Brazil: crisis of modernity and, 69–72; Euclides da Cunha and, 69–74; exception in colonial history, 68–69; national culture and, 70–74
Brown, Richard Harvey, 185n1, 194n7
Buck-Morss, Susan, 19
Bunge, Octavio, 151

Calhoun, Craig, 61, 127, 133–34, 148, 193n15 (chap. 3), 193n2 (chap. 4)
Cândido, Antônio, 188n2
Canedo, Gabriela, 170
Canetti, Elias: "momentum and sting" and, 126
Canudos War: da Cunha and, 69–72; millenarian movement and, 69; nation and, 73–74
catachresis, 54, 91, 116, 186n3; Cicero and, 87; vs. metaphor, 86–87; Parker and, 87; representation of reality and, 36; Spivak and, 86, 192n9; subalternity and, 87; transformation into metaphor and, 32–34
category of totality, 49, 51
Céspedes, Augusto, 153
Chakrabarty, Dipesh, 94–95, 158, 179; anticolonial counterdemand of the "now" and, 110; historicism and, 110; humanism and, 143, 168; the "not yet" and, 101, 110, 112; political modernity and, 98, 138–39; social imaginary and, 143; uncharted waters and, 143, 158, 168; waiting room of history and, 23, 110, 190n3
Chimbote (Peru), 30–34
Cioran, E. M., 1, 13, 21
civil society, 9, 59, 95, 98, 157, 180
Cochran, Terry, 105, 107, 109, 139
colonialism, 3, 23, 44, 56, 79; national culture and, 72
coloniality: colonial difference and, 52, 184n7; colonial differentiation and, 139–40; coloniality of knowledge and, 139; colonial wound and, 3; decolonization and, 140; ex-centrism and, 4; historical-structural complexity and, 5; modernity and, 3, 19, 52, 55, 73, 95, 183n3, 189n5; nation-state and, 99
colonial matrix of power, 3, 4, 55, 99, 183n1. *See also* Quijano, Aníbal
colonial wound, 3, 184n6, 185n8. *See also* Fanon, Frantz
communalism, 9, 10, 11, 118

Conselheiro, Antonio, 70, 73, 89, 91, 92
contact zones: Mary Louise Pratt and, 64
contemporaneity of the non-contemporaneous, 4–5, 23, 48, 55, 145, 168, 193n1; horizon of expectations and, 39, 53. *See also* Bloch, Ernst
"contingent we," 163, 165
Cornejo Polar, Antonio, 29–34, 83–84, 185n1, 189n7
Coronil, Fernando, 22, 191n5; crisis of historical time and, 14–15; leftward turn and 6, 15; utopian thinking and, 14
Costa-Lima, Luiz, 66
Creación de la pedagogía nacional (Tamayo), 151–53
Critique of Modernity (Touraine), 134
Croce, Benedetto, 78
"crowd, the": da Cunha and, 58; Mariátegui and, 58
Crowds and Power (Canetti), 126
culture of integration, 167, 170, 180; agapism and, 133–34; common good and, 134; conflict between collective needs and individual profit, 134; historicism and, 133; immanence and transcendence and, 133–34; postsecular public reason and, 133; public sphere and, 127, 133, 136; translation of religion into the secular and, 127–28, 132, 135–36. *See also* Lehm, Zulema; Taylor, Charles

Dabove, Juan Pablo: banditry and, 91–92; constituent power and, 90; imagined community and, 189n6
da Cunha, Euclides, 26, 68, 90–92, 95, 188n2; Canudos War and, 69–70; crisis of modernity and, 68–74; "the crowd" and, 58; ethnicity and, 58, 88; multitude and, 88–89; nation and, 58, 88, 189n6; "the people" and, 58; rectilinear time and, 5–6; subalternity and, 58, 88
Darwin, Charles, 106–7
decolonial turn, 23; leftward turn and, 11
decolonization: essay and, 23–24; ex-centrism and, 12; progress and, 12, 181;

rhetoric of modernity and, 55. *See also* Mignolo, Walter
Deleuze, Gilles, 185n8
Descartes, René, 2; and rationalism, 105
deterritorialization, 85–86, 89–90, 92; dimension of, 143–44, 167–68; nation-state and, 159–60, 168
"Development of Underdevelopment, The" (Gunder Frank), 194n10
Devil and Commodity Fetishism in South America, The (Taussig), 114
Diez de Medina, Fernando: authoritarian discourse and, 156–57, 182
Dirlik, Arif, 169, 171, 178
Duara, Prasenjit, 155

El peso de la noche (Jocelyn-Holt Letelier), 190n1
El Tiempo (newspaper), 78
embers of the past, 5, 10, 24–25, 35, 47, 52–53, 180, 191n5; metaphors of flowing and, 164; past as a resource for the present and, 54–55, 100–101
Empire (Hardt and Negri), 85
end of history, 5, 14–15, 41. *See also* Fukuyama, Francis
essay: decolonization and, 23–24; literary Americanism and, 16; national culture and, 149–51; nation building and, 16, 19, 20, 26, 149–50, 156; other literary genres and, 15–16; philosophy of history and, 13, 14, 18, 22–23, 27, 110; social imaginary and, 149–50; transgression and, 15–24
Estermann, Josef, 191n7
ethnicity: Hegelian philosophy of history and, 84; identity and, 8, 18, 32, 59–60, 61; multitude and, 84; nation and, 26–27, 57–63, 72–73, 76, 84, 88, 93, 144–49; nationalism and, 59, 149; "the people" and, 84; subalternity and, 84
"Evolutionary Love" (Peirce), 105–6
ex-centrism, 4, 12, 15, 18, 21, 102–3, 122
experience of the past, 33–34, 46, 48, 52; end of history and, 41; horizon of expectations and, 35, 37, 38–42, 44; Monte-

experience of the past (*cont.*)
negro and, 44; tradition and, 38–39; utopianism and, 41. *See also* Koselleck, Reinhart

Fabian, Johannes, 187n8
Fabricant, Nicole, 7–8
Facundo (Sarmiento), 66, 188n2
Fals Borda, Orlando, 169
Fanon, Frantz, 3–4, 17, 103, 184n3
Flores Galindo, Alberto, 74
flowing, metaphors of, 143–45, 157, 162–63, 166, 175, 180; embers of the past and, 164; the here and the now and, 164
"Forma clase y forma multitud en el proletariado minero en Bolivia," (Zavaleta Mercado), 195n13
"Forma multitud de la política de las necesidades vitales" (Gutiérrez, Linera, and Tapia), 164
Foucault, Michel, 25
Fox from Up Above and the Fox from Down Below, The (Arguedas, José María), 25; migrants in, 29–34; mythic past in, 30–33; transculturation in, 15
French Revolution, 3, 42–43, 59; civic nation and, 147; horizon of expectations and, 35, 38. *See also* revolution
Freyre, Gilberto, 188n2
Frye, Northrop, 87
Fukuyama, Francis: end of history and, 5

Galilei, Galileo, 2
García Calderón, Francisco, 68, 76
García Linera, Álvaro, 8–9; "multitude form" and, 164–67
gaze of the other, 46, 48–49, 52, 54
Gellner, Ernest, 61, 63, 147
genealogy of nations, 62
Gilly, Adolfo: time and modernity and, 48, 53, 141
Gobetti, Piero, 78, 80
González Prada, Manuel, 75, 82
Gramsci, Antonio, 77–79, 86, 88, 93
Guamán Poma de Ayala, Felipe: khipus and, 129

Guha, Ranajit, 75, 92; "dominance without hegemony" and, 138; nation and, 65; nationalism and, 61; "politics of the people" and, 87–88; print capitalism and, 65; subalternity and, 61, 65, 88
Gunder Frank, André, 194n10
Gustafson, Bret, 7–8
Gutiérrez, Raquel: "multitude form" and, 164–67

Habermas, Jürgen, 127, 193n14
"hard boundaries," 155, 157, 162
"hardening" of the present, 185n8
Hardt, Michael, 26, 85–86, 89–90, 95
Harootunian, Harry, 193n1; noncontemporary temporal registers and, 145
Harris, Olivia, 119, 122
Hegel, Georg Wilhelm Friedrich, 4, 12, 77, 102, 111, 188n8; civil society and, 95; specularity and, 104. *See also* Hegelian philosophy of history
Hegelian philosophy of history, 2, 12, 104, 111; colonial matrix of power and, 4; essay and, 13, 14, 18, 22–23, 27; ethnicity and, 84; historical-structural heterogeneity and, 5–6; logocentrism and, 77; utopianism and, 57
"high culture": Anderson and, 63–64, 193n4; imagined communities and, 63–64; nation building and, 61
highway, metaphor of, 174–79
Hinkelammert, Hans, 185n7
"historical we," 151, 153–54
history: "enchanted" vs. "disenchanted," 113–14; end of history and, 5, 14–15, 41; Hegelian linearity and, 103–4; the here and now and, 101–3, 185n2; historical agency and, 105–6, 109–10; historicism and, 100–110, 144; minor histories and, 97; Newtonian universe and, 113–14; pasts that resist historicization and, 97; questions of translation and, 113–14; time-space notion of "pacha" and, 111–12
Hobsbawm, Eric, 60–61, 146–47

horizon of expectations, 14, 46, 48, 52–53, 101; experience of the past and, 35, 37–42, 44; modernity and, 23; Montenegro and, 44, 51; nation and, 65, 148; notion of progress and, 45, 47; prognosis and, 148; utopianism and, 38, 39. *See also* Koselleck, Reinhart

"Humanism in a Global World" (Chakrabarty), 143

Husserl, Edmund, 184n5

Hylton, Forrest, 186n4

Idea of Nationalism (Kohn), 193n2

imagined communities, 48, 109; da Cunha and, 74, 189n6; essay and, 21; high culture and, 63–64; indigenous peoples and, 26; linear time and, 65; nation and, 61–64, 95, 144, 147; national culture and, 72; nation-state and, 26; Peru and, 75; print capitalism and, 61; social heterogeneity and, 63–64; utopianism and, 64. *See also* Anderson, Benedict

immanence, 85; transcendence and, 133–34

indigenismo, 17, 23; Mariátegui and, 26, 77–79, 81, 92, 94; mystical wager and, 81–83; peasantry and, 79, 82–83, 93–94

indigenous peoples: decolonization and, 10, 12; imagined communities and, 26; "integrating (re)territorialization" and, 169; interculturalism and, 7; modernity and, 99–100, 104, 169; movements and, 8, 27, 104, 135–38, 169, 172, 186n4, 195n14; nation-state and, 24, 27, 99, 141, 172; temporal categories and, 11, 25, 53

"integrating (re)territorialization," 169–71

interculturalism, 7, 9, 11

jagunços, 26, 70–71; multitude and, 89–90

Jakobson, Roman, 64

Jay, Martin, 104–5

Jocelyn-Holt Letelier, Alfredo, 190n1

Johnson, Ariana, 92

Katari, Tomás, 186n4

Katari, Tupac, 186n4

Klein, Étienne, 187n6

Kohn, Hans, 193n2; civic and ethnic nation and, 148

Komadina Rimassa, Jorge, 184n4; nature as legal subject and, 172, 179

Koselleck, Reinhart, 25, 55, 101, 145, 147; experience of the past and, 35, 37, 39, 46–47; horizon of expectations and, 14, 35, 37, 39, 46–47

Kundera, Milan, 190n3

Lacan, Jacques, 27

Laclau, Ernesto, 48, 190n2; "the people" and, 26, 84–88

Lander, Edgardo: coloniality of knowledge and, 139

Larson, Brooke, 151, 193n6

La ciudad de los cholos: Mestizaje y colonialidad en Bolivia, siglos XIX y XX (Soruco Sologuren), 194n8

La literatura en la historia de las emancipaciones latinoamericanas (Vidal), 193n3

La nación clandestina (Sanjinés, Jorge), 185n8

La utopía arcaica (Vargas Llosa), 184n6

Le Bon, Gustave, 151, 190n2

leftward turn: alternative modernization and, 9; Coronil and, 6, 15; decolonial turn and, 11; García Linera and, 8; Latin American countries and, 6, 15

Lehm, Zulema: anticolonialism and, 135; culture of integration and, 136; historicism and, 138; intercultural encounter and, 136; messianism and millenarianism and, 135, 191n4; millenarian search for a "land without evil" and, 135–37; modernity and, 138; past as a resource for the present and, 135; public sphere and, 136, 138; secular and supernatural and, 135–37; utopianism and, 135

letrados, 66–68, 76, 79, 102, 149, 156, 190n2

Lewkowicz, Ignacio, 162–63, 165

literary Americanism, 16–17

lloqlla, 32–43, 54

logocentrism, 139, 172, 174, 189n4; Hegelian philosophy of history and, 77; modernity and, 62, 190n3; Newtonian universe and, 114

Lomnitz, Claudio, 63

Lo pluri-multi o el reino de la diversidad (Toranzo Roca), 160–61

L'Ordine Nuovo (newspaper), 78

Los universos narrativos de José María Arguedas (Cornejo Polar), 29

Lukács, Georg: essay and, 22; "reification" and, 192n10, 192n12

MacCormack, Sabine, 119; Andean vs. Eurocentric pasts and, 128–32; ayllu and, 130–32; chronology in Western thought and, 132; colonial documentation replacing community knowledge and, 129–30; historicism and, 138; khipus and, 128–32; modernity and, 138; modes of conceptualizing history and, 128; oral tradition and, 132; subaltern pasts and, 129–31; time of the gods and, 130; translation problems and, 128–32, 137

Machiavelli, Niccolò, 89–90

Mallon, Florencia, 75–76

Mannheim, Karl, 35, 39–42, 45, 54, 101, 185n2

Mariátegui, Jose Carlos, 4, 20, 134, 184n6, 189n7; colonialism and, 79, 82; "the crowd" and, 58; decolonization and, 12; ethnicity and, 58, 88; Gramsci and, 78–79, 93; historical time and, 80, 84, 110–11; indigenismo and, 26, 77, 78–83, 92, 94; José María Arguedas and, 50–51; Marxism and, 26, 77–83, 93–94, 184n6; Montenegro and, 50–51; mystical wager and, 81, 83; myth and, 80–82; nation and, 58, 88; national culture and, 76; past as resource for the present and, 81; "the people" and, 58, 94; revolution and, 82–83, 93–94; Sorel and, 80; subalternity and, 58, 88, 94; utopianism and, 81

"Mariátegui y su propuesta de una modernidad de raíz andina" (Cornejo Polar), 189n7

Martí, José, 16–17, 70, 112

Marxism, 7, 49, 109–10, 167, 189n8; Mariátegui and, 26, 77–83, 93–94, 184n6; Peirce and, 106; subalternity and, 86, 88; Taussig and, 116, 118–27

Mateo Montemayor (Diez de Medina), 156

Mayorga, Fernando, 144–45, 147, 155

Mazzotti, José Antonio, 189n8

Merleau-Ponty, Maurice, 184n5

mestizaje, 8, 17–18, 29–30, 92, 158, 185n1; "cult of anti-mestizaje" and, 150–51, 155, 193n6, 194n8; "ideal mestizaje" and, 153–55, 157, 194n9; "multiple mestizajes" and, 161–63; nation and, 148, 150–51, 154–55

Mestizaje Upside-Down (Sanjinés, Javier), 193n5

Mignolo, Walter, 3–4, 183n3, 184n7, 187n8

migrants: Cornejo Polar and, 30; cultural conflict and, 30–32; *The Fox from Up Above and the Fox from Down Below* and, 29–34; spatial-temporal displacement and, 30

Milenarismo y movimientos sociales en la amazonía boliviana (Lehm), 135

Minima Moralia (Adorno), 20

Mockus, Antanas: amphibian metaphor and, 169–70

modernity: alternative modernization and, 8–10, 11, 27; Cartesian method and, 2; colonial deterritorialization and, 168; coloniality and, 3, 19, 52, 55, 95, 183n3, 189n5; conservatism, liberalism, and socialism and, 3; crisis of, 1, 11, 13, 15, 46–49, 53, 69–72; decentering of, 7, 9, 12, 53–54, 56, 85, 183n2; differentiation and, 139–40; enchanted pasts and, 98, 115, 128; Enlightenment and, 3, 98–99, 102; historical time and, 2–6, 13, 16, 18, 23–25, 29, 33–36, 45–50, 55–58, 65, 84, 100–101, 109–10, 139; indigenous peoples and, 99–100, 104, 169, 180; logocentrism and, 62, 190n3; nation and, 60, 62, 68–74, 77,

82, 91–92, 94; nationalism and, 59, 138; nation-state and, 99; paradox of, 100, 102; Peru and, 77, 189n7; philosophy of history and, 2, 13, 23; race and, 3, 100; revolution and, 38, 40, 42, 51; rhetoric of, 3, 5, 18, 55; secularism, empiricism, and individualism and, 140; societies on the move and, 27; time of the now and, 112; tradition and, 144–45; translation of the religious into the secular and, 135; utopianism and, 2, 57

Molina Barrios, Ramiro, 144–45, 147, 155

Montenegro, Carlos, 25, 40, 193n5; "historical we" and, 153; "ideal mestizaje" and, 153–54; José María Arguedas and, 50–51; literary genres and, 44, 45, 49, 154; Mariátegui, 50–51; nation building and 44; national culture and, 50; nation vs. anti-nation and, 154–55; revolutionary nationalism and, 44, 49, 153, 155; social suture and, 153

multitude, 10, 26, 52, 84, 88, 95; deterritorialization and, 86, 89, 167; immanence and, 85; jagunços and, 89–90; "multitude form" and, 164, 166–68; nation and, 89–90; vs. people, 85, 87, 190n9; vs. subaltern, 86, 89, 190n9. *See also* Hardt, Michael; Negri, Antonio

Multitude (Hardt and Negri), 85

Müntzer, Thomas, 186n2

mystical wager, 81–83

mythic past, 168; José María Arguedas and, 30–33

Nacionalismo y coloniaje (Montenegro), 25, 40, 46, 50–51, 194n10; "historical we" and, 153; "ideal mestizaje" and, 153, 154; literary genres and, 44, 45, 49; nation vs. anti-nation and, 154; revolutionary nationalism in, 44

¿Nación o naciones en Bolivia? (Rojas Ortuste), 161

narratemes, 18–19

Nash, June, 122

nation, 103; anti-nation and, 44, 154; "civic" and "ethnic" and, 27, 144–48, 152–55, 158; coloniality and, 73; deterritorializing dimension and, 153; developmentalist and pedagogical dimension of, 143–44, 155, 156, 168–69; discourse of, 19, 57–59, 61, 65, 67; ethnicity and, 58, 62; historical time and, 65; imagined community and, 26, 61–62, 64, 74, 95, 144, 147, 189n6; legitimization of power and, 146–47; mestizaje and, 148; "modernist" vs. "primordialist" and, 147; modernity and, 60–61, 73, 146–47; multitude and, 89–90; narrative of, 88, 97, 107, 149; national epic and, 21, 22, 24; nation vs. anti-nation and, 154; Pérez Vejo and, 146

national culture, 34, 37, 57, 109; Bolivia and, 150; Brazil and, 70–74; colonialism and, 72; cultural difference and, 72–74; Diez de Medina and, 156; essays and, 149; imagined community and, 72; lettered culture and, 66–69, 76; logic of diffusionism and, 67; Mariátegui and, 76; Montenegro and, 50; narratives of identity and, 149; national narrative and, 149; Peru and, 76; rationalizing model and, 67

nationalism: Anderson and, 58, 62; "civic" and "ethnic" nation and, 147–48; decolonization and, 8; deterritorialization and, 168; discourse of, 59–60, 65, 88, 107; indigenous, 75–76; modernity and, 138; Peru and, 75; print capitalism and, 58; productivist, 8–9; revolutionary, 44, 49, 153, 155–56, 158, 162, 182

nation building, 43, 46, 53, 57–58, 64, 66, 92, 109; essay and, 16, 19, 20, 26, 149; ethnicity and, 61; "high culture" and, 61; Montenegro and, 44; national culture and, 149; Peru and, 74

nation-state, 6, 54, 55, 91–92, 94, 103, 190n3; Bolivia and, 27, 143–44, 157, 159, 177, 180; civic nation and, 147; collapse of, 163–64; coloniality and, 99; deterritorialization and, 159, 169; developmentalist and pedagogical dimension of, 143–44, 159,

INDEX 215

nation-state (*cont.*)
169; essay and, 15, 24; ethnicity and, 60; "hard boundaries" and, 155, 157; "historical we" and, 151, 153–54; imagined communities and, 26; indigenous peoples and, 24, 26–27, 99, 141; modernity and, 99, 145; nation and, 74; plurinationality and, 11, 157; tradition and, 145

Nayjama (Diez de Medina), 156

negative dialectics, 19, 109

Negri, Antonio, 26, 85–86, 89–90, 95

neoliberal project, 7–8

Nightmares of the Lettered City (Dabove), 189n3; banditry and, 91–92; constituent power and, 90; da Cunha and, 90, 91

novel: construction of nation-state and, 46, 154; temporal categories and, 25–26, 29–33; transgression and, 15

O'Donnell, Guillermo, 153

"Of Mimicry and Man: The Ambivalence of Colonial Discourse" (Bhabha), 187n7

On Populist Reason (Laclau), 85

"On the History of the History of Peoples *without* History" (Rabasa), 190n9

ordered flow of identities, 145, 155, 162–64, 169

Origin of Species (Darwin), 106–7

Os sertões: Campanha de Canudos (da Cunha), 5, 69–74, 89–92, 188n2, 189n6

pachakuti, 33–34

paradigm other, 12, 184n7

Paris, Robert, 80, 93

Parker, Patricia: catachresis and, 87

Pascal, Blaise, 18, 80

past as resource for the present, 51, 54–55, 97–98, 100–101, 131; Mariátegui and, 81; political movements and, 33–35, 135. *See also* embers of the past

Patzi, Félix, 186n4

Paz, Sarela, 176

Peirce, Charles Sanders, 103, 142; agapism and, 105, 122, 124–25, 133; analytic philosophy and, 105; critique of Darwinian theory of evolution and, 106–7; energetic projaculation and, 124; historical agency and, 105–6, 139–40, 141; Marxism and, 106; modern theory of semiotics, and, 105; moral improvement and, 106

"people, the," 26, 92–95; da Cunha and, 58; historical time and, 85; Laclau and, 84–85; Mariátegui and, 58; vs. multitude, 85, 87, 190n9; nationalist discourse and, 88; vs. subaltern, 86–87, 190n9

Pérez Vejo, Tomás: nation and, 146; nation-state and, 147

persistence of "then" within "now": Ernst Bloch and, 13, 58; Peru and, 77, 83

Peru: Chimbote and, 30–34; national culture and, 76; nation building and, 74–75

philosophy of history. *See* Hegelian philosophy of history

Platt, Tristan, 121

plurinationality, 8, 11, 24, 48, 53, 168; Bolivia and, 157, 162, 167, 172–74, 177–78, 180–82

Poetic for Sociology, A (Brown), 194n7

"politics of the people," 87, 92–93

"Porcelain and Volcano" (Deleuze), 185n8

postcapitalism, 8–9

postcolonial societies, 23; imagined communities and, 26

postliberalism, 9, 10, 27

postliberal stage, 6, 8–9

poststatism, 9, 10

Pratt, Mary Louise: contact zones and, 64–65

"primitive, the," 187n8

print capitalism: essay and, 149; Guha and, 65; imagined communities and, 61, 63–65; nation and, 61, 193n4. *See also* Anderson, Benedict

progress, 1; Cartesian method and, 2; coloniality and, 3; da Cunha and, 71–72; decolonization and, 12, 181; essay and, 23–24; Hegelian philosophy of history and, 4–5, 12, 18–19; historical time and, 13, 107, 109, 111; nation and, 146, 148;

notion of, 24, 45, 47; rhetoric of modernity and, 5; temporal categories and, 25
proletariat, 110, 161; indigenous peoples and, 51, 82–83; Mariátegui and, 77, 79, 82–83, 93; proletariat's consciousness of itself and, 33, 164; subalternity and, 33, 88; Taussig, 114–20, 125
Propp, Vladimir, 18
Provincializing Europe: Postcolonial Thought and Historical Difference (Chakrabarty), 103
Pueblo enfermo (Arguedas, Alcides), 150–51
Puma de Ayala, Waman, 184n3

Quijano, Aníbal, 55, 99, 100, 183n11

Rabasa, José, 95, 183n2, 185n9, 189n9
Rawls, John, 127
Reflections on Exile (Said), 21
Religion in the Andes: Vision and Imagination in Early Colonial Peru (MacCormack), 130
"Repensando el mestizaje en Bolivia" (Toranzo Roca), 161
resource of the other, 48, 101; time of the now and, 53
revolution, 54, 107; Bolivia and, 36, 43–44, 46, 158, 160, 178; destruction of the past and, 37; history of the future and, 42–43; Mariátegui and, 82–83; modernity and, 51–52; republicanism and, 43; Siles Salinas and, 43; temporalization of history and, 46; tradition and, 36–37, 52; utopianism and, 37, 38. *See also* French Revolution
Rimbaud, Arthur, 185n9
Rodó, José Enrique, 70, 76
Rojas Ortuste, Gonzalo, 161
Rosas, Juan Manuel de, 66–67
Rosenzweig, Franz, 104
ruins of the past. *See* embers of the past

Said, Edward, 15, 17, 19–21, 149
Salazar-Soler, Carmen, 121
Sanjinés, Javier, 193n5

Sanjinés, Jorge, 185n8
Sarmiento, Domingo Faustino, 16, 50, 66, 76, 188n2
Scholem, Gershom, 104, 111
Secular Age, A (Taylor), 133
"Sermon to the Princes," (Muntzer), 186n2
Serulnikov, Sergio, 186n4
Seven Interpretive Essays on Peruvian Reality (Mariátegui), 50, 77, 79–80
Siles Salinas, Jorge, 43–44; tradition and, 36, 40–41
Smith, Adam, 113
Smith, Anthony, 61–62, 147
Social Darwinism, 69, 73, 91, 122, 151, 194n6, 194n12
social imaginary, 143, 144, 149–50, 153
societies on the move, 14; Bolivia and, 10, 143; essay and, 21; Hegelian philosophy of history and 6; modernity and, 27, 56
"Some Aspects of the Southern Question" (Gramsci), 79
"Some Thoughts on Comparability and the Space-Time Problem," (Hartoonian), 193n1
Sontag, Susan, 151
Sorel, Georges, 78, 80, 184n6, 189n8
Soruco Sologuren, Ximena, 194n8, 194n9, 194n12
space of experience. *See* experience of the past
spatialization of time, 145, 193n1
Spivak, Gayatri Chakravorty, 86, 88, 90, 192n9
Stefanoni, Pablo, 158–59, 194n11
subalternity, 61, 84–85, 141, 153; Beverley and, 86, 89; Chakrabarty and, 94; consciousness and, 33; constituent power and, 90–91; culture and, 52; da Cunha and, 58, 88; decolonization and, 55; deconstruction and, 86, 88; deterritorialization and, 90; dominance without hegemony and, 138; enchanted pasts and, 97–98; Gramsci and 88; Guha and, 61, 65, 88; Mariátegui and, 58, 88; Marxism and, 86, 88; vs. multitude, 89,

INDEX 217

subalternity (*cont.*)
190n9; nation and, 65; nationalist discourse and, 65; vs. "the people," 190n9; Spivak and, 86, 88, 90, 192n9; subaltern pasts and, 97, 98, 102, 113, 119–20, 122, 128–29; ungovernability and, 95; violent "now" and, 101, 110

Taine, Hippolyte, 190n2
Tamayo, Franz, 17, 68, 156, 161, 193n5, 194n8; "ideal mestizaje" and, 153; national pedagogy and, 151–53
Tapia Mealla, Luis: "multitude form" and, 164–67
Taussig, Michael, 26, 191n6, 192n11; complementarity in, 120, 122–23; demoniacal as an illumination and, 117–18, 126; devil and, 114–18, 120, 123–24; dialectical interaction between supernatural precapitalism and secular capitalism and, 117; linear history and, 119–22; Marxist theory of value within Andean modernity and, 118–27; "moment of danger" and, 114–15; neophyte proletarian and, 114–20; Pachamama and, 119–24, 192n13; reciprocity in, 115, 118–20, 123–24, 126; supernatural figure of "Tío" and, 114–15, 118–27, 191n8, 192n13; translation of supernatural into secular terms and, 114–18, 128
Taylor, Charles, 124, 139; agape and, 133–34; common good and, 134; conflict between collective needs and individual profit, 134; immanence and transcendence and, 133–34
teleological view of history, 13, 57, 84–85, 112, 178, 189n8, 191n5; alternative modernization and, 9; essay and, 23; indigenous people and, 33; Mariátegui and, 80–81; Montenegro and, 44; persistence of "then" within "now" and, 77; revolution and, 37, 39–40
temporal categories: indigenous peoples and, 11, 25, 53
temporalization of history: concept of revolution and, 46; modernity and, 46; notion of progress and, 45
"Theses on the Philosophy of History" (Benjamin), 53, 104, 107–8, 114, 135, 191n5, 192n11
Thomson, Sinclair, 186n4
time: chronological, 39, 45, 148; cyclical, 65; historical, 2, 6, 11–18, 24–26, 29, 33–36, 48, 55, 58, 65–66, 73, 82, 95, 101–3, 107, 112, 122, 139, 148; homogeneous and empty, 63, 65, 109, 113, 147–48; horizon of expectations and, 23, 148; indigenous consciousness and, 35; kronos and kairos, 73; noncontemporary temporal registers and, 145; of the "other," 47; prognosis and, 148; rectilinear, 5, 15, 22, 27, 101; space and, 1, 2, 5, 9, 23, 25, 27, 55, 111–12, 145–46, 187n8; time-space notion of "pacha" and, 111–12. *See also* embers of the past; Koselleck, Reinhart; spatialization of time; time of the now
Time and the Other (Fabian), 187n8
time of the now, 53, 108, 110, 141; agency of the supernatural and, 97; Andean culture and, 112; enchanted spaces and, 102; historical time and, 112; recollection and 112; "time of the gods" and, 97, 102, 113–14, 130–31, 171, 174; utopia and, 112
Toranzo Roca, Carlos, 159–64
Touraine, Alain, 134, 142
tradition: experience of the past and, 35, 38–39; insurrectional, 52; modernity and, 144–45; nation and, 147; revolution and, 35–37; Siles Salinas and, 36, 40–41
transculturation: *The Fox from Up Above and the Fox from Down Below* and, 15, 29
Trouillot, Michel-Rolph, 191n5

ungovernability: subalternity and, 95
utopianism, 44, 49, 53–54, 111–12, 135, 168, 180; essay and, 14, 16, 22–24; experience of the past and, 41; historical time and, 66; horizon of expectations and, 38–40, 148; imagined communities and, 64; lettered city and, 68; Mariátegui and, 81;

modernity and, 2, 5; nation building and, 57; past as, 19; resistance to, 36; revolution and, 37, 38

Valcárcel, Luis E., 79, 82
Vargas Llosa, Mario, 70, 184n6
Vasconcelos, José, 17, 77
Vidal, Hernán, 193n3; "historical we" and, 151, 153–54; narratives of identity and, 149, 153

Walsh, Catherine, 174
Wanderley, Fernanda: political mobilization and, 179–80
War of the End of the World (Vargas Llosa), 70

White, Hayden, 54
Without History: Subaltern Studies, the Zapatista Insurgency, and the Specter of History (Rabasa), 183n2

Ya es otro tiempo el presente: Cuatro momentos de insurgencia indígena (Hylton, Patzi, Serulnikov, and Thomson), 186n4
Yawar fiesta (Arguedas, José María), 51

Zavaleta Mercado, René, 166, 195n13
Zibechi, Raúl: "multitude" and, 10; nation-state and, 10; "societies on the move" and, 6, 14, 56, 143

INDEX 219

www.ingramcontent.com/pod-product-compliance
Lightning Source LLC
Chambersburg PA
CBHW071817230426
43670CB00013B/2485